Crop and Bleed

This book is number 1 in the Series on
Critical Book, Publishing, and Literacy Studies,
Robert D. Montoya, editor.

Crop and Bleed

A Selection on Boundaries in Critical Print and Visual Culture

Edited by
Sean E. Pessin and Robert D. Montoya

Litwin Books
Sacramento, CA

Published in 2026 by Litwin Books.

Litwin Books
PO Box 188784
Sacramento, CA 95818

http://litwinbooks.com/

This book is printed on acid-free paper.

Publisher's Cataloging in Publication
Names: Pessin, Sean E., editor. | Montoya, Robert D., editor.
Title: Crop and bleed : a selection on boundaries in critical print and visual culture / edited by Sean E. Pessin and Robert D. Montoya.
Description: Sacramento, CA : Litwin Books, 2026. | Includes bibliographical references and index.
Identifiers: LCCN 2025939694 | ISBN 9781634001403 (acid-free paper)
Subjects: LCSH: Literacy--Social aspects. | Literacy--Political aspects. | Visual literacy – Social aspects. | Visual literacy – Political aspects. | Library science – Moral and ethical aspects. | Book industries and trade. | Books – History.
Classification: LCC LC149 C76 2025 | DDC 302.2244--dc23
LC record available at https://lccn.loc.gov/2025939694

Contents

Introduction
Cropping, Bleeding, and Possible Futures

The general impetus for this collection arose from our collective work coordinating and expanding UCLA California Rare Book School (CalRBS), a continuing education program that offers courses throughout the world on print culture, book history, librarianship, and related fields. The first order of business in this task was to assess how a continuing education program could foster forward-thinking directions for the field, while also maintaining the core needs of the field. In examining the landscape of book history courses throughout the world—including ad hoc courses embedded in the various departments within universities—it became clear that, however print culture is operationally defined within the discipline, there was room for growth, expansion, and diversification with regard to the subjects we teach in print studies, the geographies and cultures we tend to prioritize, and of the material forms beyond the most charismatic or familiar. For CalRBS and the purposes of this collection, the term print culture is used in an incredibly broad fashion. Studying print culture and its attendant relevancies includes conversations with and between many other areas of study, including bibliography, book history, library history, and archives. The minute differences between what each of these subfields might historically represent is less important to us than providing avenues to facilitate dialogue between the many scholars of print. Further, as noted in our call for papers, as recent discussions of the global nature of the book have taken shape among bibliographical and print culture scholars there is ample momentum to rethink the role of print culture in the power-based, oppressive structures that have facilitated the many social ills currently being experienced across the globe today. The study of print and visual is tantamount to the study of how knowledge, language, and culture have impacted our epistemic, economic, political, and environmental spaces. As a primary vehicle for language and semiotic meaning, print culture has played a central role in the struggle to control the social mechanisms of power that, invariably, have led to the epistemic and social oppression of various societies and communities throughout history.

In thinking about the main title of this collection—*Crop and Bleed*—we wanted to think through how we define, navigate, and digress from what we might call the disciplinary boundaries of print culture. Of course, in a literal sense, 'to crop' in the publishing world means to trim down some object (image, graphics, etc.) to, for example, fit the space of the page. Crop marks are small line indicators on a page that tell printers where to trim pages once printing has been completed. The act of cropping is the subtraction of space to fit the needs of a final print or digital object. Space is an important concept here because in terms of a page (whether that page be digital or physical) space is limited and valuable. 'Bleed,' on the other hand, is the extension of some design element beyond the area intended to crop. We often crop what bleeds beyond our trim lines ("bleeding into the margins") to limit or erase the amount of empty space at the edges of a page. We can also bleed into the gutter, placing image and text into the space between pages, extending the visual space over multiple surfaces. Bleeding is an act of extension beyond some designated space of activity. This distance between trimming and expansion can be seen as analogous to the space between erasure and representation. What we choose to print and what we choose to omit in the course of our collective scholarship is often a political decision, even in its most basic form.

These metaphors align with some of the constraints and possibilities we see in the field of print culture. Disciplinarily, and within universities and other organizations, print culture can be defined expansively and through an artificially narrow lens. Such arrangements are often institutionally inherited and difficult to change. We can think about how difficult it is for any university department to 'change the canon,' so to speak, and to steer itself into radically new directions. In thinking about the CalRBS curriculum, it was our goal to broaden the possible spaces available to study print culture and to include these new investigatory modes side-by-side with more traditional course offerings. There is nothing wrong with tradition, to be clear, unless that very tradition actively stifles the passions of emerging scholars with new theories and practices. One of the exciting things about print culture is that it bleeds into multiple disciplines. We find practitioners doing the work of print culture in numerous university departments (Information Studies, English, Art History, etc.). It is this vast landscape of activity that makes studying print culture so exciting. Of course, a historical fact is that print culture, like so many other disciplines, has been cropped in multiple respects. Certain Western geographies, languages, cultures, and forms have taken center stage. The traditional canon of print culture or bibliography has historically been decidedly un-diverse, and until recently efforts to engage in new areas of study were often met with pushback, or worse. This is not a healthy reality for any discipline, so it's a great sign for the future of print studies that we are witnessing more diverse engagements than in most any other moment. Practitioners are engaging with new critical theories, playing with form, and focusing on historically underrepresented cultures. It is a renaissance moment in the study of print culture and we should celebrate that reality.

One important thing to note is that universities are not the only spaces for engagement with print culture. If engaging with CalRBS has taught us anything, it is that print culture is an increasing area of focus for independent scholars, artists, activists, and creatives. In 2022, while scouting new sites for the CalRBS Italy course, we were lucky enough to come across the scholarship and artworks of Shubigi Rao in the Singapore Pavilion at the Venice Biennale. Rao's multi-year project, *Pulp: A Short Biography of the Banished Book,* illustrates perfectly the extent to which print culture is the centerpoint of many such multi-format projects that focus on print's role in the building of collective memory, identity, and cultural celebration, and emphasizes the destruction of print objects is an indicator of cultural genocide. The project is textual and film based, performative and limitless. The wandering expanse of Rao's *Pulp* project is staggering and, to our minds, points to at least some avenues for future potentials in the study of print that purposefully break the boundaries of traditional approaches to scholarship. The long tradition of artists' books and fine press publishing—as both mediums of production and modes of collaboration—are a prime example of the importance of artistic activity in book studies. Of late, more artists and community activists are taking CalRBS courses than ever before. The initiation of the Radical Librarian Institute (RLI) at CalRBS is a good example of this recent trend. The RLI specifically targets public activist and artist librarians that work directly with the community to create publications that intersect with the kinds of activity often taking place in maker or zine spaces. In the future, more formal collaborations between universities and artists is essential, as is an emphasis on local community spaces that highlight the lived experience of print as it relates to the long tradition of scholarship within the academy.

Lastly, when thinking about community and local publishing, small press publishing is an area of the print world that is in dire need of attention. As most who study print history are certainly aware, small publishing circuits are integral to community building, as well as community protest. Small presses have historically been vital spaces for political activity and anti-oppressive sentiments. Magalí Rabasa's ethnographically-based text, *The Book in Movement: Autonomous Politics & the Lettered City Underground*, points to the importance of underground publishing networks in Latin America to "emerging alternative political-economic praxis" (7). These autonomous modes of publishing, however, are disappearing in the United States at an alarming rate. We type this introduction on the heels of the closure of the largest non-profit small press distributor in the United States, Small Press Distribution, leaving countless small presses without inventory and without a main mode of distributing their works. This is an alarm bell for anyone interested in the history of print, especially as this history intersects with political activism and community engagement.

This collection facilitated conversations that are fomenting new partnerships, new CalRBS courses, and new directions for examination. The process of collecting these works was a process of crossing institutions and practices and proved incredibly beneficial to the practice of our work. We are thankful to the many conversations we have had during this process, and to Hanna Davis for her contribution to editing. What follows is a brief selection of individuals whose past, current, and inevitable future thinking we admire and who are engaging in projects with aims that align with necessary critical directions. There are limitless other topics that could have been included here and this collection is by no means complete, nor could it ever be. Each of these essays touches upon themes mentioned above, whether it be the critical nature of print culture, the emerging global histories of the book, importance of small printing, a concerted focus on pedagogy, or artistic interventions. Future collections of essays in the works will certainly continue to expand into other areas and we are always ready for whatever new partnerships may come from this and future projects.

Sean E. Pessin, CSUN/UCLA/Colburn School
Robert D. Montoya, UCLA
2024–2025

Critical Print Culture Studies
A Conceptual History

Jonathan Furner, UCLA

> *In every problem we need hard, detailed inquiry and negotiation. Yet we are coming increasingly to realize that our vocabulary, the language we use to inquire into and negotiate our actions, is no secondary factor, but a practical and radical element in itself.*
>
> Raymond Williams, *Culture and Society*

Introduction

This chapter is unabashedly definitional in nature. In other words, the goal is to identify and interrogate definitions of terms like *culture*, *print culture*, and *critical print culture studies*. But that does not mean that the chapter also seeks to prescribe certain individual definitions. Instead, a range of definitions is presented in each case, from which readers are invited to choose in accordance with their own preferences. The potential ramifications of such choices are explained. The intended outcome is for readers to feel empowered to write their own works that effectively use, invert, and subvert the various meanings assigned to terms in the past by different authors.

Another way of characterizing the chapter would be to describe it as an application of conceptual analysis—that is, as an example of the use of a method of analyzing concepts like *culture* in order to establish the necessary and sufficient features that candidates should have if they are to be deemed as instances of any given concept. In the sense that a diachronic approach is taken to telling stories about the emergence and divergence of particular meanings of a concept, the chapter could at the same time be characterized as a work of intellectual or conceptual history.

The chapter is divided into five sections as follows: this brief introduction; three sections successively examining *culture*, *print culture*, and *critical print culture studies*; and a conclusion.

Culture

> *Culture is one of the two or three most complicated words in the English language. This is so partly because of its intricate historical development, in several European languages, but mainly because it has now come to be used for important concepts in several distinct intellectual disciplines and in several distinct and incompatible systems of thought.*
>
> Raymond Williams, *Keywords*, 87

In its earliest uses, from the fifteenth century onwards, the English word *culture* referred to a process—that by which plants or animals were cultivated.[1] In the sixteenth century, this meaning was extended by metaphor to the cultivation of the individual human mind,[2] and the metaphorical sense gradually became dominant. By the seventeenth century, a third sense had emerged in which the products of the process—"the works and practices of intellectual and especially artistic activity ... music, literature, painting and sculpture, theatre and film" (Williams 1976, 90)—were the referent.[3]

The history of the word since the late eighteenth century is marked by developments within two main traditions, or categories of use: (a) one that has been variously called humanistic, literary, critical, prescriptive, evaluative, absolutist, or ethnocentric; and (b) another called scientific, anthropological, descriptive, relativist, or ethnographic. The first tradition stems from Enlightenment assumptions about the

1 "The cultivation of land" (*OED* 2023, I). "The most generic sense of the word 'culture'—in Latin and in all the languages which have borrowed the Latin root—retains the primary notion of cultivation or becoming cultured" (Kroeber & Kluckhohn 1963, 66–67). Cf. *agriculture*.

2 "The cultivation or development of the mind, faculties, manners, etc.; improvement by education and training" (*OED* 2023, III.5.a). This is also the older meaning of *civilization*.

3 "[T]he arts and other manifestations of human intellectual achievement regarded collectively" (OED 2023, III.6).

universality of the values of European intellectuals; the second originates in the objections to those same assumptions expressed by early critics of the Enlightenment project.

The Humanistic Tradition

The single most important twentieth-century contributor to the theory of culture is Raymond Williams,[4] renowned as one of the founders of an influential British school of cultural studies.[5] Central to the latter project is a series of books in which Williams traces the history of the idea of *culture*: *Culture and Society: 1780–1950* (1958/1963), *The Long Revolution* (1961), *Keywords* (1976/1983), and *Culture* (1981). In particular, *Culture and Society* is an account of the relationship between changes in the meaning of the English word *culture* since the late eighteenth century and changes in English society during the same period. The methodological thesis underlying this account is that we may examine changes in the ways words are used, in order to explain the ways in which the referents of those words develop. In other words, changes in the meanings of words provide evidence of changes in social, economic, and political life. "The development of the word *culture* is a record of a number of important and continuing reactions to these changes ... and may be seen, in itself, as a special kind of map by means of which the nature of the changes can be explored" (Williams 1963, 16). In concrete terms, Williams identifies a trajectory in which, "[w]here culture meant a state or habit of the mind, or the body of intellectual and moral activities, it means now, also, a whole way of life" (Williams 1963, 18).

Some might say that the humanistic tradition begins with Enlightenment historians' equating of *culture* with an older meaning of *civilization*, viz. a universal process of an individual human mind's becoming civilized or cultivated.[6] By the nineteenth century, *civilization* would come to denote the ordinary progress of society, in contrast with *culture* which signifies the pursuit of perfection. But Williams' history of

---

4 Welsh critic Raymond Henry Williams (1921–88), sometime professor of drama at the University of Cambridge.

5 Other primary contributors to British cultural studies include English academic Herbert Richard Hoggart (1918–2014), English historian Edward Palmer Thompson (1924–93), and Jamaican-born British sociologist Stuart Henry McPhail Hall (1932–2014).

6 The most renowned of Enlightenment writers on history is the Frenchman François-Marie Arouet (1694–1778), better known by the pen-name Voltaire.

the idea of *culture* begins with an examination of the thought of Edmund Burke in the late eighteenth century,[7] and his influence on the Romantic poets—for example, William Wordsworth, who drew heavily on Burke's social theory in arriving at his conception of "the People."[8] For Wordsworth, "the People" signified, not actual readers, but "an Ideal Reader, a standard that might be set above the clamour of [a] writer's actual relations with society" (Williams 1963, 51). It is this ideal of a "true standard of excellence ... the court of appeal in which real values were determined" (Williams 1963, 52) that would eventually be called *culture*. In the meantime, Samuel Taylor Coleridge used *cultivation* to signify "the harmonious development of those qualities and faculties that characterise our *humanity*" (Coleridge 1830, 43),[9] leading Williams to assert that "it is from the time of Coleridge on ... that the idea of Culture enters decisively into English social thinking" (Williams 1963, 74). John Stuart Mill is one of the first to use the word *culture* instead of Coleridge's *cultivation* to indicate "the highest observable state of men in society" (Williams 1963, 77).[10] Ultimately, then, "[i]t is from Coleridge ... that the construction of 'Culture' in terms of the arts may be seen to originate" (Williams 1963, 83).

This is the tradition on which Matthew Arnold builds in the 1860s,[11] popularizing the literary use in English of *culture* where others previously talked more commonly of *civilization*. Influenced by Burke, Coleridge, Carlyle, and Newman (amongst others),[12] Arnold is today remembered both for his poetry and for his works of social criticism, of which the "minor prose classic" *Culture and Anarchy* (1869) is the prime example (Collini 1988, 2). The latter comprises six essays originally published as articles in the *Cornhill Magazine*, the common goal being "to recommend culture as the great help out of our present difficulties" (Arnold 2006, 5). Arnold offers *culture* as the alternative to *anarchy*, and in so doing "at last gives the tradition a single watchword and a name"

---

7 Anglo-Irish statesman and economist Edmund Burke (1729–97), widely regarded in the twentieth century as the founder of conservatism.

8 English poet William Wordsworth (1770–1850).

9 English poet and critic Samuel Taylor Coleridge (1772–1834).

10 English philosopher and politician John Stuart Mill (1806–73).

11 English poet and critic Matthew Arnold (1822–88).

12 Scottish historian and essayist Thomas Carlyle (1795–1881); English theologian John Henry Newman (1801–90).

(Williams 1963, 124). A significant quality of this tradition is that culture "is not ... an activity concerning individuals alone, or some part or section of society; it is, and must be, essentially general" (Williams 1963, 124).

Arnold identified the "besetting sins" of English public life in the 1860s as "parochialism, complacency, and ... philistinism" (Collini 1988, 9).[13] Together, these amounted to the "bad civilization" of the English middle class, contributing to the "intellectual, aesthetic, and emotional narrowness" of English society (Collini 1988, 78). Arnold defines *culture* as "a pursuit of our total perfection" by two means: (a) "getting to know, on all the matters which most concern us, the best which has been thought and said in the world;" and (b) "through this knowledge, turning a stream of fresh and free thought upon our stock notions and habits, which we now follow staunchly but mechanically, vainly imagining that there is a virtue in following them staunchly which makes up for the mischief of following them mechanically" (Arnold 2006, 5). That is, "culture is, or ought to be, the study and pursuit of perfection"; and "of perfection as pursued by culture, beauty and intelligence, or, in other words, sweetness and light, are the main characters" (Arnold 2006, 53).[14] By pursuing perfection, "bad civilization" would be transformed: "In contrast to the parochial, second-rate kinds of art and literature favoured by current middle-class taste, culture would hold up the standard offered by the very greatest achievements of the human spirit in its long history... [C]ulture would act as a unifying force, replacing the parochial with the universal, the sectarian with the national, the exclusive with the inclusive. This idea of the capacity of culture to unify and heal the divisions in society has been ... one of Arnold's most potent legacies" (Collini 1988, 87–88).

This is culture in the sense of the classical Greek concept of *paideia* (roughly, the education of the ideal member of society), and as such is "not only ethnocentric, often avowedly Hellenocentric; it is absolutistic" (Kroeber & Kluckhohn 1963, 61). For Arnold, "[c]ulture is right knowing

---

13 Arnold borrowed the term *philistinism* from German poet and critic Christian Johann Heinrich Heine (1797–1856). Heine was also responsible for naming the two tendencies of Hellenism (concerned with beauty and knowledge) and Hebraism (concerned with duty and selflessness) that Arnold uses to characterize a perennial tension both in Western society and in every individual. Arnold asserts that Victorian England was dominated by Hebraism, and advocates for Hellenism.

14 Arnold borrowed the phrase "sweetness and light" from Anglo-Irish satirist Jonathan Swift (1667–1745), writing in *The Battle of the Books* (Swift 1704, 251).

and right doing" (Williams 1963, 134): i.e., knowing the best ideas and texts, and acting on their basis. The assumptions are that some ideas and texts are objectively better than others, and that intellectuals have privileged access to knowledge of such rankings. Under Arnold's influence, this understanding of culture as limited to what we might today call "high" culture (as opposed to "popular" culture) was common in English literary discourse until well into the twentieth century.

In his introduction to Arnold's life and work, English literary critic Stefan Collini argues that it is important to characterize Arnold's "distinctive style" or voice, in order to bring out "what is so seductive but also sometimes so irritating" about the experience of reading him (Collini 1988, viii). "Less original than Coleridge, less prophetic than Carlyle, less profound than Newman, less analytical than Mill, less passionate than Ruskin, less disturbing than Morris—Arnold is more persuasive, more perceptive, more attractive, and more readable than any of his peers" (Collini 1988, 1).[15] Collini continues: "since he wrote to be read and not just to be cited in other men's footnotes, his prose is usually lively, often amusing, always accessible" (Collini 1988, 22). Moreover, he has "indisputably" exercised "an immense, perhaps decisive, influence over our whole way of talking about 'culture'" (Collini 1988, 46). Already by the 1880s, Arnold was recognized as "England's premier man of letters" (Collini 1988, 23), and in the 1920s and 1930s, T. S. Eliot, I. A. Richards, and F. R. Leavis all invoked Arnold in emphasizing the role of literature as an agent of cultural regeneration.[16] "[U]ntil about 1960 it continued to be possible to believe that the dominant forms of 'criticism' carried on within university departments of English ... still belonged within a tradition that could, without too much violence to the facts, be traced back to Arnold more than to any other single figure" (Collini 1988, 114).

Yet, more recently Arnold has been the target of some "unusually violent" criticism. The general sense is that, while his irony and self-deprecation can be entertaining, his snobbery and sneering are distasteful. More substantively, the charge is that Arnold's "prescriptive ideal" of culture "derives from and reinforces a pattern of relations between

---

15 English art critic and polymath John Ruskin (1819–1900); English designer and craftsman William Morris (1834–96).

16 American-born British poet and critic Thomas Stearns Eliot (1888–1965); English critic Ivor Armstrong Richards (1893–1979); English critic Frank Raymond Leavis (1895–1978).

classes, sexes, and races that is fundamentally unjust" (Collini 1988, 115). The concept of culture as the canonical product of a privileged élite necessarily ignores the value of the contributions of other social groups.

In the humanistic/literary tradition, Williams sees the next leap forward in the development of the concept of *culture* coming with T. S. Eliot. Eliot reviews the meanings of *culture* "in rather a school-masterish way" (Kroeber & Kluckhohn 1963, 61) in *Notes towards the Definition of Culture* (1948): "The term *culture* has different associations according to whether we have in mind the development of an *individual*, of a *group* or *class*, or of a whole *society*" (Eliot 1948, 21). Williams sees the "major importance" of Eliot's book being "its adoption of the meaning of culture as 'a whole way of life,' and the subsequent consideration of what we mean by 'levels' of culture within it" (Williams 1963, 229).[17] Eliot had been at least casually influenced by twentieth-century anthropology (see below), which provided us with new illustrations of an alternative way of life: "In common thinking, the medieval town and the eighteenth-century village have been replaced, as examples, by various kinds of recent simple societies." (Williams 1963, 229).

Reiterating his primary thesis, Williams concludes that "[t]he history of the idea of culture is a record of our reactions, in thought and feeling, to the changed conditions of our common life" (Williams 1963, 285).

The Scientific Tradition

The origins of the scientific tradition of thought about culture can be traced to Herder's unfinished *Ideen zur Philosophie der Geschichte der Menschheit* [*Outlines of a Philosophy of the History of Man*] (1784–91).[18] Here Herder grappled with the assumption typically made by the historians of the Enlightenment (taking their cue from Voltaire) that the process of civilization was necessarily universal, leading in all cases to the high point represented by eighteenth-century European culture. Herder believed, in contrast, that it was more appropriate to speak of "cultures," plural—namely, "the specific and variable cultures of different nations and periods, [as well as] the specific and variable cultures of social and economic groups within a nation" (Williams 1983, 89).

17 "The distinctive ideas, customs, social behaviour, products, or way of life of a particular nation, society, people, or period" (*OED* 2023, III.7.a).

18 German philosopher and critic Johann Gottfried von Herder (1744–1803).

In his *Allgemeine Kulturgeschichte der Menschheit* [*General Cultural History of Mankind*], 10 vols. (1843–52), Gustav Klemm outlined a theory of human evolution through three developmental stages—savagery, domestication, and freedom—and used *Kultur* to indicate a particular "way of life" that was characteristic of a people, group, or period.[19] This was the sense picked up in English by Edward Tylor in his *Primitive Culture: Research into the Development of Mythology, Philosophy, Religion, Art, and Custom*, 2 vols. (1871).[20] Tylor was concerned to identify the differences between "primitive" society and "civilized" society, defining *culture* or *civilization* as "that complex whole which includes knowledge, belief, art, law, morals, custom, and any other capabilities and habits acquired by man as a member of society" (Tylor 1871, vol. 1, p.1).

Eighty years later, two American anthropologists, A. L. Kroeber and Clyde Kluckhohn,[21] undertook a monumental review of 164 scientific definitions of *culture* that was originally published in 1952 as vol. 47, no. 1, of the *Papers of the Peabody Museum of American Archaeology and Ethnology, Harvard University*.[22] Kroeber and Kluckhohn assert that the usage of *culture* with "its modern technical or anthropological [i.e., scientific] meaning" was established in English by Tylor in 1871, and characterize culture as "a state or condition ... in which all human societies share even though their particular cultures may show very great qualitative differences" (Kroeber & Kluckhohn 1963, 13–14). In contrast to the humanistic view, this scientific view is relativistic, in that "in place of beginning with an inherited hierarchy of values, it assumes that every society through its culture seeks and in some measure finds values, and that the business of anthropology includes the determination of the range, variety, constancy, and interrelations of these innumerable values" (Kroeber & Kluckhohn 1963, 61). "Most Western humanists," note Kroeber and Kluckhohn (1963, 60), are dissatisfied with "the

19 German anthropologist Gustav Friedrick Klemm (1802–67), sometime director of the Royal Library at Dresden. Having been borrowed from the French, the word *culture* was spelled *Cultur* in eighteenth-century German, *Kultur* in the nineteenth.

20 English anthropologist Edward Burnett Tylor (1832–1917), sometime professor of anthropology at the University of Oxford.

21 Alfred Louis Kroeber (1876–1960), sometime professor of anthropology at the University of California, Berkeley, who received his Ph.D. under German-born American anthropologist Franz Uri Boas (1858–1942) at Columbia University in 1901; and Clyde Kay Maben Kluckhohn (1905–1960), sometime professor of anthropology at Harvard University.

22 This work was reissued in 1963 as *Culture: A Critical Review of Concepts and Definitions* (New York: Vintage).

anthropological habit of extending 'culture' to encompass the material, humble, and even trivial."

Kroeber and Kluckhohn bemoan "[t]he lack of mooring of the concept of culture in a body of systematic theory" as "doubtless one of the reasons for the shyness of the dictionary makers" in including scientific definitions of *culture* in their works (Kroeber & Kluckhohn 1963, 70). As a contribution to such theory, Kroeber and Kluckhohn devise a classification scheme consisting of seven categories across which they distribute their 164 definitions of *culture*: "Enumeratively descriptive," "Historical," "Normative," "Psychological," "Normative," "Genetic," and "Incomplete." Although at one point they admit that the classification is "useful for heuristic purposes only" (Kroeber & Kluckhohn 1963, 78), they conclude by proposing that each category "points to something legitimate and important" (Kroeber & Kluckhohn 1963, 308). In other words, "culture is a product; is historical; includes ideas, patterns, and values; is selective; is learned; is based upon symbols; and is an abstraction from behavior and the products of behavior" (Kroeber & Kluckhohn 1963, 308). Again, at one point they specifically refuse to add a 165th definition of their own (Kroeber & Kluckhohn 1963, 307), but later cannot pass up the chance to summarize the "central idea [as] now formulated by most social scientists" (Kroeber & Kluckhohn 1963, 357) as follows:

> Culture consists of patterns, explicit and implicit, of and for behavior acquired and transmitted by symbols, constituting the distinctive achievement of human groups, including their embodiments in artifacts; the essential core of culture consists of traditional (i.e., historically derived and selected) ideas and especially their attached values; culture systems may, on the one hand, be considered as products of action, on the other as conditioning elements of further action. (Kroeber & Kluckhohn 1963, 357)

Print Culture

> *When people talk of 'print culture' I wish I had a revolver to reach for.*
>
> Nicolas Barker, "In Praise of Manuscripts," 329

In his 2007 essay that surveys responses to his earlier classic, "What Is the History of Books?" (Darnton 1982), American cultural historian

Robert Darnton specifies that book historians should ask three main questions: "How do books come into being? How do they reach readers? What do readers make of them?" (Darnton 2007, 495) These correspond, of course, to the three phases in the communication process (or *communication circuit*, as Darnton calls it) that respectively involve production, distribution, and reception. Already in 1982, Darnton had characterized book history as "the social and cultural history of communication by print" (Darnton 1982, 65), which "arose from the convergence of several disciplines on a common set of problems, all of them having to do with the process of communication" (Darnton 1982, 65). The basic concern with the communication process is also reflected in Darnton's statement of book history's purpose: "to understand how ideas were transmitted through print and how exposure to the printed word affected the thought and behavior of mankind during the last five hundred years" (Darnton 1982, 65).

Darnton's 1982 essay is well-known for its proposal of "a general model for analyzing the way books come into being [i.e., production] and spread through society [i.e., distribution]" (Darnton 1982, 67). In this model, Darnton identifies six stages in the life cycle of printed books: He sees the first phase of production as one that, in successive stages, involves authors, publishers, and printers; the second phase of distribution involves shippers and booksellers; while the third phase of reception involves readers. This circuit "transmits messages, transforming them en route, as they pass from thought to writing to printed characters and back to thought again" (Darnton 1982, 67). The field of book history "concerns each phase of this process and the process as a whole, in all its variations over space and time and in all its relations with other systems, economic, social, political, and cultural, in the surrounding environment" (Darnton 1982, 67).

In a 1993 book chapter (Adams & Barker 1993), American librarian Thomas R. Adams and British book historian Nicolas Barker propose a "new model" designed to supplant Darnton's. This model identifies five "events," adding publication and survival to the central triumvirate of manufacture, distribution, and reception. In this way, Darnton concedes, Adams and Barker "shift attention from the people who made, distributed, and read books to the book itself" (Darnton 2007, 504), and in so doing are able to capture "the metamorphoses of texts as they pass through successive editions, translations, abridgments, and compilations" (Darnton 2007, 504). Along the way, however, Adams and Barker "underplay the role of authors" (Darnton 2007, 504).

One way of exploring print culture is by considering different senses in which the medium of print may be said to have founded a culture. Australian literature professor Harold Love identifies several such senses (Love 2003).

First, Love cites Walter J. Ong for his theory that a new form of consciousness—that is, a new structure of beliefs and perceptions—emerged as a result of the introduction of print.[23] For Ong, new kinds of cognitive experience arose from the encounter with the printed page.[24] The print culture that this new consciousness comprises may be distinguished from other cultures defined in the same way, such as oral culture, scribal culture, and digital culture.

Second, Love identifies conceptions in which print culture is characterized as "a sequencing of actors and activities which can be modelled as a continuously evolving, ever-repeating cycle" (Love 2003, 57). He adds stages of reconstitution, authorship, and commissioning/enabling to the foundational three of production, distribution, and consumption,[25] and cites D. F. McKenzie for his concern with the ways in which "the activities involved in the manufacture and distribution of printed records became productive in their own right of textual or paratextual meaning" (Love 2003, 56).[26] Further, Love cites American researchers John Seely Brown and Paul Duguid for their work showing that "the social relationships generated by printed records [i.e., between authors, publishers, readers, etc.] are as important as the content of the records" (Love 2003, 58),[27] and makes the crucial point that "to become a print author is to acquire a new kind of social identity which did not exist before Gutenberg" (Love 2003, 59). With *The Nature of the Book* (Johns 1998), Love maintains, British historian Adrian Johns has produced "[t]

---

23 American cultural historian Walter Jackson Ong (1912–2003), known for his *Orality and Literacy: The Technologizing of the Word* (1982).

24 Love summarizes these as (a) "'a shift from sound to visual space,'" (b) "a sense of 'tidiness and inevitability,'" (c) "the reduction of language to a thing-like status with a consequent 'commodification of the word,'" (d) "a reduction of living knowledge to 'cold non-human facts,'" (e) "the imposition upon discourse of a sense of closure," and (f) "the replacement of a speech-like sense of presence characteristic of the handwritten text with a mechanistic impersonality" (Love 2003, 54).

25 Reconstitution is what occurs when "the fruits of reading are digested and reformulated in personal and group experience prior to their being employed in new acts of writing" (Love 2003, 59).

26 New Zealand bibliographer Donald Francis McKenzie (1931–99), known for his *Bibliography and the Sociology of Texts* (1986).

27 Cf. Brown and Duguid (2000).

he closest we have to ... an examination [of the full revolution of the print life cycle] ... for a particular class of writing produced in a particular country over a fairly narrow span of time" (Love 2003, 60).

Third, Love formally extends the consideration of production and distribution as stages in a print life cycle to include reception and organization, and suggests that our understanding of print culture should encompass "a body of practices arising from the social relationships of reading and information management" (Love 2003, 46).

Fourth, Love invokes the fact that print culture is a part of "a larger informational entity" originating in "a perception of relationships between transmitters and receivers" (Love 2003, 60) in positioning print culture as "a specialised field of study within the wider discipline of Communication" (Love 2003, 46).

Fifth, "print culture" is used when slicing intellectual history into chronological segments. This conception assumes not just that the invention of printing led to social change, but that there was an "age of print" distinguishable from other information ages. That age is currently reaching its final days. What criteria should be used to distinguish the age of print? We have already seen that Ong believes that print erodes "presence" from the textual record. Elizabeth Eisenstein argues that print allows for improvements in the speed and volume of information flow.[28] Johns suggests that print leads to a reduced confidence in the veracity of public information.

Print culture is often spoken of as if it were the equivalent of intellectual culture generally. But "no reader or writer of the early modern period was ever 'within' print culture without also being within oral culture, scribal culture, a culture of symbolic images, a culture of the use of signs and graphics, a culture of physical performance and bodily self-presentation, numerous cultures of expert practice passed on through visual, tactile, and kinaesthetic demonstration, and ... a culture of response to ambient sound" (Love 2003, 51). For this reason, concludes Love, "the notion of an Age of Print and an all-enveloping Print Culture with stable attributes becomes untenable as a way of interrogating the everyday realities of communication" (Love 2003, 53).

---

28 American historian Elizabeth Lewisohn Eisenstein (1923–2016), known for her *The Printing Press as an Agent of Change*, 2 vols. (1979).

In her "orientation to studies in book and print culture" (Howsam 2006), Canadian book historian Leslie Howsam identifies three major scholarly approaches to print culture studies, each with an emphasis on a different aspect of books. One (literary studies) focuses on books as written texts; a second (bibliography) focuses on books as material artifacts; while a third (history) focuses on books as cultural transactions. Literary studies is about "a particular set of peculiar events that take the form of written works" (Howsam 2006, 9). Bibliography recognizes that works in the abstract "cannot be separated from the material forms in which they appear, are used, and survive" (Howsam 2006, 11). History uses the analytic categories of power, agency, and experience to explain how print culture changes over time. As Howsam explains, each perspective has its own theoretical assumptions and methodological practices; but the lesson of all three is that "texts change, books are mutable, and readers make of books what they need" (Howsam 2006, x).

Howsam imagines the three fields taking their places at the points of a triangle, with other, more specialized areas of inquiry located on the triangle's sides according to their different emphases. The meeting of literary studies and bibliography supposedly results in the sociology of texts, authorship studies, and readership studies; the meeting of literary studies and history produces literary history and reception theory; and the meeting of bibliography and history is reflected in publishing history, book-trade history, and imprint bibliography. Even if some of the placements might be challenged, the model works as a way of cataloging the many and varied flavors of print culture studies.

In addition to Howsam's literary studies, bibliography, and history, we should take into account four other fields of inquiry that are closely related to one another in several respects (including content and methods), but that are characterized by more-or-less separate histories, different sets of practitioners, and different associations and journals. These four fields are communication studies, media studies, information studies, and cultural studies.

Communication studies

The *OED* (2023) defines *communication* as "The transmission or exchange of information, knowledge, or ideas, by means of speech, writing, mechanical or electronic media, etc." Three aspects worthy of note are (a) the identification of communication with "transmission or exchange," (b) the recognition that "information, knowledge, or ideas" are what is communicated, and (c) the specification of media as the means by which communication takes place. The field of communication studies is consequently seen to focus on the *process* of communication: on the ways in which and the means by which people communicate, and on the various contexts in which communication occurs. Historically, many studies have been undertaken of interpersonal communication and mass communication.

Media studies

The *OED*'s definition of *media* is "The main means of mass communication, esp. newspapers, radio, and television, and (from the later 20th century) content accessed via the internet, regarded collectively" (*OED* 2023). Media studies, therefore, focuses on the media that are used to communicate "information, knowledge, or ideas," and on their impact—both on the production, distribution, and consumption of these messages, and on society and culture in general.

Information studies

Information is notoriously hard to define in a way that convincingly retains the distinctions between *information* and *knowledge* on the one hand, and between *information* and *data* on the other. The *OED* (2023) goes with "Knowledge communicated concerning some particular fact, subject, or event," essentially equating information with knowledge of the specific kind that has been, is being, or is to be communicated.[29] Unsurprisingly, the field of information studies focuses on information in the form of messages (often characterized as *documents*), and on the production, organization, retrieval, preservation, and use of such messages.

Cultural studies

For the *OED* (2023), culture is "The distinctive ideas, customs, social behaviour, products, or way of life of a particular nation, society, people, or period." According to the most mundane conception, then, cultural studies may be said to focus on the development of such ideas, practices, artifacts, etc., on the social, political, and economic contexts in which such ideas, etc., are produced, distributed, and consumed, and on the reciprocal impact of such ideas, etc., on society.

---

29 We have to stop somewhere so it may as well be here; but, for those expecting to take one step further, the *OED*'s relevant definition of *knowledge* is "the state or condition of knowing fact or truth" (*OED* 2023). *Knowledge studies* is seldom used; *epistemology* is the preferred term.

Print culture studies

Print culture is not defined in the *OED*, but it is possible to derive a definition using the template provided by the definition for *culture* simplex: "The distinctive ideas, practices, products, or way of life of producers, distributors, or consumers of books, newspapers, magazines, etc." From there, we might go on to describe a print culture studies that focuses on the following aspects:

- the history of print *media* (books, newspapers, magazines, etc.), and of their production, distribution, and consumption;
- the development of printing *technologies*;
- the *relationship* between print culture and the cultures associated with other forms of communication, such as oral culture, scribal culture, and digital culture;
- the social, political, and economic *contexts* in which printed materials have been produced, distributed, and consumed;
- the *impact* of print media on society, culture, and literary and intellectual history (cf. the sociology of texts);
- the impact of print media on the shaping of *values*, and on the formation of personal and national identity; and
- the ways in which printed materials have been used to create and maintain *power* structures.

Strictly speaking, *print culture studies* has the potential disadvantage of not including studies of oral culture, scribal culture, or digital culture. Similarly, on the face of it, *book history* does not appear to include newspapers, or magazines, or any other more-or-less ephemeral publications. Otherwise, the two fields may be considered roughly equivalent, and one's choice may well depend on the scope of one's personal interests.

Critical Print Culture Studies

The remaining element of *critical print culture studies* is of course the word *critical*, in the sense of "relating to criticism."[30] Here *criticism* (or *critique*) may be defined as "the art or practice of analyzing, evaluating,

30 A second sense of *critical*, deriving from *crisis*, is that of "very important."

and commenting on the qualities and character of something" (*OED* 2023). Hence, a *critical* [*social*] *theory*—as opposed to the Critical Theory of the Frankfurt School, treated below—is any theory[31] that explains the emergence of some aspect of human society by analyzing, evaluating, and commenting on its qualities and character. The act of evaluation is central to this process: normative critical theory, unlike positivistic scientific theory, examines society in relation to the ethical and political values held by critics, and identifies the social arrangements that *should be* the case.[32] British political philosopher Raymond Geuss memorably defines a critical theory as "a *reflective* theory which gives agents a kind of knowledge inherently productive of *enlightenment* and *emancipation*" (Geuss 1981, 2, emphases added). The knowledge afforded by such a theory is thus of a radically different nature from that supplied by scientific theory.

It may be argued that, since the 2000s, the field of print culture studies has taken a decidedly critical turn, producing work that is intended to be normative and reflective, enlightening and emancipatory. It does this primarily by considering how categories of empire, race, gender, sexuality, and class intersect with established components of the communication circuit, and by drawing on postcolonialism, critical race theory, feminism, queer studies, and Marxism. For example, Jesse R. Erickson (2022) identifies a Black print culture studies that pursues a number of interrelated goals:

- assessing the impact on print culture studies of its racist and colonial history, including the marginalization of Black print cultures and "the mythology that people of color, especially Black people, were incapable of producing a sophisticated print culture";
- centering Black culture in book and printing history;
- understanding the material conditions of Black literature;
- analyzing the reception of printed books and ephemera by Black readers;

---

31 *Theory* itself has multiple senses, but the one being invoked here is the *OED*'s 6.a.: "An explanation of a phenomenon arrived at through examination and contemplation of the relevant facts..." (*OED* 2023).

32 The dictionary compiled by David Macey (2000) is a useful reference tool for those interested in critical theory in this broad sense.

- realizing the emancipatory potential of literacy for Black communities;
- recognizing the book as an anti-Black object;
- making the changes needed in bibliographic practices to accommodate Black print culture; and
- resisting the forms of exclusion that discount, as unworthy of attention by print culture studies, "the sophisticated orality of Black vernacular" and "practices that dwell at the edges of our understanding of textuality like quilting" as well as "contemporary popular literature produced by, for, and within the Black community."

Tessa Jordan and Michelle Meagher (2018, 93) introduce a selection of papers inspired by a 2015 conference with two key questions: "What can print culture tell us about feminism's past(s), its present articulations, and its future aspirations? What role does feminist print culture ... play in the expansion of feminist politics, perspectives, and communities?" They go on to highlight three themes running through the papers: (1) "the political commitments and practical impacts of often low-budget amateur production"; (2) "the capacity for ... publishers, contributors, and readers to build and narrate communities both imagined and real"; and (3) the ways in which "frequently forgotten and marginalized texts and narratives" may be integrated into feminist histories (Jordan & Meagher 2018, 96).

Jordan and Meagher (2018, 100) note that the papers from their conference share an emphasis on "North American publications produced by and for communities composed largely of white feminists writing in English," and concede that this focus serves to obscure the print-related labors of people of color. Contrastingly, Benjamin Fagan (2016) places Black women at the center of his study of early American newspapers, enabling him to reorient his reading of an early print culture around "the presence ... of the very people such cultures tried to make invisible" (Fagan 2016, 21).

We mentioned above that critical theory (lower-case) should be distinguished from the Critical Theory (upper-case) of the Frankfurt School, which itself may be considered as a group of important and influential instances of critical theory: the relationship is thus one of genus–species. *Frankfurt School* designates several generations of social theorists based at the German Institut für Sozialforschung (Institute for Social Research), including Max Horkheimer (1895–1973), Herbert Marcuse

(1898–1979), Theodor Adorno (1903–69), and Jürgen Habermas (1929–).[33] Critical Theory extends the Marxist critique of political economy (with its emphasis on the economic *base*) to a broader, neo-Marxist critique of society and culture (with its emphasis on the sociocultural *superstructure*).[34] At the "very heart" of the Frankfurt School's Critical Theory is its criticism of *ideology* (Geuss 1981, 2–3). Raymond Geuss asserts that ideology is "what prevents the agents in the society from correctly perceiving their true situation and real interests" (Geuss 1981, 3).

Twenty-first-century scholars working in the Critical Theory tradition are keen to "reinvigorat[e] [its] political dimension" (Bronner 2017, xix), claiming that "[n]ew forms of critical theory can and should offer constructive response to new forms of authoritarian excess, institutional bigotry, religious extremism, class conflict, and various structural imbalances of power" (xx). The Marxian method of the Frankfurt School—an "unrelenting" (Bronner 2017, 1), "withering" (Bronner 2017, 3) analysis of *alienation* and *reification* in terms of "how they imperiled the exercise of subjectivity, robbed the world of meaning and purpose, and turned the individual into a cog in the machine" (Bronner 2017, 4)—remains intact, while the concept of the *culture industry* (Horkheimer & Adorno 1947) has also been developed to explain how "[a]uthentic individual experience and class consciousness [have been] threatened by the consumerism of advanced capitalism" (Bronner 2017, 4–5).

In his book *The Practice of Citizenship: Black Politics and Print Culture in the Early United States* (2019), Derrick Spires uses Critical Theory, including Habermas's idea of the public sphere, to develop his own theory of how Black writers created a "practice of citizenship" through active participation in a Black print culture, conceived as a central space in which Black writers "constituted community outside of the nation-state form" (Spires 2019, 9). The heyday of the Frankfurt School may have passed, but applications of Critical Theory are still to be found in contemporary print culture studies seeking to explain historical instances of ideological struggle.

---

33 The literature by and about members of the Frankfurt School is enormous. An anthology of English translations of the major works by Frankfurt School authors is edited by Andrew Arato and Eike Gebhardt (1978). Useful introductions to the major works include the encyclopedia entry by James Bohman (2005), and the short book by Stephen Eric Bronner (2017). Fuller histories include those by Rolf Wiggershaus (1994), and Stuart Jeffries (2016).

34 German philosopher Karl Marx (1818–83) presents his base–superstructure concept in the preface to *A Contribution to the Critique of Political Economy* (1859).

Conclusion

> *[I]t is a testament to the continued vitality of print culture methodology that new works continue to destabilize core assumptions of American literary studies in ways that invigorate the discipline.*
>
> Adam Gordon, "The Rise of the Print Culture Canon," 534

In their introduction to the fifth volume of *The Oxford History of Popular Print Culture* (*U.S. Popular Print Culture to 1860*), editors Ronald J. Zboray and Mary Sarcino Zboray explain their aversion to the term *history of the book*, which seems to them to be "too top-down, value-laden, object-centered, supply-sided, processual, and restrictive." They state a preference for *history of (popular) print culture*, which is "more bottom up, value-critical, person-centered, demand-driven, nonlinear, and fluid" (Zboray & Zboray 2019, 5). This preference is evidence of a generational shift in print culture studies, in which "critical race studies and book history ... are increasingly in dialogue" (Dietrich 2020, 8).

The turn towards social justice as a goal for print culture studies has also been reflected in the work of the University of Wisconsin–Madison's Center for the History of Print Culture in Modern America, established in 1992, and since 2011 known as the Center for the History of Print and Digital Culture. Led successively by Wayne Wiegand, James Danky, Christine Pawley, Greg Downey, and Jonathan Senchyne, the Center has followed up its publication in 1999 of *Print Culture in a Diverse America* with a series of books on Print Culture History in Modern America. The mission of the Center includes the goal of "stimulat[ing] research in the print and digital culture history of groups whose gender, race, occupation, ethnicity, and sexual preference (among other factors) have historically placed them on the periphery of power but who have used print and digital sources as one of the few means of expression available to them" (Center for the History of Print and Digital Culture 2023). Pawley (2008, 705) comments that "the center has influenced a general shift in print culture studies from texts to readers of all walks of life, and has help[ed] move the field, as Danky argues, from 'questions of aesthetics and technique' into social history."

In their introduction to the special June 2022 issue of *The Papers of the Bibliographical Society of America* on "Black Bibliography: Traditions and Futures," Jacqueline Goldsby and Meredith L. McGill ask "What Is

'Black' about Black Bibliography?" and respond with a set of principles, as follows (Goldsby & McGill 2022, 175–176):

1. The 'Black' in 'Black bibliography' is a polyvalent term.

2. Black bibliography encompasses more than books.

3. Black bibliography traverses disciplines.

4. Black bibliography is openly and pro-actively political.

5. Black bibliography embraces indeterminacy.

Critical print culture studies is emerging as a field in its own right on the basis of a similar set of principles. Its objects are diverse; its scholarship is interdisciplinary; and, most significantly, its goal is overtly political. If we were to ask "What is 'critical' about critical print culture studies?" we might point to the ways in which scholars approach their studies of components of the communication circuit—seeking to eradicate prejudice, eliminate oppression, fight injustice, and redress imbalances of power, as well as to uncover alternative perspectives and voices. Critical print culture studies is anti-racist, anti-capitalist, anti-war. Critical print culture studies is here.

Bibliography

Adams, Thomas R., and Nicolas Barker. 1993. "A New Model for the Study of the Book." In *A Potencie of Life: Books in Society: The Clark Lectures, 1986–1987*, edited by Nicolas Barker, 5–43. London: British Library.

Arato, Andrew, and Eike Gebhardt, eds. 1978. *The Essential Frankfurt School Reader*. New York: Continuum.

Arnold, Matthew. 1869. *Culture and Anarchy: An Essay in Political and Social Criticism*. London: Smith, Elder. [Reprinted as: Arnold, Matthew. 2006. *Culture and Anarchy*. Oxford: Oxford University Press.]

Barker, Nicolas. 2000. "In Praise of Manuscripts." *The Book Collector* 49, no. 3: 329–348. [Reprinted as: Barker, Nicolas. 2003. "In Praise of Manuscripts." In *Form and Meaning in the History of the Book: Selected Essays*, 27–37. London: British Library.]

Bohman, James. 2005. "Critical Theory." In *Stanford Encyclopedia of Philosophy*, edited by Edward N. Zalta. Stanford, CA: Metaphysics Research Lab, Stanford University.

Bronner, Stephen Eric. 2017. *Critical Theory: A Very Short Introduction*. Oxford: Oxford University Press.

Brown, John Seely, and Paul Duguid. 2000. *The Social Life of Information*. Boston, MA: Harvard Business School Press.

Center for the History of Print and Digital Culture. 2023. "History and Mission." Madison, WI: University of Wisconsin–Madison. http://www.wiscprintdigital.org/history-and-mission/.

Coleridge, Samuel Taylor. 1830. *On the Constitution of the Church and State, According to the Idea of Each: With and toward a Right Judgment on the Late Catholic Bill*. London: Hurst, Chance.

Collini, Stefan. 1988. *Arnold*. Oxford: Oxford University Press.

Darnton, Robert. 1982. "What Is the History of Books?" *Dædalus* 111, no. 3: 65–83. [Reprinted as: Darnton, Robert. 1990. "What Is the History of Books?" In *The Kiss of Lamourette: Reflections in Cultural History*, 107–135. New York: Norton.]

———. 2007. "'What Is the History of Books?' Revisited." *Modern Intellectual History* 4, no. 3: 495–508.

Dietrich, Lucas A. 2020. *Writing across the Color Line: U.S. Print Culture and the Rise of Ethnic Literature, 1877–1920*. Amherst, MA: University of Massachusetts Press.

Eisenstein, Elizabeth L. 1979. *The Printing Press as an Agent of Change: Communications and Cultural Transformations in Early Modern Europe*, 2 vols. Cambridge: Cambridge University Press.

Eliot, T. S. 1948. *Notes towards the Definition of Culture*. London: Faber & Faber.

Erickson, Jesse R. 2022. "Discursive Perpendicularity: Intersections of Black Print Culture Studies and Bibliography." *RBM: A Journal of Rare Books, Manuscripts, and Cultural Heritage* 23, no. 1. https://rbm.acrl.org/index.php/rbm/article/view/25502/33399.

Fagan, Benjamin. 2016. *The Black Newspaper and the Chosen Nation*. Athens: University of Georgia Press.

Goldsby, Jacqueline, and Meredith L. McGill. 2022 "What Is 'Black' about Black Bibliography?" *Papers of the Bibliographical Society of America* 116, no. 2: 161–189.

Gordon, Adam. 2014. "The Rise of the Print Culture Canon." *Early American Literature* 49, no. 2: 533–551.

Guess, Raymond. 1981. *The Idea of a Critical Theory: Habermas & the Frankfurt School*. Cambridge: Cambridge University Press.

Herder, Johann Gottfried von. 1784–91. *Ideen zur Philosophie der Geschichte der Menschheit* [*Ideas on the Philosophy of the History of Mankind*], 4 vols. Riga; Leipzig: Johann Friedrich Hartsnoch.

Horkheimer, Max, and Theodor W. Adorno. 1947. *Dialektik der Aufklärung: Philosophische Fragmente* [*Dialectic of Enlightenment: Philosophical Fragments*]. Amsterdam: Querido.

Howsam, Leslie. 2006. *Old Books & New Histories: An Orientation to Studies in Book and Print Culture*. Toronto: University of Toronto Press.

Jeffries, Stuart. 2016. *Grand Hotel Abyss: The Lives of the Frankfurt School*. London: Verso.

Johns, Adrian. 1998. *The Nature of the Book: Print and Knowledge in the Making*. Chicago: University of Chicago Press.

Jordan, Tessa, and Michelle Meagher. 2018. "Introduction: Feminist Periodical Studies." *American Periodicals: A Journal of History, Criticism, and Bibliography* 28, no. 2: 93–104.

Klemm, Gustav Friedrich. 1843–52. *Allgemeine Kulturgeschichte der Menschheit* [*General Cultural History of Mankind*], 10 vols. Leipzig: Teubner.

Kroeber, A. L., and Clyde Kluckhohn. 1952. "Culture: A Critical Review of Concepts and Definitions." *Papers of the Peabody Museum of American Archaeology and Ethnology, Harvard University* 47, no. 1: viii, 223 pp. [Reprinted as: Kroeber, A. L., and Clyde Kluckhohn. 1963. *Culture: A Critical Review of Concepts and Definitions*. New York: Vintage.]

Love, Harold. 2003. "Early Modern Print Culture: Assessing the Models." *Parergon* 20, no. 1: 45–64.

Macey, David. 2000. *The Penguin Dictionary of Critical Theory*. London: Penguin.

Marx, Karl. 1859. *Zur Kritik der Politischen Ökonomie* [*A Contribution to the Critique of Political Economy*]. Berlin: Franz Duncker.

McKenzie, D. F. 1986. *Bibliography and the Sociology of Texts*. London: British Library.

Oxford English Dictionary. 2023. Oxford: Oxford University Press. https://oed.com/.

Ong, Walter J. 1982. *Orality and Literacy: The Technologizing of the Word*. London: Methuen.

Pawley, Christine. 2008. "'Success on a Shoestring': A Center for a Diverse Print Culture History in Modern America." *Library Trends* 56, no. 3: 705–719.

Spires, Derrick R. 2019. *The Practice of Citizenship: Black Politics and Print Culture in the Early United States*. Philadelphia: University of Pennsylvania Press.

Swift, Jonathan. 1704. "A Full and True Account of the Battel Fought last Friday between the Antient and the Modern Books in St. James's Library." In *A Tale of a Tub: Written for the Universal Improvement of Mankind*, 229–278. London: John Nutt.

Tylor, Edward B. 1871. *Primitive Culture: Researches into the Development of Mythology, Philosophy, Religion, Language, Art, and Custom*, 2 vols. London: John Murray.

Wiggershaus, Rolf. 1994. *The Frankfurt School: Its History, Theories, and Political Significance*. Cambridge, MA: MIT Press.

Williams, Raymond. 1958. *Culture and Society: 1780–1950*. London: Chatto & Windus.

———. 1961. *The Long Revolution*. London: Chatto & Windus.

———. 1963. *Culture and Society: 1780–1950*, 2nd ed. London: Penguin.

———. 1976. *Keywords: A Vocabulary of Culture and Society*. London: Croom Helm.

———. 1981. *Culture*. London: Fontana.

———. 1983. *Keywords: A Vocabulary of Culture and Society*, 2nd ed. London: Fontana.

Zboray, Ronald J., and Mary Sarcino Zboray, eds. 2019. *The Oxford History of Popular Print Culture, Volume 5: U.S. Popular Print Culture to 1860*. Oxford: Oxford University Press.

Global Book History and the Library[1]

Devin Fitzgerald

Introduction

In late 2019, I began looking closely at some of the undescribed and under-catalogued Asian materials in UCLA Library Special Collections. There were books that made me feel capable. The Manchu, Mongolian, Tibetan, and Thai materials posed little problem, both because of my own training and UCLA faculty and graduate student assistance. Riding high, I paged 16 boxes of brittle palm leaf manuscripts labeled "Collection of Manuscripts in Tamil, Sanskrit, and Malayan, and Indian Palm Leaf Books, ca. 1600-1899," which arrived sometime in the 1960s. I contacted specialists and shared pictures widely. I checked the collection file, which contained a single plaintive letter from the National Library of Malaysia asking for information (as they couldn't have known that these are likely *Malayalam* not Malayan manuscripts). Almost a year later, they remain sitting on the shelves in the secure hall leading to my office, a testament to generations of institutional and curatorial neglect.

The story of these palm manuscripts is part of a broader history of the connections between racial capitalism and Euro-American institutional rare book collections, one which often elides the fact the bibliographic holdings of many "special collections" are inexorably linked to a "global book history" indebted to Euro-American imperial

1 Many thanks are owed to Peter Sachs Callopy for sharing his insights into Millikan, as well as an unpublished paper. Anabel Teh Gallop for helping me better understand the history of the Javanese manuscripts in the British Library. Lizeth Ramirez for reading an early draft. The debt owed to the editors is impossible to express. Dorothy Berry, Yael Rice, and Aaron Pratt all provided useful feedback during the last round of revisions. David James Hudson made me realize that I was trying to talk about racial capitalism. Finally, Ayesha Ramachandran and Carina Johnson helped me extensively (more than anyone should expect) as the paper first began.

expansion and settler-colonialism.[2] A consideration of library histories in conversation with global book history moves us beyond neutralized stories of individual objects "circulating" and allows us to more clearly identify the structural conditions that led to the growth and prestige of the institutions that store these materials. It helps us to see how Euro-American research libraries and their encyclopedic collections of rare books were produced by and contributed to structural shifts associated with Euro-American global domination and White supremacy.[3]

This paper discusses research library collections as they evolved from the Early Modern period to the modern period, beginning in the sixteenth century and ending in the early twentieth. Focused on Chinese books in the Bodleian Library, Oxford; English looting of Ethiopic manuscripts during the nineteenth century; and the collecting activities of the Huntington Library, San Marino, California. It investigates the global roots of book collections by exploring three values shared by most research libraries: curiosity, colonialism, and canon-formation. These values were not neutral, but rather need to be considered as part of the process which transformed the value of books-as-commodities into books as artifacts.[4] The values explored in these cases will allow us to consider how racial capitalism informed the valuations of texts in the creation of rare book collections.

Before proceeding into the body of this essay, it is necessary to outline my use of the terms "racial capitalism" and "White supremacy." Racial capitalism, as defined by Nancy Leong, is "the process of deriving social or economic value from the racial identity of another person."[5] In my case, and following Jesse Erikson's notion of ethno-bibliography, this is the process of valuing books in terms intimately connected to their stated and unstated racialized contents.[6] Capaciously conceived,

---

2 For a recent attempt at describing this new field, see the essays in: Elleke Boehmer et al., *The Global Histories of Books: Methods and Practices* (Springer, 2017).

3 This statement is particulary inspired by the research of Salvatore, who has described how North American Latin American studies emerged in the tweentith century: Ricardo Salvatore, *Disciplinary Conquest* (Duke University Press, 2016).

4 My thoughts on these transformative processes are inspired by: Arjun Appadurai and Arjun Appadurai, eds., *The Social Life of Things: Commodities in Cultural Perspective*, 1st paperback ed (Cambridge [England] ; New York: Cambridge University Press, 1988).

5 Nancy Leong, "Racial Capitalism," accessed June 30, 2021, https://harvardlawreview.org/2013/06/racial-capitalism/.

6 Jesse Ryan Erickson, "Rethinking the Library Response to Black Literacy" (UCLA, 2016), https://escholarship.org/uc/item/1023g7nx.

racial capitalism informed how early collectors and institutions determined books were valuable enough to be 'special' and/or 'rare,' and in its largest ramifications, racial capitalism also forces us to consider some of the capitalist logic behind the production of fields such as Semitics, Sinology, Latin American Studies, and the collections of research materials they rely upon.[7]

As deployed in this essay, White supremacy is understood as the super-structural hegemony that emerged in the West from settler-colonialism. It is rooted in Early Modern and contemporary negation of black lives. The growth of white supremacy, which truly began in the Early Modern period, provided justification for the growth of cultural, institutional, and political structures which treated Anglo-European culture as normative and *defined* in contrast to values from outside of this imagined tradition. White supremacy provided the institutional norms and ideologies that contributed to global empire building. White supremacy and racial capitalism are overlapping and intertwining, and I believe that by historicizing examples around the creation of 'value' in different contexts, we can begin to understand how they have informed the growth of rare book collections.

Books as Curiosities: Chinese Books at the Bodleian

Most studies about global books focus on the circulation of single objects, juxtapose book cultures, or explore the contents of a single text.[8] These studies show the global book as something that led to the "the conditions for global imagination and cosmopolitan community" by creating points of intercultural contact.[9] While these approaches are essential for reconstructing the pathways of information and processes of cultural globalization, they also raise questions about histories of collecting. If we step back from specific examples of circulation and consider books in their institutional contexts, a picture of global book history rooted in collections of texts allows us to consider how

---

7 Salvatore, Ricardo D. *Disciplinary Conquest: U.S. Scholars in South America, 1900–1945*. Durham; London: Duke University Press, 2016.

8 *For examples see*: Suarez, Michael F., and H. R. Woudhuysen, eds. *The Book: A Global History*. First edition. Oxford: Oxford University Press, 2013; The Oxford Illustrated History of the Book: Raven, James: 9780198702993: *Oxford Illustrated History* (Oxford, New York: Oxford University Press, 2020).

9 Boehmer et al., *The Global Histories of Books*, 3.

objects, institutions, and superstructures intertwined in the creation of "global book history."[10]

Before the year 1700, Chinese books arrived in Europe in a gradual trickle.[11] Early accounts of Chinese books indicate that they first arrived in Europe via the Iberian peninsula, owing to early Portuguese and Spanish exploration in East Asia.[12] Catherine of Austria, Queen Regent of Portugal, owned two Chinese books, which she displayed to curious visitors. These works left a deep impression on Bernardino de Escalante, who noted that the Chinese had been printing "for many years before" Europeans. While the characters struck him as odd, it was noteworthy that they could be used to communicate across the linguistic boundaries of different East Asian states.[13] And from Iberia, Chinese materials made their way to other parts of Europe. In his history of the world to 1545, Paolo Giovio noted,

> There are [at Canton] printers who print according to their own method books containing histories and rites [...] Pope Leo has graciously showed me a volume of this sort, given as a present with an elephant by the King of Portugal.[14]

The book described by Giovio, which has still not been identified, likely made it to Rome in 1514, along with a wide array of exotic gifts

---

10 Boehmer et al., 3.

11 Monique Cohen, *A Point of History: The Chinese Books Presented to the National Library in Paris by Joachim Bouvet S.J., in 1697.* (S.l.?, 1990); Nicolas Standaert, "Jean-François Foucquet's Contribution to the Establishment of Chinese Book Collections in European Libraries: Circulation of Chinese Books," *Monumenta Serica* 63, no. 2 (July 3, 2015): 361–424; Albert Chan, *Chinese Materials in the Jesuit Archives in Rome, 14th-20th Centuries: A Descriptive Catalogue: A Descriptive Catalogue* (Routledge, 2015); David Helliwell, "The Bodleian Library's Chinese Collection in the Seventeenth Century" (draft paper, 2016); Bert Van Selm, "Cornelis Claesz's 1605 Stock Catalogue of Chinese Books," *Quaerendo* 13, no. 4 (January 1, 1983): 247–59, https://doi.org/10.1163/157006983X00218.

12 Much of this sesction is based on chapter five of my dissertation: Devin T. Fitzgerald, "The Ming Open Archive and the Global Reading of Early Modern China" (PhD Thesis, Harvard University, 2020).

13 Bernardino de Escalante, *Discurso de la navegación que los portugueses hazen a los reinos y provincias del oriente, y de la noticia que se tiene del reino de China* (Sevilla: en casa de la biuda de Alonso Escriuano, 1577), 62: "Esta mesma orden tienen en sus emprentas, de las quales usaron muchos años antes que en Europa. Destos sus libros de molde que tratan de sus historias, avia dos en poder de la Sereniss. Reina de Portugal doña Catalina, que oy bive."

14 Cited in Thomas Francis Carter, *The Invention of Printing in China and Its Spread Westward*, 2nd ed. (New York: Ronald Press Co, 1955), 164–65.

presented by the Portuguese emissary Dom Manuel.[15] Giovio's account, widely regarded as the first Western account to hypothesize about the Chinese origins of European printing, illustrates how Chinese books initially circulated as diplomatic gifts.[16]

Paired with an elephant, which captured the imagination of Europe, the pope also displayed his new book as one of many new curiosities to "his Friends." What they saw was a book made of:

> narrow and long leaves of thin and smooth Paper whereupon they write, not from the Left hand to the Right nor (like the *Hebrews*) from the Right to the Left, but from the Bottom to the Top.[17]

The book, or books like it, were seen by later visitors, such as Michel de Montaigne, who in his travel journal to Italy made special note of the rare books and manuscripts he saw in the Vatican library. He was shown a Chinese book printed in "outlandish characters, the leaves of some material much softer and more pellucid than our paper."[18]

These descriptions show that when they arrived in sixteenth century Europe, Chinese books were some of the many objects that contributed

---

15 On the arrival of the elephant and greater context see: Silvio A. Bedini, *The Pope's Elephant* (Penguin Books, 2000); *Imagining the Americas in Medici Florence* (Penn State Press, 2016), 13 describes the arrival of a Mesoamerican codex at the papal court, combined with other curios from the Americas.

16 Donald Lach, *Asia in the Making of Europe*, vol. 2, bk. 1, *The Visual Arts* (Chicago: The University of Chicago Press, 1994), 41.

17 Translation from: Guido Panciroli, *The History of Many Memorable Things Lost, Which Were in Use Among the Ancients and an Account of Many Excellent Things Found, Now in Use Among the Moderns ... Written Originally in Latin ... and Now Done Into English ... with Several Additions (Etc.)* (London: John Nicholson, 1715), 342. The 1599 edition of Panciroli does not have a section on typography. The first in-depth discussions of Chinese books are seen in the 1602 edition. Panciroli's observations both cite Mendoza (see below) and his personal experience, as noted in Guido Panciroli, *Rerum memorabilium, iam olim deperditarum: & contrà recens atque ingeniosè inuentarum: libri duo, à Guidone Pancirollo: ... Italicè primùm conscripti, nec unquam hactenus editi: Nunc verò & Latinitate donati, & notis quamplurimis ... illustrati per Henricum Salmuth: Noua reperta siue Rerum memorabilium, recens inuentarum, et veteribus plane incognitarum Guidonis Pancirolli IC. Liber secundus* (Ambergae: typis Forsterianis, 1602), 585: "Ad scribendum arctas & oblongas adhbiente e levi admodum ac tenui papyro pagellas: neque versus ab leva ad dextram, ut Greaci, neque ab dextram ad laevam, ut Hebraei; sed ad imum ab summon preducunt. Cuius generis impressum voluen, atque inde transmissum Romae in Vaticano, itemque in Lautentiana Philippi Regis bibliotheca videre me memini."

18 Michel de Montaigne, *Journal du voyage de Michel de Montaigne en Italie, par la Suisse & l'Allemagne en 1580 & 1581, 1* (Paris: chez Le Jay, 1774), 145, cited in Charles Ralph Boxer, *South China in the Sixteenth Century: Being the Narratives of Galeote Pereira, Fr. Gaspar Da Cruz, O.P. [and] Fr. Martín de Rada, O.E.S.A. (1550-1575)* (London: Kraus Reprint, 1953), lxxxvi.

to the relativization of European experience.[19] The books, like many curiosities, were likely fondled by visitors. Possession of these books did as Daston and Park have noted of collections of wonder:

> [They] represented (and, in part, constituted) the wealth and power of those who owned them; on a more abstract level, their rarity or uniqueness reflected the rarity and uniqueness of their proprietors, conceived in terms of nobility and cultivation.[20]

Chinese books in the Vatican, the Escorial Library, and the Herzog August Bibliothek all indicate that these texts circulated in rarified circles as part of the European desire for curiosities.[21]

Chinese books were also collected at Oxford.[22] Most of the books were donated to the collection by English savants. The earliest books, one of which was given to the library by Thomas Bodley, likely was traveled to Europe on a Dutch East India company ship—and interest in Chinese books was substantial enough that there was even an auction in Holland in 1605. Since most Chinese books are composed of multiple thin volumes, the auction appears to have broken multi-volume works for resale as individual units, as in the case with the volumes donated by figures such as Archbishop William Laud (1573-1645).[23] Other books, like the Southern Ming calendar in the possession of Robert

---

19 In discussing the impact of knowledge from the New World on European epistemologies, I have been particularly influenced by Jorge Cañizares-Esguerra, *How to Write the History of the New World: Histories, Epistemologies, and Identities in the Eighteenth-Century Atlantic World* (Stanford, CA: Stanford University Press, 2001); Daniela Bleichmar, "Painting the Aztec Past in Early Colonial Mexico: Translation and Knowledge Production in the Codex Mendoza," *Renaissance Quarterly* 72, no. 4 (2019): 1362–1415.

20 *Wonders and the Order of Nature 1150–1750*, 2001, 68, https://press.princeton.edu/books/paperback/9780942299915/wonders-and-the-order-of-nature-1150-1750.

21 For a discussion of the many locations of Chinese books see chapter 5: Fitzgerald, "The Ming Open Archive and the Global Reading of Early Modern China"; The literature on curiousity is extensive. For an introduction to recent research see: R. J. W. Evans, *Curiosity and Wonder from the Renaissance to the Enlightenment* (Routledge, 2017).

22 For an indepth consideration of this, see chapters 4-8 of my dissertation: Fitzgerald, "The Ming Open Archive and the Global Reading of Early Modern China."

23 For a discusson of the collection and its history see: Helliwell, "The Bodleian Library's Chinese Collection in the Seventeenth Century"; For a more general consideration of the value of Chinese materials at Oxford see: Timothy Brook, *Mr. Selden's Map of China: Decoding the Secrets of a Vanished Cartographer* (Bloomsbury Publishing USA, 2013).

Boyle, were gifts given to English merchants before eventually being donated the library.[24]

After entering the library, Chinese books were gradually rebound in limp vellum, so that they could stand in Archive Cabinet A in the European style. The Chinese books at Oxford remained little known until the summer of 1687. Michael Shen Fuzong (d. 1691), a Chinese Jesuit, traveled to Oxford at the request of Thomas Hyde (1636-1704) to describe the collection, thus producing the first catalog of Chinese books in the collection.[25] For a brief moment, as William Poole has shown, intellectuals in England turned to Shen for information about China.[26] After Shen left, the books returned to Archive Cabinet A, where they would have to wait likely until the nineteenth century to transform back from curios into books.

The case of Chinese books at Oxford provides insight into an early period of the "research library"—which we might call the pre-European hegemonic period—that saw the development of 'Oriental studies' as a diffuse activity spread among scholars of different sorts reliant on lavishly sponsored collections or fortuitously procured texts.[27] Chinese books were curios, but curiosity frequently served European intellectual ends; the two were not mutually exclusive. Jesuits convinced European readers that Chinese books could be evidence for research into biblical chronology, or, in the cases of John Webb and Athansius Kircher, research projects to reconstruct languages lost after the Tower of Babel collapsed.[28] While curious objects could challenge European assumptions about the world, more often than not, as the mystique

24 William Poole, "'All Mr Boyl's Pieces': Robert Boyle and the Bodleian Library," *On the Boyle*, no. 10 (Spring 2017): 14–17.

25 William Poole, "The Letters of Shen Fuzong to Thomas Hyde, 1687-88," *The Electronic British Library Journal*, January 1, 2015, 1; 146 Cécile Leung, *Etienne Fourmont, 1683-1745: Oriental and Chinese Languages in Eighteenth-Century France* (Leuven University Press, 2002), Arcadio Hoang was another Chinese scholar in Europe shorlty after Shen Fuzong. He catalogue books for the Royal Library in Paris.

26 Poole, "The Letters of Shen Fuzong to Thomas Hyde, 1687-88."

27 For details related to Arabic see: Alexander Bevilacqua, *The Republic of Arabic Letters: Islam and the European Enlightenment* (Belknap Press of Harvard University Press, 2018).

28 John Webb, *The Antiquity of China Or an Historical Essay: Endeavouring a Probability That the Language of the Empire of China Is the Primitive Language, Spoken Through the Whole Word, Before the Confusion of Babel*, 1678; David E. Mungello, *Curious Land : Jesuit Accommodation and the Origins of Sinology* (Honolulu: University of Hawaii Press, 1989), 179; For a discussion of the tensions this introduced to how the Chinese were depicted see: Eun Kyung Min, "China between the Ancients and the Moderns," *The Eighteenth Century* 45, no. 2 (2004): 115–29.

of the "curio" was stripped away, they contributed to a sense of Western superiority as Europeans used them to confirm their own biases.[29]

Colonial Expansion and Looted Book Collections

Despite Europeans' long-standing interest in collecting "Oriental" books, the Early Modern period also saw the intentional erasure of some textual cultures at the hands of European empire builders: the fires of New Spain, for instance, burned uncounted Latin American codices.[30] Those fires augured enlightenment chauvinism, which saw the maturation of European views of "other" cultures as not only alien, but also inferior. Such nascent notions of Western superiority combined with the very real need to deal with colonial governance in Persian, Malay, and other languages. Libraries transformed into more than symbolic centers: they became repositories for materials which could provide a foundation for exerting rule over subject populations.[31]

During the nineteenth century, a global plundering of libraries transferred textual wealth to a number of European libraries and museums. As John Hodgson has noted:

> Institutional collections at the heart of empire continually reaffirmed—indeed re-enacted—British conquests (military, political and cultural). Manuscripts thus functioned as instruments of colonial intelligence gathering and control...[32]

While it is certainly true that libraries around the world and through most periods of time have always been targets for theft and destruction,

---

29 On the rise of Sinophobia see: Ashley Eva Millar, "Revisiting the Sinophilia/Sinophobia Dichotomy in the European Enlightenment through Adam Smith's 'Duties of Government,'' *Asian Journal of Social Science* 38 (2010): 716–37.

30 Elizabeth Hill Boone, *Cycles of Time and Meaning in the Mexican Books of Fate* (University of Texas Press, 2013), 1-5.; For a consideration of Arabic language manuscripts in Europe see: Bevilacqua, *The Republic of Arabic Letters.*

31 Here it is important to note the ambiguous place of rare book collections. Sitting somewhere between archives and museums, their political implications are only now being explored. The following two articles are useful places to begin thinking through convergences and divergences: Gina Athena Ulysse, "Skin Castles," *Third Text* 33, no. 4–5 (September 3, 2019): 521–39, https://doi.org/10.1080/09528822.2019.1654780; Jennifer R O'Neal, "'The Right to Know': Decolonizing Native American Archives," *The Right to Know*, 2015, 19.

32 John R. Hodgson, "'Spoils of Many a Distant Land': The Earls of Crawford and the Collecting of Oriental Manuscripts in the Nineteenth Century," *The Journal of Imperial and Commonwealth History* 48, no. 6 (November 1, 2020): 1011–47, https://doi.org/10.1080/03086534.2020.1765532.

what occurred during the nineteenth century far surpassed previous levels.[33] Examples of lootings abound. Consider, for example, the case of Indonesia. In 1812, Anglo-Indian troops sacked the palaces of Yogyakarta on the island of Java, an event precipitated by the arrival of the English in Indonesia as part of the Napoleonic wars.[34] After the battle, the prize commission did as they were designed to do, auctioning loot to the highest bidders.[35] The palace was stripped of valuables, through four whole days of "an unending stream of booty being carried to the Residency and on ox-carts and on the backs of porters," the palace archives and its manuscripts were specifically targeted by John Crawfurd (1783-1868) and several other British agents.[36]

Looted manuscripts from Yogyakarta left Java with British officers. These materials included not only manuscripts, but also a large number of archival documents which would later end up in several English collections. The manuscripts that belonged to Thomas Stamford Raffles were given to the Royal Asiatic Society in 1830; most of John Crawfurd's manuscripts were sold to the British Museum in 1840.[37] Crawfurd's asking sum of £526 was deemed too high for what was deemed the "lowest class of oriental literature," and he eventually accepted the price of £250.[38] In their new home, removed from their original context, the Javanese manuscripts remained mostly neglected. Their recent digital repatriation has allowed for a new generation of scholars to explore their significance.[39]

---

33 Joshua Ehrlich, "Plunder and Prestige: Tipu Sultan's Library and the Making of British India," *South Asia: Journal of South Asian Studies* 43, no. 3 (May 3, 2020): 478–92.

34 Peter Carey, in *The Power of Prophecy: Prince Dipanagara and the End of an Old Order in Java,* 1785-1855 (Brill, 2007), 261–344.

35 Margot C. Finn, "Material Turns in British History: I. Loot," *Transactions of the Royal Historical Society* 28 (December 2018): 17.

36 P. B. R. Carey, *The Power of Prophecy: Prince Dipanagara and the End of an Old Order in Java, 1785-1855* (Kitlv Press, 2007), 350.

37 405 Th C. van der Meij, *Indonesian Manuscripts from the Islands of Java, Madura, Bali and Lombok* (Brill, 2017).

38 Peter B. Carey and Annabel Gallop, "The Origins of the John Crawfurd Collection of Javanese Manuscripts in the British Library: An Overview," *The Archive of Yogyakarta; Volume I: Documents Relating to Politics and Internal Court Affairs*, 8, accessed January 9, 2021, https://www.academia.edu/43066387/The_Origins_of_the_John_Crawfurd_Collection_of_Javanese_Manuscripts_in_the_British_Library_An_Overview.

39 For background on the India Office library and its many roles see: Rajeshwari Datta, "The India Office Library: Its History, Resources, and Functions," *The Library Quarterly: Information, Community, Policy* 36, no. 2 (1966): 99–148.

While the fall of Yogyakarta and the looting of its manuscripts never much interested English reading publics, the fall of Maqdala, in Ethiopia, and the looting of its library, was discussed in the news.[40] Like the collection in Yogyakarta, the manuscripts in Maqdala were collected from across Ethiopia to support the self-legitimating agenda of Emperor Tewodros II (r. 1855-1868).[41] Manuscripts for the library were collected from Gondar, which foreign observers claimed Tewodros plundered for "prayer-books, their other old documents" before setting the churches on fire, as well as other locations.[42]

The British invaded Ethiopia because emperor Tewodros imprisoned several missionaries in frustration after years of seeking British support to quell rebellions. The English expedition saw the captives released without harm but resulted in Tewodros committing suicide to avoid capture. When Maqdala was taken by the English in April 1868, the English found the "plunder collected by the King," including "tons of Geez and Amharic manuscripts" in the treasury.[43] These materials were gathered by prize officers.[44] When the manuscripts were put up to auction by the prize agent, Richard Rivington Holmes, who was the official "archeologist" appointed by the British museum, bid aggressively to secure as many manuscripts as possible.[45]

One interesting aspect about Holmes and the prize-auction of the manuscripts is that they represented the result of an intentional policy of systematic manuscript collection. Even before the campaign was launched, officials had determined that Ethiopic manuscripts were of interest to the empire. In 1867, John Winter Jones (1805-1881), the Principal Librarian of the British Museum wrote to the Secretary of the State of India (who was in charge of the operation), noting the importance of Ethiopic sources to "various branches of learning." He wrote that:

---

40 For an interesting example of an anti-looting view written by an American reporter see: *Public Opinion*, 1868, July 18. pg 68.

41 Metikou Ourgay, "Libraries in Ethiopia before 1900," *International Library Review* 23, no. 4 (December 1, 1991): 395, https://doi.org/10.1016/0020-7837(91)90009-O.

42 Rita Pankhurst, "The Library of Emperor Tewodros II at Mäqdäla (Magdala)," *Bulletin of the School of Oriental and African Studies, University of London* 36, no. 1 (1973): 15.

43 Sir Clements Robert Markham and William Francis Prideaux, *A History of the Abyssinian Expedition* (Macmillan, 1869), 358.

44 Pankhurst, "The Library of Emperor Tewodros II at Mäqdäla (Magdala)," 17–18.

45 Pankhurst, 19–20.

> Abyssinia, moreover, possess one of the oldest Christian Churches in the East, and it may be reasonably anticipated that numerous ancient manuscripts must have been preserved there....the Trustees are desirous to recommend to her Majesty's Government that a competent archaeologist accompany the force ... to collect inscriptions, coins, gems, manuscripts, ethnographical and other objects, and, as occasion might offer, transport them to England, for the trustees of the British Museum.[46]

While the campaign into Ethiopia was considered excessively expensive over a matter of 'honor,' for Jones and the trustees, it was an opportunity for bibliographical acquisitions.

When Holmes returned to England with the nearly 300 manuscripts he acquired, they were turned over to Orientalist William Wright (1830-1889) of the British Museum, who became professor of Arabic at Cambridge in 1870. Wright's career illustrates how, whether they liked it or not, even arm-chair Orientalists were beneficiaries of empire. Born in India, the Scotsman's first positions was as a Professor of Arabic at the University College London, where part of his duties included training future colonial officers in Persian, an important language for governing India. From 1861-1869, he worked for the British museum in the manuscripts section.

When the Maqdala manuscripts arrived at the British Museum, there was initially excitement that they might contain texts lost in other Christian tradition. The importance of the Maqdala manuscripts in England had nothing to do with an attempt to better understand Ethiopia or its important place in history. [47] Instead, they became part of the grand Protestant tradition of seeking to excavate a truer version of Christian history from allegedly ancient documents. Wright vied for the privilege of cataloging the manuscripts: he soon discovered that the looted manuscripts were not sufficiently "ancient" to be of substantial scholarly interest beyond the field of semetics, as he noted in

---

46 Great Britain Parliament House of Commons, *Accounts and Papers of the House of Commons* (Ordered to be printed, 1868), 370.

47 Richard Ovenden, *Burning the Books: A History of the Deliberate Destruction of Knowledge* (Harvard University Press, 2020), 180 provides a nuanced reading of the Magdala manuscritps. For a discussion of digital repatriation of the Javanese manuscripts from Yogyakarta see: "Javanese Manuscripts from Yogyakarta Digitisation Project Completed–Asian and African Studies Blog," accessed March 2, 2021, https://blogs.bl.uk/asian-and-african/2019/04/javanese-manuscripts-from-yogyakarta-digitisation-project-completed.html.

his preface.[48] Indeed, he described the project as "wearisome, laborious, and thankless work, for which even those who profit by it never seem thankful."[49]

While Wright's letters and his own scholarship are generally devoid of much political content, part of the reason for his ultimate lack of enthusiasm for the collection was because they failed to play into his fantasies of an ancient and unchanging Ethiopic church. Like many of his generation, we could generously call Wright "paternalistic" in his views of non-Whites, and when contemporary realities intruded on his love of antiquity, he was generally displeased—as when he called the Shah of Qajar Iran a "dirty mushroom" and reflected on the "great misfortune" of the "sudden emancipation" of enslaved Black Americans, noting "this race is not prepared for unrestrained freedom."[50] Blackness in antiquity was perhaps not a problem for Wright, or even the British Museum's manuscript collections, but contemporary Blackness left much to be desired.

The looting of libraries for political prestige was, of course, not a new phenomenon in world history. As Joshua Ehrlich has described, Tipu Sultan built a library of symbolic importance from the collections of defeated rivals, which it maintained even after being dissected by the English.[51] In the late sixteenth century, Toyotomo Hideyoshi's invasion of Korea likewise saw the pillaging of Korean books for Japanese collections.[52] Yet, the global-imperial context of the nineteenth century made this looting qualitatively different. Libraries and museums in metropoles became charged spaces both for displaying conquests and researching conquered peoples. Earlier "looters" built libraries of books that they did not see as having been produced by

---

48 British museum : Department of Oriental printed books and manuscripts and William Wright, *Catalogue of the Ethiopic Manuscripts in the British Museum Acquired Since the Year 1847* (Gilbert and Rivington, 1877).

49 Bernhard Maier, *Semitic Studies in Victorian Britain: A Portrait of William Wright and His World through His Letters* (Würzburg: Ergon-Verl., 2011), 56 He mentions vying for the catalog in a letter from 1872 (220) and by 1875, refers to the work as "stupid" (228).

50 Maier, 85, 83.

51 Ehrlich, "Plunder and Prestige."

52 Peter Kornicki, "Books in the Service of Politics: Tokugawa Ieyasu as Custodian of the Books of Japan," *Journal of the Royal Asiatic Society (Third Series)* 18, no. 01 (January 2008): 71–82; Peter Kornicki, "Korean Books in Japan: From the 1590s to the End of the Edo Period," *Journal of the American Oriental Society* 133, no. 1 (January 2013): 71–92. It is not surprising that a hagiographic tradition was quick to establish itself. This tradition attributed superhuman qualities to Tokugawa Ieyasu (1543–1616).

inferior "others." They were part of the traditions they looted in conquest. In Europe, looted materials put into libraries were monuments to European superiority—and the display of loot in sponsored catalogs and as gifts to the Queen played a symbolic function, even if the objects themselves never went on view.[53] European empires engaged in what Carey has described as "intellectual booty capitalism in its purest form, invaluable for subsequent Western scholars, deeply impoverishing for those non-European societies who fell victim to its depredations."[54] Looted books became the stuff of a narrowly-defined body of "scholarship" that did not recognize traditions of scholarship outside of Anglo-American orientalist standards. As Yirga Gelaw Woldeyes has noted, imperial looting divorced texts from their communities by burying them in Western institutions.[55]

Canon-Formation and "Our Book History"

In the United States, the relationships between settler-colonialism, White supremacy, and research libraries are intertwined with a patently American institutions, such as land-grant universities and privately established research libraries. Anglo-Americans, who for a long time imagined themselves on the frontiers of Western civilization, did not engage in the systemic collection of materials from other cultures until arriving, in the twentieth century, at new notions of the role of the United States in the world. Area studies libraries and non-Western rare book collections were usually only a consideration after securing strong collections that exemplified the values of Anglo-American Whiteness.[56]

---

53 Here I ask the reader to consider the function of the detailed cataloging and publication of Ethiopic manuscripts. In this case, I believe that we could argue that a bibliography is an important symbolic text for signaling ownership and control: British Museum. Dept. of Oriental Printed Books and Manuscripts, and William Wright. *Catalogue of the Ethiopic Manuscripts in the British Museum Acquired since the Year 1847.* [London], 1877.

54 Carey, *The Power of Prophecy*, 352.

55 Yirga Gelaw Woldeyes, "'Holding Living Bodies in Graveyards': The Violence of Keeping Ethiopian Manuscripts in Western Institutions," *M/C Journal* 23, no. 2 (May 13, 2020), http://www.journal.media-culture.org.au/index.php/mcjournal/article/view/1621. As the Other of Europe, a land "enveloped in the dark mantle of night" was supported by Western states as it justified their colonial practices (Hegel 91).

56 For a consideration of related topics see: Salvatore, Ricardo D. *Disciplinary Conquest: U.S. Scholars in South America, 1900–1945.* Durham ; London: Duke University Press, 2016; and, Salvatore, Ricardo D. "Progress and Backwardness in Book Accumulation: Bancroft, Basadre, and Their Libraries." *Comparative Studies in Society and History* 56, no. 4 (2014): 995–1026.

One of several North American research libraries explicitly designed to celebrate Western civilization was the Huntington Library, which was built from the private collection of Henry E. Huntington and opened to the "public" in 1925.[57] Through the late nineteenth century, Henry Huntington (1850-1927) amassed his wealth in railroads and eventually property development. His wealth was built on the American conquest and colonization of the American West, which enabled the Huntington family to amass wealth in the railroad industry, light-rail, and property development.[58]

As Huntington's riches grew, his passion for books grew into an obsession. After 1900, he began collecting in earnest, spending an estimated $61,180.91 (over $2,000,000 today) on books between 1901 and 1905.[59] After 1905, he began spending even more on books, and his purchasing habits also included buying complete libraries. One of the crowning acquisitions of Huntington's collection was the purchase of the Bridgewater Library in 1917. Founded by Thomas Egerton (d. 1617), the library grew to more than 8,000 printed books and 13,000 manuscripts; its acquisition was lauded as "one of the literary treasures of America," transferring a small piece of England to California.[60] The Bridgewater Library was, in many respects, a perfect acquisition to celebrate the canon of English language and literature. Egerton and

57 "Public" merits quotes because the Huntington Library reading room is, in most cases, only open to readers with advanced degrees. This discussion of the Huntington Library could also include consideration of the Morgan Library, the Folger Shakespeare Library, and others.

58 For a consideratiion of the sanguinary roots of Huntington's wealth see: Manu Karuka, *Empire's Tracks: Indigenous Nations, Chinese Workers, and the Transcontinental Railroad* (Univ of California Press, 2019).

59 James Thorpe, *Henry Edwards Huntington: A Biography* (University of California Press, 1994), 261. A connoisseur of fine art, a horticulturist, and a philanthropist, Henry Edwards Huntington is perhaps best known as the founder of the world-renowned Huntington Library, Art Gallery, and Botanical Gardens in San Marino, California. James Thorpe's comprehensive biography of Huntington tells the richly human story of the man who became America's greatest book collector and was a leading figure in the development of southern California. Henry Edwards Huntington was born in New York State in 1850. He began working at the age of 17, eventually moved to California, and in later years was hailed for his vision in developing the street railway system that created the structure of the Los Angeles area. Always a lover of books, Huntington acquired many spectacular volumes—among them the complete Gutenberg Bible on vellum and the library of the Earl of Bridgewater. He also built a splendid art collection and established a grand botanical garden on the grounds of the buildings that would house his art and books. Then, in an act of philanthropy seldom equaled, he gave these great treasures to the public. The intimate side of Huntington's life appears in these pages, too. Thorpe has culled a vast trove of private letters, diaries, and other documents that reveal Huntington's exceptional personal qualities. The author's well-rounded biography of this unassuming yet gifted American is also richly evocative of the times in which Henry Edwards Huntington lived.

60 William Newnham Chattin Carlton, *Notes on the Bridgewater House Library* (Priv. print., 1918), 18.

his heirs new. The library had its own copy of Shakespeare's first folio and quartos printed from when he was still alive; an important Caxton; and a wide variety of manuscripts. One of the most important acquisitions in the library was undoubtedly the Elsmere Chaucer, which sits on permanent display in the Huntington's Library Exhibition Hall—feet away from a vellum Gutenberg bible and another few feet away from the necessary ode to Shakespeare. Its symbolic placement in the Exhibition Hall leaves little doubt about the importance of Anglo-American literature to the library's mission.

The Huntington Library that opened in 1925 was part of something much bigger: it was an institution that grew with explicit ties to White supremacy in the contested spaces of early California. Its first board consisted of friends of Henry Huntington, including the famed George E. Hale as well George S. Patton, father to the general of the same name.[61] Patton was a close friend of Huntington, and frequent partner in his business dealings in Southern California.[62] As a member of the Southern gentry who emigrated to California after the Civil War, he was also committed to making California a "vanguard of Aryan civilization."[63] The Library was part of this vision. He noted in a letter to Hale in 1925, that the "the intellectual development of the race" was furthered by the "establishment in California of research institutions like the Huntington Library."[64]

The library and its English books were imagined as a cultural fortress that would defend Anglo-European culture on the Western frontier. This vision was also articulated by one of the library's other early trustees, Robert Andrews Millikan (1868-1953), a towering figure in Southern California history who was appointed to the Huntington Library board of trustees in 1925. Millikan's responsibilities on the board were manifold, but as a prominent humanist-scientist, he was committed to a

---

61 On the first board and later boards see: Godfrey Davies, H. E. Huntington, and Max Farrand, "The Huntington Library as a Research Center, 1925-1927," *Huntington Library Quarterly* 11, no. 3 (1948): 293–306, https://doi.org/10.2307/3815951; For a note on Hale's fundraising activities see: Garland E. Allen, "The Eugenics Record Office at Cold Spring Harbor, 1910-1940: An Essay in Institutional History," *Osiris* 2 (1986): 263.

62 Anthony M. Platt and Cecilia Elizabeth O'Leary, *Bloodlines: Recovering Hitler's Nuremberg Laws from Patton's Trophy to Public Memorial* (Routledge, 2015), 19.

63 Platt and O'Leary, 113.

64 Platt and O'Leary, 113.

teleological vision of the history which placed White, Western civilization at the pinnacle of development.

Before Millikan's appointment to the Huntington board, his views on the superiority of "Nordic" races were already in print. In his 1924 *Science and Life*, he noted:

> And if you wish to see the practical result of this changing of "the way men think," look at the difference between our own civilization and the static civilizations of Asia... in certain sections of the world, primarily those inhabited by the Nordic race, a certain set of ideas have got a start in men's minds, the ideas of *progress* and of *responsibility*...[65]

An examination of Millikan's papers from his time on the board of the Huntington illustrates that he was not alone in his enthusiasm for promoting the unique achievements of the "Nordic" or Anglo-Saxon race. Instead, he, the executive board, and librarians all worked together to make the Library, which was "at the furthest outpost of Arian Nordic civilization" (as Milliken called Los Angeles), a center to celebrate and better the White race.[66]

A 1927 framing document produced by the first director of the library, Max Farrand, described the importance of the Huntington in similar terms. Farrand congratulated the board and Huntington for creating a library dedicated to "the development of Anglo-American civilization." The mission was, he crowed, "greater than that which controls the Library of Congress or even the British Museum."[67] Similar sentiments were echoed by Louis B. Wright in 1932, when he noted the centrality of studying the English Renaissance for understanding modern American society.[68] Voiced by several members of the Huntington's board,

65 Robert Andrews Millikan, *Science and Life* (Pilgrim Press, 1924), 11.

66 Quotation cited in Peter Sachs Collopy, "Caltech and Eugenic Sterilization: Science and Power Entwined" (July 2020), 7.

67 CalTech Archives, Robert A. Millikan papers. Reel 13.300

68 CalTech Archives, Robert A. Millikan papers .Reel 13.504

such statements demonstrate the symbolic importance of the library in broader White supremacist agendas.[69]

The Library's White supremacy sometimes crept into public view, too. Millikan, along with other members of the Huntington Board of Trustees, joined a campaign to keep San Marino White.[70] In February 1942, when race restrictions on property ownership were set to expire, the San Marino Civic Betterment Association wrote to Millikan and other Huntington trustees to ensure their support for the restrictions. The restrictions read:

> No portion or part of said lots or parcels of land shall ever at anytime be used or occupied by or permitted to be used or occupied by any person whose blood is not entirely of the White or Caucasian race exception that persons not of the White or Caucasian race may be kept thereon by such White or Caucasian occupant strictly in the capacity of servants or employees of such occupant.[71]

Since the Huntington Library could never be sold, Millikan and the board of trustees saw no need to sign the covenant. However, the financial arm of the Huntington estate, the Huntington Land and Improvement Co. was advised by Millikan that it was in a different situation.[72]

The case of the Huntington Library may not seem to be in same genealogy as imperial looting or curio collecting. But if we consider the funding for libraries like the Huntington, we see how powerful forces combined financial and symbolic commitment to make libraries which would reflect an idealized America. The American "industrialist" could build libraries because of profits from America's imperial violence.[73] Much like the collection in the British Museum, the wealth generated by American settler colonialism and chattel slavery (especially in

---

69 Importantly Millikan also joined the board of the Pasadena-based Human Betterment Foundation in 1938—an institution founded in 1928 to research and advocate for mass sterilization efforts—of which he spoke glowingly See: Collopy, "Caltech and Eugenic Sterilization: Science and Power Entwined."

70 Platt and O'Leary, *Bloodlines*, 129.

71 CalTech Archives, Robert A. Millikan papers Reel 13.944

72 Platt and O'Leary, *Bloodlines*, 130.

73 On the soruces of Huntington's wealth see also: William Friedricks, "Henry E. Huntington and Real Estate Development in Southern California, 1898-1917," *Southern California Quarterly* 71, no. 4 (1989): 327–40, https://doi.org/10.2307/41171454; William B. Friedricks, *Henry E. Huntington and the Creation of Southern California* (Ohio State University Press, 1992).

the case of several important university library special collections) supported library building. The values of settler colonialism, including White supremacy, inspired American elites and library boards to build collections of rare books.

The multiculturalism of a metropolitan collection like the British Museum was a danger on the frontier of California, and this can be seen in recent controversies surrounding the acquisition of the Octavia Butler papers, in which readers of color have felt excluded.[74] Rather than acquiring curiosities or through conquests, Huntington and his board attempted to create and fortify identities valued primarily in terms of their proximity to Whiteness. Even with well-intentioned curators, White supremacist legacies still define many collections, and as Jesse Erikson has noted, its ghosts are haunting the "gentleman's study" design of many reading rooms.[75]

Conclusion

While varied in their specifics, the cases outlined in this essay are all framed by the context of Euro-American global hegemony as it developed from the early modern period into modernity. Each of these values—curiosity, colonialism, and canon—are indelibly linked to intellectual values generated by White supremacy as they have manifested in special collections libraries in the West. Using these terms as they intertwine with concepts of Racial capitalism, we can see how identities associated with the producers of books shaped their value for collecting repositories. In the case of Chinese books—simple commercial imprints became ciphers for Europeans to ponder—and their material features made them curiosities to be marveled at. The Maqdala manuscripts tapped into European beliefs that a somehow more primitive Africa had preserved lost texts. Once this proved untrue, their value

74 Cecilia Caballero, "Mothering While Brown in White Spaces, Or, When I Took My Son to Octavia Butler's Exhibit," mysite, August 23, 2017, https://www.chicanamotherwork.com/single-post/2017/08/23/mothering-while-brown-in-white-spaces-or-when-i-took-my-son-to-octavia-butler-s-exhibit. Owing to early complaints around the acquisition of the papers, the library has established fellowships to provide support for new users.

75 Jesse Ryan Erickson, "The Gentleman's Ghost: Patriachrchal Eurocentric Legacies in Special Collections Design," in *Archives and Special Collections as Sites of Contestation*, ed. Mary Kandiuk (Sacramento, CA: Library Juice Press, 2020), 121–59. It should be noted that in the last decade the Huntington Library has been engaged in critically reassesing its historically problematic collecting practices. Especially important in this regard has been its continued work with Chinese American communities under the curatorial guidance of Li Wei Yang.

diminished in the eyes of both their cataloger and the British museum. Finally, the Huntington Library was built explicitly to celebrate White Western achievements. Even as the institution has changed, the permanent exhibition hall still tells this story.

I think it should now be clear that to some extent all rare book collections are products of ideology—one that is often solidified in collection development policies. The fantasy of a collecting institution where "learning" is free from political entanglements needs to be abandoned. The decision to collect any rare book within an institutional framework has always been both a financial and symbolic decision. It costs money, time, and effort to acquire, catalog, and preserve books, and it's critical to remember that collecting priorities are intellectual and political ones priorities that derive many of their ideas of value from racial capitalism. The fact that UCLA's collection of palm leaf manuscripts remains uncatalogued, neglected as a legacy acquisition that doesn't quite "fit," speaks to the tensions of racial capitalism as it contributed to developing global book histories. "We'll take it" we say, while never really imagining what to do with these acquisitions. The curio made possible by a hegemonic, colonial world, gets shunted into a storage room. While global book history shows us how individual books could be objects with global histories, and how more broadly defined book cultures are interdependent, these histories have yet to reckon with how institutional trends in collecting can reveal systemic changes that reflect how White supremacy and racial capitalism have helped to constitute encyclopedic collections of rare books in the West.

Bibliography

Allen, Garland E. “The Eugenics Record Office at Cold Spring Harbor, 1910-1940: An Essay in Institutional History.” *Osiris* 2 (1986): 225–64.

Appadurai, Arjun, and Arjun Appadurai, eds. *The Social Life of Things: Commodities in Cultural Perspective*. Cambridge University Press, 1988.

Bedini, Silvio A. *The Pope’s Elephant*. Penguin Books, 2000.

Bevilacqua, Alexander. *The Republic of Arabic Letters: Islam and the European Enlightenment*. Belknap Press of Harvard University Press, 2018.

Boehmer, Elleke, Rouven Kunstmann, Priyasha Mukhopadhyay, and Asha Rogers. *The Global Histories of Books: Methods and Practices*. Springer, 2017.

Boone, Elizabeth Hill. *Cycles of Time and Meaning in the Mexican Books of Fate*. University of Texas Press, 2013.

Brook, Timothy. *Mr. Selden’s Map of China: Decoding the Secrets of a Vanished Cartographer*. Bloomsbury Publishing USA, 2013.

Caballero, Cecilia. “Mothering While Brown in White Spaces, Or, When I Took My Son to Octavia Butler’s Exhibit.” mysite, August 23, 2017. https://www.chicanamotherwork.com/single-post/2017/08/23/mothering-while-brown-in-white-spaces-or-when-i-took-my-son-to-octavia-butler-s-exhibit.

Carey, P. B. R. *The Power of Prophecy: Prince Dipanagara and the End of an Old Order in Java, 1785-1855*. KITLV Press, 2007.

Carey, Peter. “The End of the Beginning;: The Last Months of the Franco-Dutch Government and the British Rape of Yogyakarta, 1811-1812.” In *The Power of Prophecy*, 249:261–344. Prince Dipanagara and the End of an Old Order in Java, 1785-1855. Brill, 2007. https://www.jstor.org/stable/10.1163/j.ctvbqs55t.12.

Carey, Peter B., and Annabel Gallop. “The Origins of the John Crawfurd Collection of Javanese Manuscripts in the British Library: An Overview.” *The Archive of Yogyakarta; Volume I: Documents Relating to Politics and Internal Court Affairs*. Accessed January 9, 2021. https://www.academia.edu/43066387/The_Origins_of_the_John_Crawfurd_Collection_of_Javanese_Manuscripts_in_the_British_Library_An_Overview.

Carlton, William Newnham Chattin. *Notes on the Bridgewater House Library*. Priv. print., 1918.

Chan, Albert. *Chinese Materials in the Jesuit Archives in Rome, 14th-20th Centuries: A Descriptive Catalogue: A Descriptive Catalogue*. Routledge, 2015.

Cohen, Monique. “A Point of History: The Chinese Books Presented to the National Library in Paris by Joachim Bouvet S.J., in 1697.” *Chinese culture* 31.4 (Dec. 1990), pp. 39-48.

Collopy, Peter Sachs. “Caltech and Eugenic Sterilization: Science and Power Entwined.” CalTech report. July 2020. https://inclusive.caltech.edu/documents/18182/CNR_Report_FINAL.pdf. If you look at the bibliography (page 76), the referenced report is only cited as in possession of the committee. We can get alrification from author when they review proofs.

Commons, Great Britain Parliament House of. *Accounts and Papers of the House of Commons*. Ordered to be printed, 1868.

Daston, Lorraine, and Katharine Park. *Wonders and the Order of Nature, 1150-1750*. New York, NY: Zone Books, 2012.

Datta, Rajeshwari. "The India Office Library: Its History, Resources, and Functions." *The Library Quarterly: Information, Community, Policy* 36, no. 2 (1966): 99–148.

Davies, Godfrey, H. E. Huntington, and Max Farrand. "The Huntington Library as a Research Center, 1925-1927." *Huntington Library Quarterly* 11, no. 3 (1948): 293–306. https://doi.org/10.2307/3815951.

Ehrlich, Joshua. "Plunder and Prestige: Tipu Sultan's Library and the Making of British India." *South Asia: Journal of South Asian Studies* 43, no. 3 (May 3, 2020): 478–92. https://doi.org/10.1080/00856401.2020.1739863.

Erickson, Jesse Ryan. "Rethinking the Library Response to Black Literacy." UCLA, 2016. https://escholarship.org/uc/item/1023g7nx.

———. "The Gentleman's Ghost: Patriachrchal Eurocentric Legacies in Special Collections Design." In *Archives and Special Collections as Sites of Contestation*, edited by Mary Kandiuk, 121–59. Library Juice Press, 2020.

Evans, R. J. W. *Curiosity and Wonder from the Renaissance to the Enlightenment*. Routledge, 2017.

Finn, Margot C. "Material Turns in British History: I. Loot." *Transactions of the Royal Historical Society* 28 (December 2018): 5–32. https://doi.org/10.1017/S0080440118000026.

Fitzgerald, Devin T. "The Ming Open Archive and the Global Reading of Early Modern China." PhD Thesis, Harvard University, 2020.

Friedricks, William. "Henry E. Huntington and Real Estate Development in Southern California, 1898-1917." *Southern California Quarterly* 71, no. 4 (1989): 327–40. https://doi.org/10.2307/41171454.

Friedricks, William B. *Henry E. Huntington and the Creation of Southern California*. Ohio State University Press, 1992.

Helliwell, David. "The Bodleian Library's Chinese Collection in the Seventeenth Century." Draft paper, 2016.

Hodgson, John R. "'Spoils of Many a Distant Land': The Earls of Crawford and the Collecting of Oriental Manuscripts in the Nineteenth Century." *The Journal of Imperial and Commonwealth History* 48, no. 6 (November 1, 2020): 1011–47. https://doi.org/10.1080/03086534.2020.1765532.

"Javanese Manuscripts from Yogyakarta Digitisation Project Completed–Asian and African Studies Blog." Accessed March 2, 2021. https://blogs.bl.uk/asian-and-african/2019/04/javanese-manuscripts-from-yogyakarta-digitisation-project-completed.html.

Karuka, Manu. *Empire's Tracks: Indigenous Nations, Chinese Workers, and the Transcontinental Railroad*. University of California Press, 2019.

Kornicki, Peter. "Books in the Service of Politics: Tokugawa Ieyasu as Custodian of the Books of Japan." *Journal of the Royal Asiatic Society (Third Series)* 18, no. 01 (January 2008): 71–82.

———. "Korean Books in Japan: From the 1590s to the End of the Edo Period." *Journal of the American Oriental Society* 133, no. 1 (January 2013): 71–92.

Leong, Nancy. "Racial Capitalism." Accessed June 30, 2021. https://harvardlawreview.org/2013/06/racial-capitalism/.

Leung, Cécile. *Etienne Fourmont, 1683-1745: Oriental and Chinese Languages in Eighteenth-Century France*. Leuven University Press, 2002.

Maier, Bernhard. *Semitic Studies in Victorian Britain: A Portrait of William Wright and His World through His Letters*. Würzburg: Ergon-Verl., 2011.

manuscripts, British museum : Department of Oriental printed books and, and William Wright. *Catalogue of the Ethiopic Manuscripts in the British Museum Acquired Since the Year 1847*. Gilbert and Rivington, 1877.

Markey, Lia. *Imagining the Americas in Medici Florence*. Penn State Press, 2016.

Markham, Sir Clements Robert, and William Francis Prideaux. *A History of the Abyssinian Expedition*. Macmillan, 1869.

Meij, Th C. van der. *Indonesian Manuscripts from the Islands of Java, Madura, Bali and Lombok*. Brill, 2017.

Millar, Ashley Eva. "Revisiting the Sinophilia/Sinophobia Dichotomy in the European Enlightenment through Adam Smith's 'Duties of Government." *Asian Journal of Social Science* 38 (2010): 716–37.

Millikan, Robert Andrews. *Science and Life*. Pilgrim Press, 1924.

Min, Eun Kyung. "China between the Ancients and the Moderns." *The Eighteenth Century* 45, no. 2 (2004): 115–29.

Mungello, David E. *Curious Land : Jesuit Accommodation and the Origins of Sinology*. University of Hawaii Press, 1989.

O'Neal, Jennifer R. "'The Right to Know': Decolonizing Native American Archives." *The Right to Know*, 2015, 19.

Ourgay, Metikou. "Libraries in Ethiopia before 1900." *International Library Review* 23, no. 4 (December 1, 1991): 391–99. https://doi.org/10.1016/0020-7837(91)90009-O.

Ovenden, Richard. *Burning the Books: A History of the Deliberate Destruction of Knowledge*. Harvard University Press, 2020.

Pankhurst, Rita. "The Library of Emperor Tewodros II at Mäqdäla (Magdala)." *Bulletin of the School of Oriental and African Studies, University of London* 36, no. 1 (1973): 15–42.

Platt, Anthony M., and Cecilia Elizabeth O'Leary. *Bloodlines: Recovering Hitler's Nuremberg Laws from Patton's Trophy to Public Memorial*. Routledge, 2015.

Poole, William. "'All Mr Boyl's Pieces': Robert Boyle and the Bodleian Library." *On the Boyle*, no. 10 (Spring 2017): 1–25.

———. "The Letters of Shen Fuzong to Thomas Hyde, 1687-88." *The Electronic British Library Journal*, January 1, 2015, 1.

Public Opinion, 1868.

Salvatore, Ricardo. *Disciplinary Conquest*. Duke University Press, 2016. https://doi.org/10.1215/9780822374503.

Salvatore, Ricardo D. "Progress and Backwardness in Book Accumulation: Bancroft, Basadre, and Their Libraries." *Comparative Studies in Society and History* 56, no. 4 (2014): 995–1026.

Selm, Bert Van. "Cornelis Claesz's 1605 Stock Catalogue of Chinese Books." *Quaerendo* 13, no. 4 (January 1, 1983): 247–59. https://doi.org/10.1163/157006983X00218.

Standaert, Nicolas. "Jean-François Foucquet's Contribution to the Establishment of Chinese Book Collections in European Libraries: Circulation of Chinese Books." *Monumenta Serica* 63, no. 2 (July 3, 2015): 361–424.

Suarez, Michael F. *The Book: A Global History*. OUP Oxford, 2013.

The Oxford Illustrated History of the Book. Oxford Illustrated History. Oxford University Press, 2020.

Thorpe, James. *Henry Edwards Huntington: A Biography*. University of California Press, 1994.

Ulysse, Gina Athena. "Skin Castles." *Third Text* 33, no. 4–5 (September 3, 2019): 521–39. https://doi.org/10.1080/09528822.2019.1654780.

Webb, John. *The Antiquity of China Or an Historical Essay: Endeavouring a Probability That the Language of the Empire of China Is the Primitive Language, Spoken Through the Whole Word, Before the Confusion of Babel*, 1678.

Woldeyes, Yirga Gelaw. "'Holding Living Bodies in Graveyards': The Violence of Keeping Ethiopian Manuscripts in Western Institutions." *M/C Journal* 23, no. 2 (May 13, 2020). http://www.journal.media-culture.org.au/index.php/mcjournal/article/view/1621.

Distributed and Conditional Documents

Conceptualizing Bibliographical Alterities

Johanna Drucker

To conceptualize a future history of the book we have to recognize that our understanding of the bibliographical object of the past is challenged by the ontologically unbound, distributed, digital, and networked conditions of the present. As we draw on rich intellectual traditions, we must keep in view the need to let go of the object-centered approach that is at the heart of book history. For this reason, this seems an apt moment to emphasize scholarship of books in the period of colonial expansion and cross-cultural encounter (particularly, though not exclusively, that of the 17th and 18th centuries). In part because of the character of the works they study, scholars working in this area put ideas of performative materialities into the context of networked environments as a basic framework for their analysis. We know that classic studies in bibliography have emphasized the understanding that textual artifacts are frequently constituted through complex processes and received through the parallax of varying cultural, social, or historical perspectives. Taken to their logical extension, such approaches suggest that cultural artifacts are constituted within cycles of circulation where lines between production and reception blur.[1] But in book history, an object-centered approach persists, even, as we shall see, in revisionist models of the field. We have to shift outside its modern or Western frames to grasp an alternative conception—in which a *book is conceived as a distributed object*, not a

1 See McKenzie, 1986; McGann, 1983.

thing, but *a set of intersecting events, material conditions*, and *activities*. Books, documents, textual artifacts can no longer be thought of as autonomous objects that circulate in a context, but must be reconceptualized as event spaces within an ecology of changing conditions.

My argument begins, therefore, with a few assertions. First, that we have much to learn from the scholarship on Old and New World contact that touches on bibliography, document studies, and book history for formulating a non-object centered conception of what a book is. Why begin with scholarship focused on artifacts composed three or four hundred years ago? Because contact experiences unsettled every certainty that had been in place in the Renaissance, shaking the foundations of historical, religious, geographical, and philosophical knowledge across nearly every domain. The importance of these exchanges has registered in theoretical and critical writings with increasing frequency in recent decades. Second, that the insights from these studies can be usefully combined with a theory of the "conditional" document to develop the model of the kinds of distributed artifacts we encounter on a daily basis in the networked conditions of current practices.[2] Finally, I would suggest that this model provides a different conception of artifacts (books, documents, works of textual or graphic art), one in which reception is production and therefore all materiality is subject to performative engagement within varied, and specific, conditions of encounter.

Twenty years ago, in his groundbreaking book, *The Darker Side of the Renaissance*, Walter Mignolo argued that European colonization in the Renaissance was replicated by scholarly practices up into the present because they assessed "other" cultures' textual practices from a Western perspective. One of his examples was standard account of writing systems, derived from the work of such well-respected scholars as Ignace Gelb and David Diringer.[3] Mignolo's argument was that these performed their "colonization" by normalizing the history of inscriptions on the basis of Western alphabetic scripts. In their accounts, writing systems "developed" through a series of "progressive" stages from "proto-writing" in pictures and signs to an advanced "true" alphabetic script, which was taken to be the highest level of achievement in this technological matrix.

2 The phrase *conditional document* is mine.

3 See Mignolo, 1995; Diringer, 1948; Gelb, 1963.

We should keep in mind, *pace* Mignolo, that Diringer and Gelb, among others in the early and mid-20th century, were still piecing together the archaeological evidence on which such a master narrative could be constructed. Well into the 19th century, a figure like the British cleric and scholar, Charles Forster, was still tracking the "one primeval" language and attributing the invention of writing to a divine origin.[4] Chronologies of human history were based on biblical accounting, and only went back 4-5,000 years until geological evidence to the contrary made its way into scientific and historical perception. Thus the "modern" formulation of progress has to be seen in its own historical frame. Still, as Mignolo points out, the typology of the Diringer/Gelb approach, which underpins current studies of the history of writing and the alphabet, enforced a binaristic hierarchy in which the writing systems of the New World, in particular, were always subject to a prejudicial judgment and characterized as inferior, inadequate, or undeveloped: writing systems in Mayan glyphic inscriptions and Aztec codices never "reached" the alphabetic stage.

Not only is it impossible to fit these non-Western materials into a standard model of textual production and bibliographical studies, but, in the larger point Mignolo makes, a confrontation between that standard model of writing, literacy, and books can be staged on the basis of a fresh encounter with these indigenous materials and their conditions of production and use. In essence, Mignolo is launching an attack on the *fundamental coloniality of knowledge in the realm of bibliographical studies* and suggesting that it be rethought (Mignolo, 1995).

If we take this seriously, the challenge is to think about what a future history of the book would look like if it began its formulation with New World examples of writing included from the outset. Rather than add (or try to add) indigenous glyphs, signs, quipu, and wampum as anomalies or exceptions to a "normative" bibliography, we would formulate a broader, more inclusive field of practices and works on which bibliographical studies could be constructed. Similar sentiments and impulses can be found in the small but growing literature that scholar Jesse Erickson designates with the term "ethno-bibliography" and that Jason Hewitt also called to my attention within his study of "fundamental semiosis," which examines the emergence of signs within

4 See Foster, 1851-1854.

human cognition and culture.[5] Inspired by their comments and the work of Mignolo, my argument takes up studies by Robert Fraser, Birgit Rasmussen, Betty Booth Donahue, D.F. McKenzie, Jared Diamond, Jerome McGann, and Phillip Round, and others, to make a general proposal about how to put this changed concept of "the book" into dialogue with the prevailing/current models of book history and to think through the implications of this for our collective approach to pedagogy in the field.[6]

In his work on encounters between old and new world cultures, Jared Diamond makes the point that "guns, germs, and steel" and "alpha-numeric notation" were not "superior technologies" to those found among the indigenous people, but they were embedded in a technological system that allowed "instrumentalization of control" in a way that shifted and skewed power relations from the outset (Diamond, 1998). In other words, a techno-ecology, not technology, is what we have to examine if we are to understand the contact encounters—and more important, learn from them. The imprint of the "technology" model—the core of which is what Mignolo is pointing to in his analysis of the "progressive" version of writing systems "advancing" towards the alphabetic—is still so present and prevalent that we barely see it. The naturalization of colonial power in knowledge production—*ours*—successfully conceals its workings. How to undo this?

Before I answer that question by turning to the work of some of the authors mentioned above, let me pause to situate the argument I will make within the intellectual traditions in which book historians have developed a well-articulated series of successive paradigms for the field. Each builds on and extends (sometimes contests) the other: from the bibliographical attention to descriptions of objects; the reconstruction of their production; authentication of their intellectual content; study of their impact and effects; analysis of their lineages and genealogies.[7] "Histories of the book" usually map the development of writing, early codes for recording speech or language acts, and the sequence of technologies from sticks to clay to brushes, papyrus, leather,

---

5 Jesse Erickson and Jason Taksony Hewitt, both in conversations within the context of their doctoral studies at UCLA. I'm indebted to both Erickson and Hewitt for their contributions to my education in this area, and to the future directions their work suggests for the fields of information studies and bibliography/book history.

6 See Fraser, 2012; Donahue, 2011; Round, 2010; McKenzie, 1985; Mignolo, 1995.

7 Douglas McMurtrie's *The Book: The Story of Printing and Bookmaking* (1943) is the classic.

vellum, parchment, paper, and print (and recently, electronic formats and digital files). From wall and monument to tablet and scroll to codex and screen, the technological developments march along and with them a well-marked history of milestones in publication methods, major figures, important works, and shifts in the controls over intellectual property, production means, and distribution networks.

The narrative version of the "history of" is complemented by a statistical, sociological methodology associated with the French Annales school.[8] Not content with the description of physical artifacts, knowledge of their makers, or conditions of production, the Annales historians added considerable breadth by extending the field to studies of commerce, politics, economics, and other aspects of book history that would not be immediately extractable from the object, but required analysis of account books, documents and records, and other historical materials. The very act of periodization, such as that performed by Roger Chartier in his attention to the "break" between scroll and codex, and then manuscript and print, for all its benefits and virtues, reinforces certain assumptions that are readily undone when points of continuity, rather than over-determined notions of difference, are brought into play (Chartier, 1992). A historical approach based on changes in technology (manuscript to print) does not necessarily map onto shifts in practices (e.g. publishing), for instance, while the study of numbers of readers, book sellers, copies in circulation offers yet other insights.

In addition to adopting techniques from the broader field of social history, book historians have created specific models for analysis in their domains. These successive models have built a series of useful intellectual frameworks for analysis in the field, beginning with Robert Darnton's "What is the History of Books?" published in 1982. Darnton's "communications circuit" emphasized the interconnection of the many agents (author, printer, binder, bookseller, etc.) in the lifecycle of a book—but the book is an autonomous object moving through this circuit. In 1993, Nicolas Barker and Thomas Adams proposed an alternative version emphasizing the dynamic "events" in that lifecycle

8 The French "Annales" School brought social history methods into play from its founding in the late 1920s to its ascendance in the 1950s-60s. Its principles and methods, a broad social history, had an impact on the history of the book. Works by Lucien Febvre had a large influence by introducing quantitative methods to complement (or even displace) narrative and descriptive historial analysis. Lucien Febvre and Henri-Jean Martin, *The Coming of the Book, the Impact of Printing 1450-1800*, (First published, Paris: Editions Albin Michel, 1958; first English edition, NY: Verso, 1976).

(publication, distribution, etc.), stressing social processes over individual human agents as the crucial elements of a book's existence (Barker and Adams, 1993). A decade later, Michael Suarez's thoughtful "Historiographical Problems and Possibilities," published in *Studies in Bibliography*, laid out the many complexities that continue to plague the development of the field of book history, including those of periodization, gaps in knowledge, the multiple dimensions of the sociology of bibliography (Suarez, 2003-2004). The bibliographical context of his publication is significant, as it signals an effort to keep critical issues from that field in dialogue with book history. Suarez's analysis exposes the difficulties of periodization in particular, and demonstrates the need for more complex and less reductive approaches. A subtle and exemplary set of studies by Adrian Johns offers a useful demonstration of historical methods, much of it dispensing earlier myths about the impact of printing technology (Johns, 1998). In *The Nature of the Book*, Johns put forward detailed individual cases that show the extent to which exceptions to generalized rules further complicate any "models" we create. The summary effect of these and other contributions to the field is to provide a highly useful set of analytic approaches that reveal different facets and aspects of objects under investigation.

Each, however, assumes the existence of a *book* as an *object, a priori*. But for works outside the Western tradition (or even within it, I will argue) the object constituted by the historical and theoretical inquiry may be an *event space*. There may not be an *object* in play at all, only a distributed condition of literacy and/or semiotic communication across physical traces and inscriptional or productive apparatus. Rather than relying on a forensic, descriptive, object-based approach for their analysis, such works may have to be conceived from a performative approach. Even where actual books are part of this alternative legacy, they call for reading of the polysemous field of their composition and conception and its performative dimensions, rather than assuming its literal, physical, or textual self-identity. Production, in other words, may not always result in an *object*, but even where it does, reception produces a performatively constituted event in response. Thus the cultural parallax described in D.F. McKenzie's still dazzling study of the "Treaty of Waitangi" has to be expanded beyond the discussion of two crossed gazes, each from a different cultural perspective, misunderstanding each other's foundations and assumptions about the symbolic and literal value of an object, a treaty. It needs to be expanded into a model in which recognition of constitutive processes replaces the assumption of an a priori object that is misread (McKenzie, 1986).

Marking, making, inscribing, reading, are all aspects of a system of social and cultural production. A semiotic object does not sit inside it, like a gem in a setting, in a context-based model of object and conditions. Instead, the object is constituted, like an organism in a medium, as an effect of the very conditions that bring it into being. In the same way that cell walls and chemical/physical/biological processes create the conditions of semi-autonomy that define a living organism in an ecological system, the semiotic "object" is an effect of constitutive conditions in the culture of which it is an integral part. Its reception is a secondary act, provoked by the material traces of production, but reception is a primary act in so far as it constitutes a text or artifact as an event, a performative reading or engagement.

If we return to the contact studies, we can see how such an approach is required. When Mignolo describes the cultural politics of encounter between Mayans and Spanish, he points to the asymmetry present from initial contact (Mignolo, 1995). The 16th century Jesuit José de Acosta "ranked writing systems according to their proximity to the alphabet," in spite of the recognition that the indigenous people had a highly developed literate culture (4). This included vocabulary designating Incan men of letters, "quipu camoyan," scribes, "tlacuilo," and surfaces for painted narratives "amoxtli" (75). Mignolo insists that we move beyond cultural relativism, particularly the sort based on comparative approaches privileging old world norms and conventions as standards on which terms of comparison are established. With rare exceptions, Mayan literacy has always been conceived from the European perspective (76). Among the exceptions, the aforementioned Acosta, who observed of the quipu that "in every bundle of these, as many greater and lesser knots and tied string [...] in short, as many differences as we have" (83).

Acosta recognizes *difference* as the basis of signs. His recognition of the fundamental non-equivalence of these semiotic systems is equally striking. He knows that the bibliographic practices based in alphabetic literacy are inadequate for addressing literacy conceived in a fundamentally different mode. Each sign systems may be as complicated as the other, but they cannot be put into a relation of reciprocity. In Nahutl, emphasis is placed on the connection between spoken words and an agent, Mignolo continues, and the Mexicans "had a set of concepts to outline their semiotic interactions"(103). If their "Sages of the Word," were resident in the "amoxtli" or surfaces, learning was located in the body of elders, transmitted orally. The Christian philosophy of the word, conceived in connections between the archetypal book (of God) and the metagraphic book (of communication), was embedded in the Franciscan view of writing and book (106). Mignolo makes clear that this distinction doesn't transfer to Nahuatl practices. None of these indigenous inscriptions is self-evident, each has to be read within the cultural ecology of signs, practices, event spaces, and knowledge technologies. How is this different from alphabetic writing, really? Is the semiotic code of alpha-numeric writing any more self-evident than quipu knottings? Any less dependent on the act of reading for its productive of significance? The differences reside in their specifics at a more fundamental level.

Perceived asymmetries and cultural obstacles to equivalence have been recognized for decades. But the implications of these contact moments of the 16th and 17th century are still present at the deeper level—in the still unarticulated recognition of the ways cultural semiotic systems emerge, organize the cultural world, and then pass themselves off as natural, erasing the process by which semiotic *conception* occurs. In other words, Mignolo's argument is not that we need better "translations" across sign systems, but that we need a way to understand *difference* and *specificity* at the level of original semiosis—in attending to the emergence and structuring effects of the formation of sign systems. The ways signs and literacy are thought, conceived, and acted are distinct in these contact zones, and the bibliographic requirements for this alternative ecology of signs can't be developed—or turned into a critical or pedagogical method—as a simple appendix or corrective.

When Mignolo discusses later developments in the 17th and 18th century exchanges and the philosophical foundations of their attitudes towards signs, writing, and history, he shows how the cross currents of belief in the "universal history" of humankind were—and are—at odds with contact experience and exchanges. Boturini Benaducci, the 18th century ethnographer, for example, in his study of quipu, undercut the idea that the alphabet was the sole authority for the historical record (151-161). Mignolo emphasizes the paramount importance of attending to description and discourse as well as objects—because the objects are constructed by the discourses of inquiry and scholarly attention precisely in so far as they align with the conceptual principles on which the discourse itself operates. In classic post-structuralist parlance, the object of knowledge is constituted, not perceived, by the discourse.

As long as difference is construed as otherness, the asymmetry of these colonializing discourse persists. To move beyond this dilemma in book history, we can rely on a few concrete examples in scholarship of the last two decades to show the way.

Elizabeth Hill Boone, whose edited volume, *Writing Without Words* was published in 1994 (also 20 years ago), was aware that she was working after two decades in which post-structuralism and deconstruction had shaken up the authority of text and power relations. Jacques Derrida's reformulation of the primacy of "writing" over the authority of "voice" was at odds with the literacy studies formulated by Jack Goody, Walter Ong, and the Canadian media theorists around Marshall McLuhan beginning in the 1960s.[9] But theoretical ambitions had a difficult time getting traction on material realities. Bibliography remained book-based, antiquarian in its attention to physical facts of collation, misprint, wrong-font and crooked sheets with overprints and recycled dingbats, cuts, or initial letters even if "grammatology" reformulated attitudes towards inscription. Bibliography met critical textual studies in the work of Jerome McGann (1993, 2001) and Dennis Tedlock (1983). Their performative concept of the text and the book, had a strong emphasis on the codependence of conditions of production and circumstances of use.[10] From these, as well as the other strains of intellectual thought already mentioned, we can begin to see both the limits of traditional bibliographical models for an encounter with "alterity" and to sketch an approach that is not "post-colonial"—i.e. a task of corrective recovery and retrospective inclusion of new examples to an old paradigm—but "de-colonizing," to use Mignolo's term, a project of rethinking the fundamental frameworks that constitute the object of inquiry at the center of our field. On what foundations, then, do we conceive

9 See Derrida, 1976; Goody, 1987; Ong, 1982; McLuhan, 1967; McLuhan, 1962.

10 McKenzie, *op.cit.* The distinction between a sociology of texts, in which the social institutions of production and value are brought to attention, and a social production of texts, in which the object is considered as a product of many processes, should be kept in mind. The first deals with an object in circulation, but finished and complete, to which value accrues through social practices. The second takes apart the autonomy and completeness of the textual object by exposing its production across many moments, persons, practices, and circumstances. The first is focused on reception history, the second on production. They complement each other. I'm attempting to fuse the two in a more radical constructivist approach that argues for constitution of the object in practice, rather than of an object that precedes apperception. Reception *is* production. I believe McGann would agree.

of the "book" that comes to figure on such grounds? What, in fact, is a "book" in this shifted frame?

The contact zones of the 16th and 17th century are places in which the assumptions underpinning Western bibliography are exposed and their limitations revealed because many of the textual and inscriptional practices are distributed in character and/or highly contingent, dependent on circumstances of use in ways that make it impossible to ignore qualities that pass with less notice in the bibliographical traditions that take the book object for granted. Literal, forensic, formal materialities, so crucial to bibliography, have to be extended by a performative understanding of materiality that engages bibliographical objects in terms of what they do, how they work, not just what they are (Kirschenbaum, 2008). This approach to performativity, this doing and working, is constitutive, and asserts that an object emerges from the co-dependent conditions in which it appears (Drucker, 2009, 2013). These codependencies occur at many levels—within the composition of the text, the structure of the object, its embedded condition within social practices, and across activities of editing and translation.

In her study of William Bradford's 17th century *Of Plimoth Plantation*, Betty Booth Donahue shows the extent to which the book is a record of the "indianization" of the colonists (Donahue, 2011). To cite Donahue, "In American Indian epistemology the earth is First Text, and the study of its features constitutes textual exegesis" (20). Within the frameworks of this alternative semiology, Donahue tracks Bradford's absorption of spatial constructs and directions, cosmology, and knowledge of natural history as they are encoded in Indian systems of language, work, and ceremony. Bradford absorbed the structuring principles of Native cosmologies into the language in the text. The work is constituted as a border zone which embodies the Native tribal leaders realization that they were preparing the land for a new narrative (5-18, 19-38). The outcome was not inevitable at the outset, and though its course is marked by fatal asymmetries, this re-reading and rethinking allow an alternate bibliography to take root as one aspect of a de-colonization of current epistemology.

Phillip Round opens his book on printing in "Indian Country," *Removable Type*, with a study of the volume commonly known as the "John Eliot Bible." He says, "In their stubborn materiality and monumental presentation, however, books were [...] useful signs of the 'visible civility' Eliot demanded from his Native parishioners" (25). He goes on to paraphrase the work of Matthew Brown, a scholar whose work emphasizes the ways "the culture of the book in Puritan New England provides us with ample opportunities to explore Euro-American settlers' representations of imagined Native peoples," and all the asymmetries that implies. But, as Round goes on to say, Brown, like many scholars, refuses to view "the books in the Indian Library as 'ethnographic facts drawn from the contact zone or as neutral sources of Algonkian expression'" (25). Round asserts, instead, that the Indian Library "actually grew out of a fundamentally unstable bicultural communicative field." Round takes apart each step of the composition of the Indian Bible, demonstrating that its translation, orthography, composition, and design function as a "crucial mediating semiotic in New England's colonial middle ground." Eliot was dependent on collaboration with Christian Indians "to work up a syllabic orthography of the Massachusett language" (26). James Printer, the "Nipmuck convert," and Job Nesuton worked closely with Eliot to produce the Bible: "The physical properties of the 1663 *Mamusse wunneetupanatamwe up biblum God* [...] reveal the collaborative, bicultural social horizon from which the Native print vernacular emerged" (27). Round goes on to note all of the details in layout, typography, and design that differentiate the Algonquian Bible from the English one, stressing the impossibility of translation: "the Algonquian vernacular cannot stretch to accommodate many of the underlying ideological principles of either Protestant doctrine or book culture that inform the Bible's production." And, "In the Algonquian edition, the concept of 'book' itself is untranslatable." Thus the pages are peppered with a kind of hybrid Algon-ish, with "words 'Booke,' 'Bibleut,' 'Chaptersash,' 'Bookut,' and 'Bookash'" (29).

Contact encounters erased the literacies and practices of indigenous people. We *know* this, but revisiting the way these encounters have been written and assessed forces a reconceptualization of bibliographical studies. This is only becoming apparent in more recent work. In *Queequeg's Coffin*, for instance, Birgit Rasmussen recounts debates about relations between knowledge, recording practices, and sign systems in the literate cultures that existed in the New World at the time of contact (2012, 2). Her argument focuses on ways that the concept of "literacy" is a colonizing discourse that has to be dismantled and rebuilt if the full inventory of non-Western notational frameworks are to factor into it. Among other indigenous forms of literacy, for instance, she discusses the practices by Indian warriors of putting public postings along their routes, in waterproof ink, as a distributed information system across the landscape (3). Native languages included terms for writing and grammar. Wampum was its own system of encoded information, never meant to be separated from the context in which it was used, and served as the foundation of oral recitation and performance. Such artifacts have to be approached through a revised bibliographical mode, not as static objects under examination, but as transactional objects whose very identity is constituted through exchange. The erasure of these practices has been systematic, Rasmussen demonstrates over and over again, through the repeated assertion that Native peoples lacked writing—or lacked "real" writing. The painful history of the Mayan and Aztec codices is too familiar to need repetition, but rethinking the still extant and remarkable documents produced by Bernardino de Sahagún, with his Native scribes, along with that of Guaman Poma and his *Nueva corónica and buen gubierno*," the Popul Vuh narratives of the Guatemalan highlands, the Chilam Balam (Mayan works from the 17th and 18th centuries) as an "inter-animated" semiotic exchange, she offers a way to think through a "decolonizing" scholarship in and through bibliographic practice (28-29).

In our current moment, this has tremendous relevance for the ways we will apprehend digital artifacts. Their identity is dependent on a complex of conditions. They are, in essence, contingently configured in the dynamic flux of multiple co-dependencies in ways print artifacts only hint at, but which the distributed character of landscape signs, wampum performance, and quipu knowledge approach. Coming to terms with conditional texts and ephemeral documents whose "conditionality" is always shifting within the lifecycle of their production and use brings us right up against the recognition that these "artifacts" are not entities but events, not things "discovered" by an inquiry but objects constituted by it. With such an insight, we realize that we need not only to have the skills and techniques for practicing bibliography, but for reading bibliographically, taking the traces of material into their indexical and contingent relations and situated-ness, and then producing them through a reading across these distributed factors. This is what Armando Petrucci suggested as a method in *Public Lettering*, when he argued that the "spaces" of Rome are the *effect of signage and written traces*, not merely surfaces and sites whose identity is anterior to the inscriptional acts (Petrucci, 1993).

Contact zones characterize 16th and 17th century encounters between the old world of the European "west" and the New World cultures (whose established communication and semiotic systems were so radically different from those of the colonizers that they disturbed their epistemological belief systems—and were thus distorted, rejected, ignored, or subject to repression or eradication). These exchanges, so important to the philosophical formulations of the late Renaissance and early Enlightenment, where the questions about peoples, identities, universal history, language, religion, civilization, and humanity all came up for question, are particularly useful as the start point for thinking about bibliographical work now and for the future. Why? Because the systems-ecological approach to the semiotics of biblio-literacy exposed in those encounters have implications that have been engaged only somewhat to date in the field of book history and bibliography.

As we engage with the pedagogical challenge of formulating future histories of the book, we have to move beyond connoisseurship and antiquarianism, into this realm of meta-bibliographical description and performative, constitutive practices. We need to defamiliarize our own practices, which take for granted their forensic attention to production histories and reception histories, and attend instead to the assumptions on which they work. By shifting our frameworks from Western-based conceptions of bibliography to ones grounded in an ethnographic alterity we can reformulate the foundations on which we work.

So far my argument has drawn on approaches to this question informed by the study of books, literacy, writing, and inscriptional forms of knowledge and communication that broaden the traditions of bibliographical study. The future of book history will be altered substantially by including such works in a bibliographical approach that starts with these diverse forms as part of the field, rather than adding them as "other" to its "mainstream" traditions. Such a shift has wider implications for ways diversity is understood within intellectual and historical frameworks. Instead of registering "otherness" in relation to a normative "sameness," we can construe all forms of identity as alterities. Thus our conception of a book shifts from that of an autonomous object that "contains knowledge" and to the notion it is part of a "knowledge ecology" and exists in a co-dependent relation to the cultural systems of production/reception in which it functions. The point is not merely to extent bibliographical or historical frameworks to include previously little studied or marginalized works, but to reconsider the foundations on which such frameworks established their own "colonizing" approaches to bibliographical knowledge, and to undo them in a way that takes up the call for "de-colonization" in other intellectual realms. This is the decolonialization called for by Mignolo, which cannot be accomplished by extending the existing epistemologies to include "other" objects. It has to begin with dismantling the foundations of these epistemologies and rebuilding them with the full field of objects/practices in view.

What makes this so timely is that a bibliographical approach grounded in this alterity proves to be highly relevant to understanding documents produced in networked and digital environments. The ideas of conditional texts and ephemeral documents have their roots in a wide array of communities, including the creative realms of poetics and printing with their direct understanding of composition and production, academic structuralist and post-structuralist discourses, and encounters between digital humanities and theories of critical editing.[11] Textual scholars and bibliographers have long struggled with the difficulties of establishing the authority of texts, extracting versions from material witnesses, seeking any one of several elusive objects, each of which might be elusive differently—the intention of an author, or in the case of sacred or canonical texts, the "first," most complete, or least corrupted version. Like an asymptote that never reaches the limit of the original, these vectors of inquiry expose the impossibility of certainty, and the conditional character of textuality within the larger problems of bibliographical study.

In the editing community the notion of a fluid text, with its apparatus of critical editing comprised of codes and elaborately governed rules of application, produces its own specialized language (and debates). Attention goes to the "lemma," that sequestered figment of text arrayed with all of its variants, hints, and whispers, pulled out of its place in the weave of prose or the tightly made stanza, so that a phrase once breezily skimmed within a passage or verse is now tied with as many small strings and stakes of explanation and filiation as Gulliver in the hands of the Lilliputians.

11 None had more influence on me than the University of Virginia, where the legacy of scholarly editing was highly influential in the persons and traditions of Fredson Bowers, Thomas Tanselle, and Jerome McGann. Though each was unique and each different from the other, they shared a passion for critical editing and its legacy. In the 1990s, McGann was reflecting on the ways that editing had met the digital humanities community through a rising enthusiasm for textual markup and debates about its relation to the tension between the artifactual and textual features of documents.

The task of the scholarly apparatus is to expose the complex produced-ness of any single textual artifact. All words and phrases, it turns out, have a tendency to licentious errancy and promiscuous use that must be accounted for through revision and review. The result is not so much an ordering as a scattering, refraction of any text into a myriad of facets so that no text ever appears as a single, intact, defined phenomena, but always a result of combinatoric circumstances and happenstances. An author's ability to muster vocabulary or references, to conjure phrases as if from a store laid by or snatched from language heard passing in the street or unearthed from the rapid streams of conversation or culled from reading and gleaning published sources through a diligent porousness of mind, shows that texts are indeed *textura* weavings of threads twisted and plied, their appearance of wholistic integrity an illusion produced by the tightness with which the many borrowings and offerings come together.

Therefore temporality of textual production is not so much a question as a given. Alluded to by dates on manuscripts, the identification of a hand or condition of the writing links to a particular phase of an author's life, or even the use of a medium (*that* typewriter, piece of letterhead, or postmark on an envelope used for scrap writing). The times of these documents are used to piece together the production history of a text. Milestone dates of publication or review, galley corrections or editorial communication, second editions or later printings each and all bear their testimony in some more or less discernible, material way. However fluid the text, the documents have their own kinds of persistence and permanence, however palimpsestic and complex their relations to the streams of production in which they participate may be.

The documents remain, or appear to, and their ephemerality is no more or less poignant than our own. We therefore mark and measure the lifespan of a work by similar metrics—ones that measure the relation of relativity static things (documents) to fleeting ones (events). If we subscribe to the notion that a reading a makes a text anew in every instance, that still does not undermine our commonsense commitment to the existence of the thing/document as a thing—paper and print, ink and substrate, loose sheets or bound books or any other physical evidence.

But the conditionality of artifacts changes in networked environments, and here the tools of archival studies, informatics, digital scholarship and data curation, have to be drawn on to assist the bibliographer and textual editor. The analysis of tracking logs, click trails, and data mined results create new challenges to our conception of a document, as do text messages and mobile communications. The archivists' vocabulary of *respect des fonds*, and diplomatics, include longstanding and constantly shifting concepts of order, classification, and organization. Recently the notion of the records continuum has been described by the Society of American Archivists as "de-emphasizing the time-bound stages of the lifecycle model, recognizing that records do not 'die' but are reused and reanimated in various communities at different times." Frank Upward, among others, has been discussing "post-custodial" approach to archival work, which, though it does not disregard the care/custodianship of physical artifacts nonetheless also takes into account the need to think about the "continual transactionality" of documents (Upward, 1996). These are "fluid" to a new degree and in novel ways.

The possibilities of "new" activity are not just re-workings of the activities of quiet shelves, files in vaults, and instruments of textual accounting. The editing techniques descended from the scholars of biblical, sacred, and classical texts within erudite communities of rabbinic Hebrew, orthodox Greek, Sanskrit, and classical Latin scholars, among others, were used assiduously to assemble as complete a knowledge base as they could. These are essential, but not sufficient, to current tasks. We have not only to deal with fragmentary evidence, but with fleeting, fugitive compositions. The bright surfaces and pixel arrays of screens and devices display Twitter streams and postings according to the browser's whimsical responses. Documents are configured momentarily, in passing, on the fly. Are these audio-visual-textual offerings "documents" in any traditional sense? No WayBack machines in the world can reconfigure today's search results the same way tomorrow. The composition is dependent on what I do in the course of the day, what I have searched and will search a few moments later, but also, on the always shifting field of networked texts within range of the search engine algorithm. The "document" that is displayed as the result of a search for "topic modelling" contrasts with that of "topic modeling" (spelling variance), and each is different from the results displayed a day earlier.

This category of contingent and ephemeral documents can't be "captured" except with screen grabs, and the same is true of a host of other temporary screen configurations that are based on a set of protocols meeting query conditions and making a display. For the document specialists, these aberrations have to find their place among the envelopes and antelopes, the kitted scarves and knotted skeins, the furtively scribbled prayers thrown on a flame and the never-revealed ciphers of occult messages that have all come to stand before the dock and be deemed worthy or not to be included among the documentary elect. Other specimens of "conditional" documents exist and they also alter or trouble our understanding of, for instance, the "temporality" of a document as a feature of its ontological/inherent existence.

A conditional document is not a speculative one, not imaginative or imagined, but is produced by protocols and processes that use structured conditions as a way to run, operate, select information, and display it. It is configured as the outcome of specified process varyingly specific constraints (a filtered search in a closed data base vs. a search by Google across the WWWeb). We could argue that the protocols, processes, and constraints built into the structure and organization of the database *are* the documents. But that would only dodge the question of how we think about search results pages, for instance, as a document. Documents and means of their production are related, but not the same. The conditions are a means of conjuring that remain distinct from their creations, so merely saving the search or query protocols does not preserve the documents that arise as their results.

Revisiting other examples of conditional texts and their odd temporalities expands the range on which this argument builds: the results of data mining in a faceted search, a display of structured texts in filtered search, the results of natural language processing on a corpus, and any engagement with the ever-changing networked domain of the Web. Seeking to define a "document" in this circumstance, we can try to default to the entirety of the system, and suggest that the document depends on all the code/codes, networks, systems software/hardware, and contingencies. But then the whole ecology of the Web has to come into play, as it should, but this does not help establish limits on our already spiraling-out-of bounds definition of a document. Faceted searching in a closed system will yield repeatable results whose circularity returns us to the system itself as the "full" document. But, again, in an environment like the WWWeb, this is meaningless. The Web is too changeable, organically so, too whimsical in its shifts of information mood and weight, its zones of access and obscurity, its constant flicker of appearances and disappearances. The implications for scholarship, policy, or any activities that depend upon documentary evidence are profound. Imagine that you create a Google n-gram for a term that has had currency in a very short and recent time frame (e.g. "metadata" just had a vogue moment in popular press). If these results are used to support an argument, then what is the record of what is displayed on my screen? A print out is a surrogate that cannot satisfy the need to show the choices and results or the field from which the document is drawn. A screen shot suffices as a snapshot, but loses the interaction with the living Web. Even working within a more controlled or close environment, one faces the challenge of how to cite and display query results as a facet of a larger database.

Another good example of text documents with unstable ontological identities are those produced by Matthew Hurst's Hapax Legomenon, a natural language processor that distills of language culled from the Web between a particular start and stop date. These have no stability as enduring documents, and in fact, exist only as long as they are on view. We can conditionally configure documents, dependent on our fickle attention for their very existence, but they can vanish along the errant whimsy of our lines of attention intersecting our computational realms.

If ever the principles of a Heraclitean flux were embodied in the very ontology/phenomenology of an artifact, it is here, now, in the fleeting immediacies through which a document composes itself for our eyes only and for an instant's disregard and then vanishes. Siblings and cousins and shades of resemblance may reassemble, so like the original we mistake them, momentarily, for that earlier temporary object brought into being but our attention, but then, with regret, relief, and other realization of the subtle but significant difference between the initial document and this "new" one, we realize the perils of our connection to refresh rates. No corpses remain. The past history of the documentary field is only in the cache, very easily emptied, more difficult to preserve. Gone, not in the same way as Ozymandias's past glory, crumbling into ruins, over which we may wax romantically mournful. No, this is a profoundly new form of vanishing—without an inscription (forensics and their orthodox positivism aside). They leave no trace because there is no ground on which to register it, no way to preserve or recover the phantasm whose materiality is dependent on so many contingencies and co-dependencies of distributed hardware and related software, networks and clock speeds, protocols and display capacities. Ground and figure were/are co-dependent, and not just on each other, as smoke rings are on the density of air, but on the temporally configured conditions that produce these ephemeralities and make them available for a moment—or more—of cognition.

"Documents" have never been more material—and yet—they push against new limits of ephemerality, stretching the temporal spectrum of existence to nano-thresholds below perception and above its limits.

Questions of preservation and access follow, but the ones of ontological and phenomenal existence come first. The event spaces collapse into fleeting ephemerality possessed of a mad momentum. When I need to reference the results of a Search by referring to a temporally configured "document" that appeared on account of the precise conditions that existed at the moment of production I realize that the human universe resembles, more than before, those universes we produce in observation of quantum phenomena as well as those of the cosmos at its opposite and expanding scale.

Temporality defines documentality in these conditional circumstances, it does not merely enact specific variants of a document at different rates or speeds, its being as a document is an expression of momentary—highly fleeting—conditions whose relation to each other is temporal. The "being" of a document is always in a condition of "becoming," just that now that act is unmoored from a substrate with memory.

As we consider the relations of documents to their temporalities, we see this is an issue of the very identity in/as production of documents. Rather than the history of a document, and/or its place in a temporal continuum, now, a conditional document is a contingent configuration, a fleeting document, which is produced across a span of time. This changes the identity and status of documents, and is not just a matter of degree, but of ontology—a difference in kind and character of how a document is in and of the cultural and material world.

Bibliography and book history, in their future formulations, will have to contend with these changed conditions. The distributed character of the document includes distribution across space(s) *and* temporalities. The artifact has no singular autonomy under such circumstances (if it ever did, it now loses that illusion). A constructivist epistemology, one that takes the conditional of objects into account, as well as taking seriously the constitutive acts of engagement, can still track its allegiance to the traditions and conventions of bibliography and document studies. The requirements pressed on us for reconceptualization within the networked environments of document and text production cause us to reflect retrospectively, not just redefining our understanding of the past, but mining it for insights we were not able to have in advance of our current moment.

Bibliography

Barker, Nicolas, and Thomas Adams (1993). "A New Model for the Study of the Book." *A Potencie of Life: Books in Society.* Ed. Nicolas Barker. London: British Library.

Boone, Elizabeth Hill, and Walter D. Mignolo, eds. (1994). *Writing Without Words: Alternative Literacies in Mesoamerica and the Andes.* Durham, NC: Duke University Press.

Chartier, Roger (1992). *The Order of Books.* Palo Alto: Stanford University Press.

Darnton, Robert (1982). "What is the History of Books" *Daedalus* 111: 65-83.

Derrida, Jacques (1996). *Of Grammatology.* Baltimore: Johns Hopkins University Press.

Diamond, Jared (1998). *Guns, Germs, and Steel: The Fates of Human Societies.* New York: W.W. Norton & Co.

Diringer, David (1948). *The Alphabet: A Key to the History of Mankind.* New York: Philosophical Library.

Donahue, Betty Booth (2011). *Bradford's Indian Book: Being the True Roote & Rise of American Letters as Revealed by the Native Text Embedded in Of Plimoth Plantation.* Gainesville: University of Florida Press.

Drucker, Johanna (2009). *SpecLab: Digital Aesthetics and Projects in Speculative Computing.* Chicago: University of Chicago Press.

———. (2013). "Performative Materiality and Theoretical Approaches to Interface." *DHQ: Digital Humanities Quarterly* 7.1. http://www.digitalhumanities.org/dhq/vol/7/1/000143/000143.html.

Febvre, Lucien, and Henri-Jean Martin (1976). *The Coming of the Book: The Impact of Printing 1450-1800.* NY: Verso. [First published, Paris: Editions Albin Michel, 1958].

Foster, Charles (1851-1854). *The One Primeval Alphabet.* London: R. Bentley.

Fraser, Robert (2008). *The Book through Post-Colonial Eyes: Rewriting the Script.* London: Routledge.

Gelb, Ignace (1963). *A Study of Writing.* Chicago: University of Chicago Press.

Goody, Jack (1987). *The Interface between the Written and the Oral.* Cambridge: Cambridge University Press.

Johns, Adrian (1998). *The Nature of the Book: Print and Knowledge in the Making.* Chicago: University of Chicago Press.

Kirschenbaum, Matthew (2008). *Mechanisms: New Media and the Forensic Imagination.* Cambridge, MA: MIT Press.

Mcgann, Jerome (1983). *A Critique of Modern Textual Criticism.* Chicago: University of Chicago.

———. (2001). *Radiant Textuality: Literature after the World Wide Web.* London: Palgrave.

Mckenzie, D.F. (1986). *Bibliography and the Sociology of Texts*. London: British Library.

Mcluhan, Marshall (1962). *Gutenberg Galaxy.* London: Routledge and Kegan Paul.

———. (1967). *The Medium is the Massage*. New York: Bantam Books.

Mcmurtrie, Douglas (1943). *The Book: The Story of Printing and Bookmaking.* Oxford: Oxford University Press.

Mignolo, Walter D. (1995). *The Darker Side of the Renaissance: Literacy, Territoriality, & Colonization*. Ann Arbor: University of Michigan Press.

Ong, Walter (1982). *Orality and Literacy: The Technologizing of the Word.* London: Methuen.

Petrucci, Armando (1993). *Public Lettering: Script, Power, and Culture*. Chicago: University of Chicago Press.

Rasmussen, Birgit Brander (2012). *Queequeg's Coffin: Indigenous Literacies and Early American Literature*. Durham, NC: Duke University Press.

Round, Phillip (2010). *Removable Type: Histories of the Book in Indian Country,* 1663-1880. Chapel Hill, NC: University of North Carolina Press.

Suarez, Michael (2003-2004). "Historiographical Problems and Possibilities in Book History and National Histories of the Book." *Studies in Bibliography* 56: 141-170.

Tedlock, Dennis (1993). *Spoken Word and the Work of Interpretation*. Philadelphia, PA: University of Pennsylvania Press.

Upward, Frank (1996). "Structuring the Records Continuum–Part One: Postcustodial principles and properties." *Archives and Manuscripts* 24.2: 268-287.

The Mail/Male Room
Queer Personae of the Chicano Avant-garde

Robb Hernández

The *Los Angeles Times* declared it one of the top five "must-see" booths at Printed Matter's LA Art Book Fair in 2015 (Miranda 2015). Edging out over 300 exhibitors of independent, alternative, and underground publishers from around the world, the Maricón Collective (Spanish for "faggot") caught the attention of cultural critics, bloggers, and art journalists alike. Sporting this offensive moniker on uniform black sweatshirts, the stylish queer quintet established a local following, hosting happy-hour socials in Silver Lake, spinning records at the Tom of Finland erotic art fair, and organizing "old school" parties in backyards (Villarreal 2015). At the Printed Matter's fair, word about the collective's re-release of *Homeboy Beautiful* magazine (1978–79) traveled around the more than 30,000 attendees. The short-lived art and lifestyle digest, by gay Chicano mixed-media artist Joey Terrill, satirized the "homo-homeboy" underground of East Los Angeles, replete with Judy Garland cholo disciples and glamorously coiffed Boyle Heights "Lil' Locas." The Maricón Collective's collaboration with Terrill reintroduced his out-of-print magazine to new audiences, distributing it inside sleekly sheathed packaging with matching tote bags. As *Los Angeles Times* art critic Carolina Miranda noted, "This represents an opportunity to lay your hands on some pretty rare work—only 100 copies will be printed of each [issue]" (2015).

In bringing renewed attention to *Homeboy Beautiful*, the Maricón Collective sidesteps the ephemerality of handcrafted art publications like zines, which are most often intended to be traded or discarded after use (Thomas 2009, 34). By introducing *Homeboy Beautiful* into a contemporary art-publishing marketplace like Printed Matter, the group elevates the magazine's artistic authority as a vintage collectible. Its popular reception reflects a growing tendency for art fairs, biennials, and even studio practices to deal in what Susan Thomas calls "retro nostalgia," a preference for "obsolete technologies" that offer a screen-addicted society "relief in the printed form" (2009, 27). A project like *Homeboy Beautiful* does more than enhance the material dimensions of queer Chicano print media, however. By countering a heteronormative lineage of independent ethnic self-publishing, the Maricón Collective's reissue is politically astute and symbolically "demands a radical archive of emotion" for queer *latinidad* "in order to document intimacy, sexuality, love, and activism—all areas of experience that are difficult to chronicle through the materials of a traditional archive" (Cvetkovich 2003, 241). In constructing a "counterarchive," in queer theorist Ann Cvetkovich's terms, the Maricón Collective not only recovers the homo-homeboy for a queer millennial readership under the retro-nostalgic banner, but also reactivates a broader and more complex visual, literary, and performance-based origin story for *Homeboy Beautiful*. This must not be minimized.

Unbeknownst to the Maricón Collective, Terrill's network of art collaborators and Chicano creative circles, and, most importantly, the queer cultural landscape to which he and his friends belonged, were all resuscitated within the freshly xeroxed reissue. *Homeboy Beautiful* is indebted to the creative forces behind its original production. Together, they germinated a participatory art-making sensibility to which paper proved indispensible. Perhaps more than any other medium, paper played (and continues to play) a critical role in conveying queer Chicano visuality in the experimental art aesthetics of post-1960s Los Angeles. Also, it enabled a crucial interface through which the connective tissue between queer men cohered. Evidence of these connections pervades the pages of *Homeboy Beautiful* in Terrill's deliberate citations of conceptual art clubs, fictitious art handles, and, most especially, the alter personae that populated the Chicano avant-garde in the 1970s.

Foregrounding *Homeboy Beautiful* in my analysis, I examine the textual and visual cues to these personae in the magazine's pages. The case studies that follow include an examination of the Escandalosa Circle, Butch Gardens School of Art, Pursuits of the Penis, and Judeo Christian Ethic Universal. As examples of the queer creative configurations happening in and around *Homeboy Beautiful*, they were significant despite being little regarded in Chicano avant-garde theory and criticism. Using private archives, historical analysis, and close interpretations of image-text junctures, including a variety of print materials (art magazines, mail art, flyers, and letter correspondence), I show how these artistic personae forged queer zones of social contact based on paper. Hints of these circles expand the corporeal possibilities happening across the mail/male when queer bodies interconnect through printed matter. I thus argue for a more complex understanding of *Homeboy Beautiful*'s material agency as a forum for the Chicano avant-garde's transgressive sexualities and gender expressions.

The Escandalosa Circle

As an undergraduate at Immaculate Heart College, Joey Terrill launched his conceptual art project, *Homeboy Beautiful*, in 1977. After reading a condescending exposé on the "social problem" of East Los Angeles juvenile delinquency in *New West* magazine, Southern California's counterpart to *New York* magazine, Terrill started to wonder: what would happen if the tables were turned and the cholas themselves investigated West Side elites (2007)?[1] Riffing on *House Beautiful* at the suggestion of his classmate Skot Armstrong, his innovation denaturalizes glossy layouts of wealthy home interiors, using staged photographic vignettes, didactic metacommentary, and tongue-in-cheek self-portraits for each magazine cover (Terrill 2010). As *Homeboy Beautiful*'s resident "cover girl," Terrill himself confronts the hypermasculine diatribes in Chicano media, challenging the pervasive "straight" propaganda of chiseled Aztlán warriors, fraternal photography of barrio *carnales*, and muscular lowrider facades in car club ephemera (see Rodríguez 2009).

The second issue's lead "exposé," titled "E.L.A. Terrorism," intensifies this contrast (Terrill 1979, 15–31). Adopting an alter ego by the name of Santo ("saint" in Spanish), Terrill plays the part of a Chicano investigative journalist. A saint turned sinner, Santo navigates the perverse underbelly of the homo-homeboy underground. On the cover, he poses in a white bandana and black jacket with "East Los Angeles"

1 Additionally, in my 2010 interview with the artist, Terrill cites a *New West* story on Chicana social delinquents as a key influence. However, I could not locate any such article prior to *Homeboy Beautiful*'s release in 1978. In its January 29, 1979, issue, *New West* published an exploitation story titled "La Vida Loca: Girls in the Gangs of East L.A." (Johnston 1979). However, it followed *Homeboy Beautiful*'s initial run, contradicting Terrill's claim. Deferring to the artist's recollection of events, I preserve his account here as a part of the publication's mythology.

Figure 1

Joey Terrill, cover of *Homeboy Beautiful*, issue 2, 1979. Color photocopy, 11 Å~ 8. inches. Image courtesy of the artist.

splayed across his back (fig. 1). His stylish accouterments give the reader a "sense of place" (Hayden 1997, 12), and a collaged scrap from a road atlas centers East Los Angeles, making the location central to the viewer's reading. The mural backdrop reveals Willie Herrón's *The Wall that Cracked Open* (1972). Painted after Herrón's brother was knifed to death in an act of gang violence, the mural authenticates a barrio spatial aesthetic within a hardened urban setting (see Knight 2011). Turned slightly to the left, Santo holds a spherical mortar bomb styled like exaggerated cartoon artillery. As a queer saboteur, he upsets a significant symbol of Chicano masculinity with his self-staging, a monument to a fallen homeboy and to Herrón's *hermano*, no less, charging the City Terrace landscape with a "disidentifying" recircuitry of queer racialized demolition (Muñoz 1999). Santo literally stands apart from Herrón's mural, a mural otherwise converted and discursively reformed within the Asco corpus.[2]

Asco, the conceptual collective founded by Herrón, Harry Gamboa Jr., Gronk, and Patssi Valdez in East Los Angeles in 1972, ushered in an

2 Harry Gamboa Jr. (1998, 75, 77) cites Herrón's *Wall that Cracked Open* in his genealogy of Asco's formation. Also see Knight (2011).

innovative repertoire of performance-based interventions organized around the revolting affective structures of "disgust," as its Spanish name suggests (Gamboa 1998, 77). As a terrorist performance, Santo fits awkwardly with Herrón's symbol of *carnalismo*, cholo gang violence, and Chicano avant-garde mural experimentation. Posing with a bomb ready to fire, Terrill indicts the US military-industrial complex for its disproportionate drafting of Chicanos into the Vietnam War and its pathologizing of homosexuals as abject and sexually perverse. Simultaneously, he metaphorically stands apart from the heteronormative ideologies underlying the Chicano nationalist discourse that calls for the reclamation of Aztlán as a mythic homeland. Santo is a criminal outcast, an insurgent journalist within a "radical homeboy terrorist group" (Terrill 1979, 15). Terrill's narrative anticipates what Jasbir Puar terms "terrorist assemblage"—that discursive production of nonnormative terrorist bodies that emerged in the post-9/11 context of Islamophobia and "homonationalism" (2007, 2, xxiv). Santo illustrates "this disjuncture of the regulating and regulated queer, homosexual, gay disciplinary subjects and the queered darkening of terrorists" (xiii), nuanced from the standpoint of queer Chicano liminality—a perspective shaped at the margins of the city and Aztlán nation. An incongruent "assemblage" within East LA cultural geography and Chicano visual genealogies, Santo threatens to attack the normative subjects and symbols of the US nationstate, sabotage a racially and sexually stratified urbanity, and even bomb Los Angeles's more progressive avant-garde auxiliary, Asco.[3] As a noncompliant force, Terrill lays the groundwork for his creative destruction and the iconoclastic power of homo-homeboys. Of course, this second issue of *Homeboy Beautiful* could not have happened without the influence of his artistic conspirators in the first issue. Enter the Scans.

The Escandalosa Circle—Terrill's queer Chicano social network cultivated through gay liberation dances, "be-ins," house parties, and impromptu art events—supplied the naturally "wild" performers to take on the personae populating the covert underworld pictured in the *Homeboy Beautiful* series. The Scans, as they were known, initially came to life in the open-air corridors of Cathedral High School, a Catholic private preparatory school for young men near Chavez

3 Of late, Asco has been evaluated as a more tolerable art circuit for sexually transgressive subjects when compared to other nationalist and identitarian activist art projects in the Chicano movement, despite evidence to the contrary. Consider Jones (2011).

Ravine, northeast of Downtown Los Angeles. From 1969 to 1973 Terrill attended the school, where being thrown against lockers was a frequent occurrence (Terrill 2007). He was assailed with Spanish slurs—*puto, maricón*—giving an audibly violent texture to the predominately Mexican American male demographic of the campus. Terrill survived by striking up friendships with other young gender and sexually transgressive Chicanos, classmates who appeared in the initial issue of the magazine, among them Louis Vela and Ronnie Carrillo.

Terrill's name for his crew of homeboy courtiers, barrio debutantes, and cholo luminaries was retrofitted from a queer Chicano vernacular introduced by Richard Nieblas, an artist who attended California State University, Los Angeles. On December 18, 1975, "Escandalosa's Gallery," an ephemeral happening in Nieblas's living room in East Los Angeles, brought Terrill into contact with other convening artists, including an important faction trained at California State University, Long Beach (CSULB): Jef Huereque, Jack A. Vargas, and Teddy Sandoval.[4] Terrill's involvement with these CSULB artists, especially Sandoval, resulted in a series of philosophical dialogues and conceptual exercises, beginning with the Maricón Series of photo-based performances (1975–76), which I have discussed elsewhere.[5] *Homeboy Beautiful* was the apex of their creative exchanges and collaborative productions.

With Sandoval, Vela and Carrillo were also central to *Homeboy Beautiful*'s first issue in 1978. They come together as the "homo underground" in Terrill's cover story titled "What Really Happens on Those Hot Summer Nights in Geraghty Loma!" (Terrill 1978, 14–26). The performances were cast inside a trailer in the backyard of Vela's family's residence in East Los Angeles. The trailer was something of an epicenter for Scan expressive play: "everything from *Homeboy Beautiful*, to working out, to parties, orgies, acid, drunken debauchery, music ... it all took place here," Terrill recollects (2015). That little slice of queer East Los Angeles became a pivotal outlet for subversive Chicano creativity in a manner reminiscent of the nostalgic "backyard boogie" parties of the 1970s that the Maricón Collective strived to recreate. Their contemporary efforts echo the collaborative tenor and social atmosphere of the Scans, despite being separated from them by decades

4 Escandalosa's Gallery announcement, December 18, 1975, box 3, folder 3, The Fire of Life: Cyclona Collection, UCLA Chicano Studies Research Library.

5 For more on Terrill and Sandoval's collaborations, see Hernández (2014).

(Villarreal 2015). It is therefore not surprising that the group would reclaim and re-release *Homeboy Beautiful* to a similarly unapologetic bastion of self-proclaimed "maricón" millennials. Using the Vela trailer as the Scan home base, Terrill adds a spatial dimension that introduces another layer of authenticity. Each shot becomes "recovered" footage from East Los Angeles, unsettling presumptions of fact in print journalism and photography.

Mimicking the *fotonovela* genre, *Homeboy Beautiful* presents narrativizing and sequential pictorial frames, creating the illusion of mass, scale, and in particular, social reproducibility. Each still frame filled with anonymous cholo bodies impresses a queer corporeality into the page. Scans cover the expanse of the photographic field. Their anonymous brown flesh destabilizes and penetrates machista masculinity, making it vulnerable and "cracking" that impenetrable wall of homeboy heteronormativity. Scenes staging cholos' subversive knowledge of gay male camp, connoisseurship of all things Judy Garland, and expertise with the hanky code, that quotidian language of colored handkerchiefs used to signal preferred sexual practices and suggestive self-fashioning, blurs the line between *choloismo* and homosexuality. Pointing to homo-homeboys necking with bandanas removed from their back pockets, Santo's metacommentary informs the curious reader, "As you can see the homo-homeboys look perfectly normal on the outside. How deceiving!!!" (Terrill 1978, 23).

Homeboy Beautiful, like the temporary Chicano serials that popped up sporadically on college campuses and in community-based activist networks in the 1970s, also mirrored the infrastructural limitations of ethnic print media. Comparable to periodicals like *Regeneración* and *Chismearte* in its self-published construction and attention to Chicano photographic lexicons, *Homeboy Beautiful* participates in this "print renaissance," which, according to literary scholar Randy Ontiveros, "was in many ways the cornerstone of the cultural politics of the Chicano movement" (2014, 76). Terrill's work thus delimits Chicano serials' compulsory heterosexuality not only in its content and visual discourse but also in its material expression. What Terrill lacked in production materials and professional equipment, he made up for with self-publishing resourcefulness. This may have been fostered by his immersion in mail art, pioneered in the 1950s by Black Mountain College alumnus Ray Johnson. Johnson sent what he termed "moticos," or miniature collages, anonymously through the mail, activating a federal agency, the US Postal Service, to exhibit "the co-creative process of art-making in both embodied and disembodied forms" (Gangadharan 2009, 285–86). Terrill's handmade aesthetic combines Johnson's postal activity with performance art as he presses his body and creative labor into each hand-stapled xeroxed packet. As Alison Piepmeier (2008, 220) notes, "Paper ... is a nexus, a technology that mediates the connections not just of 'people' but of bodies." *Homeboy Beautiful*'s materiality moves Terrill's queer bodily imprint through established and emergent mail art networks and thus contests the heterosexual perception of Chicano periodicals and art publications at the time.

With a principal emphasis on mail art aesthetics, Terrill uses collaging, stenciling, commercial media clippings, type lettering, Old English typographic writing, and xeroxing. His fashion illustrations are styled after highly lauded Nuyorican art director and Warhol acolyte Antonio Lopez. The mock classifieds section from *Homeboy Beautiful*'s second issue in 1979 impresses Terrill's body further within the page. Using his signature artist rubberstamp, Terrill imprints his own visage within the textual intersections of song dedication listings and a lesbian personal ad looking for a "strong, wonderful, masterful amazon" (Terrill 1979, 40). His self-portrait augments the literary space as a bodily signifier, impressing a corporeal referent against thickly handwritten text declaring "Mail Art Wanted" (40). The addresses of participatory correspondents are listed, with Terrill registering himself alongside Johnson, John Dowd, and, most importantly, Butch Gardens School of Art. Placing himself within this mail art cohort, he also adapts a familiar protocol of mail art exhibition catalogs whereby respondents are listed in the back matter to widen postal art exchanges in what Robert Filliou called the "Eternal Network" (Held 2005, 89). In doing so, Terrill positions *Homeboy Beautiful* within that network, within Piepmeier's "paper nexus," and thus distorts the media distinctions between Chicano zine, art magazine, mail art, and performance practice. In this way, Terrill brings homo-homeboys to interconnect Chicano art and ethnic media publication with an alternative queer vision for East LA's avant-gardism.

Butch Gardens School of Art

In *Homeboy Beautiful* magazine, Butch Gardens School of Art appears in a myriad of ways as an artistic signature, homo-homeboy art, and enigmatic entity. A recognizable handle frequently found in mail art exchanges, print publications, and advertisements, Butch Gardens is sometimes assumed to be a permanent physical location. Art historical and literary discourse furthers this impression, calling it a "bar and performance space operated by Teddy Sandoval ... [where] emerging Chicano artists and musicians regularly congregated and collaborated" (Benavidez 2007, 52). Since Butch Gardens was, in fact, *also* the name of a gay bar located at 3037 West Sunset Boulevard in the Silver Lake neighborhood of Los Angeles, misperceptions abound. The Butch Gardens School of Art, which had no physical premises, was the creative vehicle of Sandoval, an elusive insignia that paid homage to the dirt, grit, and perversion of the original bar. Just as Johnson's own mail art network, the "New York Correspondence School," was a tongue-in-cheek riff on abstract expressionism's New York School, Sandoval created his own conceptual "School of Art" featuring mail art's queerer and racialized facets (Gangadharan 2009, 286).

One of Sandoval's art tactics resembled that of Johnson, who invited correspondence through letters mailed on behalf of fictitious fan clubs that were "phantoms, created entirely through rubber stamps and existing only on paper" (De Salvo 1999, 27). Butch Gardens School of Art issued communications and invitations in the name of its enigmatic persona, Rosa de la Montaña. In this, Sandoval may have been influenced by feminist artists who enacted radical personae on paper, including Judy Gerowitz, who dubbed herself "Judy Chicago," and Adrian Piper, who cultivated a racially indeterminate masculine persona or "mythic being," printed in *Artforum* advertisements in 1970 and 1972, respectively (Smith 2011; Gerhard 2011). Transmitted through the post office as an idea, queer persona, and drag show on paper, Rosa de la Montaña ("Rosie") is an androgynous personification of Butch Gardens School of Art and of the artist himself. Dragged through the mail, she is a performance expression bound by paper but also by flesh. As Michael Crane notes about mail art's collaged and xeroxed tableaus, "In a subjective sense, these media are used to create the psychological constructs of contact and support necessary for the existence of the network. Some letters and envelopes are used to create fiction, legends, and other attitudes of the mind" (1984, 20). Sandoval mediates Rosa within paper technology, crafting Butch Gardens School of Art's own iconic resident celebrity; her printed modifications become a potentially transgender fiction of self.

Her mystery is textually evident on a flyer from *Corazón Herido* (Wounded Heart), an exhibition opening on September 15, 1979, at Sandoval's downtown loft on Banning Street (fig. 2). He invites his guests at the request of "Ma[dame] Rosa de la Montana"—who is named but not

Figure 2

Teddy Sandoval, flyer for Corazón Herido, 1979. Photocopy, 11 Å~ 8. inches. Image courtesy of Paul Polubinskas.

pictured—and the “Butch Gardens School of Art.” Pairing his phantom persona with a conceptual art entity, he creates a “relational aesthetic” environment (see Bourriaud 2002). The mystique of the unseen Rosa draws queer Chicano avant-gardists together based on the power of her persona expressed through her textual authority on paper. Spirited by Nieblas’s Escandalosa’s Gallery as well as by “Nothings”—Johnson’s invitation to non-event happenings organized around empty spaces—Sandoval’s version of Butch Gardens is a temporary exhibition space instilled with the “relational” art making of its attendants (Gangadharan 2009, 286). *Corazón Herido* consisted of artist responses to Mexican surrealist Frida Kahlo. A submission by Terrill “channel[ed] an East Coast Pop Art sensibility for a burgeoning West Coast Chicano gay aesthetic,” whereby his “homage to Frida’s visage mirrored Warhol’s facial focus on Marilyn [Monroe]” (Rodríguez 2011, 475). However, the visual politics of “face-giving,” as Richard T. Rodríguez observes, could not be more contentious than in Sandoval’s withdrawal of Madame’s physiognomic dimensions (475). At *Corazón Herido*, she is a textual trace on a flyer. When she is pictured, her portrayal is equally elusive.

Sandoval’s small-scale print, *Rosa* (1976), shows a figure who is anonymous in appearance (fig. 3). More essence than drag character, she is

Figure 3 Teddy Sandoval, *Rosa*, 1976. Work on paper (non-extant, dimensions unknown). Image courtesy of Paul Polubinskas and the Estate of Teddy Sandoval.

a malleable form facing viewers over her bare shoulder with coquettish abandon. Her seductive tease is deepened by her floral wallpaper surroundings, a suggestive abstract flower motif that evokes Georgia O'Keeffe's feminist modern language. The flowering cascade is a labial shower, exuding a hyperfeminine sensibility. For Sandoval, clues about Rosa's enigmatic countenance are found in the vulva shroud surrounding her. The elusive Rosa de la Montaña is a floating signifier in a broad spectrum of feminist art, Chicano avant-garde, and American modernist traditions. Sandoval's aesthetic entwines queer racialized visibility with a gender-fluid sexual power. In its word play, subversive language, and androgyny, Butch Gardens School of Art can be seen as a direct Chicano descendent of American Dada. Sandoval's "Rosa" is a punning tribute to Marcel Duchamp's gender-transgressive persona Rrose Sélavy, made iconic in a collaborative portrait photographed with Man Ray in 1921. In fur and darkly stained lips, Duchamp's alter ego and stand-in signature becomes what Amelia Jones calls a "feminine masquerade," asserting "the radical potential of self-presentational strategies" which "enables Marcel to eschew the macho worker/painter identity in favour of an ambiguously gendered persona" (1995, 22).

Sandoval similarly unfastens the machista archetype of the Chicano street artist, loosening its close associations with community-based muralism, barrio urban realism, and anti-Eurocentric art politics (see

Latorre 2009). As Rosa, Sandoval stands in the face of this heteropatriarchal cultural worker, undercutting his macho bravado. Rejecting social realist figuration and iconography indigenous to barrio life, he challenges a romantic urban portrait, even doing away with that culture's capacity to see itself through facial recognition. By dissolving Rosa's identifiable traits, he upsets a Chicano ethnic political project based on a tenuous system of race and gender assignments. Rosa remains an evasive figure, illusive flirt, and shadowy saboteur. At *Corazón Herido*, she is there, not there, and all around us. And like the gender-defiant modernists before her, she undermines a passive feminine portrait, repudiating a heteropatriarchal desire to see, know, and ingest her.[6]

Pursuits of the Penis and Judeo Christian Ethic Universal

Just as Sandoval's work on paper allowed his alternative persona to take amorphous shape, the conscious use of postal technologies to cultivate queer affective structures between Chicano avant-garde artists and writers led to the emergence of other creative factions in and around *Homeboy Beautiful*.[7] "Pursuits of the Penis," an epistolary forum imagined by writer/poet Ronnie Carrillo, was met with return correspondence from "Judeo Christian Ethic Universal," the creation of conceptual artist Jack A. Vargas.[8] Documenting a pre-AIDS period in Los Angeles around 1976–83, these young men's art-literary exchange traveled between Carrillo's barrio home in Lincoln Heights and Vargas's Orange County suburbia. Their fictitious monikers moved through postal channels in a queer mediation of the mail/male. Together, they shared experiences with the cultural schisms, spiritual incongruities, and sexual liberationist possibilities available to young Chicano men at the time. Religion posed its own set of challenges, since Vargas was Methodist and Carrillo attended a

6 Sandoval filters through a transgender visual economy in Chicano avant-gardism advanced by the "Mija" chola gangbangers in *Homeboy Beautiful*, Robert Legorreta's live art persona "Cyclona," and Mundo Meza's "glitter queen" androgyny. On the "Mijas," see "Fashion for the Working Girl" (Terrill 1979, 11–14). On Legorreta and Meza, see Hernández (2009).

7 This section is based on private letters and ephemera of writer Ronnie Carrillo sent to the author for studying, archiving, and preservation at the University of California, Riverside, in 2014. The residual research project will result in the Jack A. Vargas digital archive (in process), creating public access to a rare queer Chicano epistolary literature, art, and performance occurring around 1976–83 between East Los Angeles and Orange County, California.

8 Vargas conceptualized the Judeo Christian Ethic Universal in May 1976. He describes this as among his "sensibility-changes." Jack A. Vargas to Ronnie Carrillo, July 4, 1977 (postmarked July 11, 1977), 5.

Catholic school. The result catalyzed image-text works, yet another paper-generated queer expression in "epistolary performance" (Longstreth 2001, 32).

Evidence of their influence appears in *Homeboy Beautiful*, with Carrillo's photo documentation as a homo-homeboy in the inaugural issue and Vargas's other mail art incarnation, "Le Club for Boys," coded into a queer cholo fashion layout in the second issue. They also symbolize the queer social fabric popular among the Scans at the time. This is especially true of Carrillo, who represents this lifestyle in the purest sense: he attends Cathedral High School alongside Terrill, imbibes boys and spirits at Circus Disco, and traverses the body traffic cruising men in Griffith Park in pursuit of his next "male muse." More than this, he is also a reflection of the unexpected connections made between artists moving in queer circles of the CSULB studio art program. Through CSULB alumnus Jef Huereque, Carrillo met Vargas at Studio One, a West Hollywood disco, around 1975, and he quickly realized Vargas's prior acquaintance with his friends Sandoval and Terrill. Vargas showed with Huereque, Sandoval, and Terrill at Nieblas's Escandalosa's Gallery that year.[9]

The pair established an immediate bond, choosing written correspondence over phone contact to allay parental suspicions. Letters offered a more discrete channel for messaging than the telephone. Vargas lived with his devoutly religious parents at the time, and in a letter to Carrillo he cites his frustration in having to sneak out of his Cypress home to service a late-night trick.[10] At first, Carrillo dismisses letters as something "trendy," but he is enticed after Vargas's original comments that "sex was absurd," a powerful indignation correlating with his own personal experience.[11] In his first letter to Vargas, he admits, "You are to be given credit for the birth of these letters ... I had strayed or taken a wrong turn from my high expectation and visions of love and life when I was still innocent. I am baffled by this spell ... [that] does not seem to weaken."[12] In a tone of self-surrender, Carrillo reassures Vargas that "what I hope to derive from these occasional

9 Ronnie Carrillo, email to author, October 29, 2014.

10 Jack A. Vargas to Ronnie Carrillo, December 30, 1976, 2.

11 "Trendy" is cited in Ronnie Carrillo to Jack A. Vargas, October 24, 1976, 1. Also, Ronnie Carrillo to Jack A. Vargas, October 31, 1976 (continuation of original letter dated October 24, 1976), 6.

12 Ronnie Carrillo to Jack A. Vargas, October 31, 1976, 6.

written revelations is short and simple none other than your friendship in long lasting terms. Please, advise me if this confines or bothers you in any way—I am ready to cope with something like this[.]"[13] He continues with twenty stanzas of untitled poetry written between June 1973 and January 1975. Carrillo shows a skillful mastery of poetic verse and metaphor, impressing Vargas: "You have so much, Ronnie, and you do write better than I, you're more precise, exacting in your descriptions. I tend to meander—I can write well <u>about</u> things (as space is <u>about</u> the earth and not a real part of it) but when I try to be exacting, I miss the mark."[14] What Vargas lacks in prose, he makes up for by proposing a new experimental language on paper. A gay polyglot, Vargas utilizes a patois spoken within his inner circle of Chicano artists. Words like "la-la's" reference an aura of "boring" uniformity, of young gay men in a phase of hedonistic frivolity.[15] "Public Hairs" names the hypervisible and audacious behavior of gay nationalists making their private parts into public parts.[16] Together, Carrillo and Vargas produce a rare queer Chicano epistolary literature, one that emerges out of a pre-AIDS period in Southern California.

Their correspondence begins with Carrillo's "Pursuits of the Penis," to which Vargas responds with letters penned under his own name as well as various pseudonyms. In a letter dated July 4, 1977, Vargas introduces the phantom persona "Judeo Christian Ethic Universal," a concept-based identity predicated on his relationship to Christ and the "sensibility-changes" he endured. These changes affected his spiritual existence and "sexual transition," an area of slippage that unfixes his sexual orientation from opposite-sex attractions.[17] Vargas's perspective is partially attributed to pathologizing discourses favoring conversion therapy for homosexuality spearheaded by family values zealot Anita Bryant, a divisive figure who nonetheless at times speaks to him and his complicated Christian beliefs.[18] According to Vargas, "the more 'real' the J.C.E. will be ... the less it will be thought

13 Ronnie Carrillo to Jack A. Vargas, October 24, 1976, 1.

14 Jack A. Vargas to Ronnie Carrillo, December 30, 1976, 3–4.

15 Jack A. Vargas to Ronnie Carrillo, September 20, 1977 (postmarked October 28, 1977), 2.

16 Ibid., 4.

17 Jack A. Vargas to Ronnie Carrillo, July 4, 1977 (postmarked July 11, 1977), 5.

18 Ibid., 8.

of as an art piece or another specialized, cult-ish publication."[19] Breaking down divides between art and life, his pursuit of the "real" evokes the way Johnson and Fluxus artists undercut the formalism of Greenbergian modern art by choosing more participatory art sensibilities.

Foregrounding literary and visual elements, the two men experiment with the epistolary form. Carrillo begins this technique in his inaugural letter. Subverting the salutatory format at the top of the page, he interjects a personal log into the opener. Male Muse, Artistic Apparition, Anti-Disco Song, and Vote are categories listed at the outset of the text. He names Vargas as his male muse, applauds Judy Garland's saucy rendition of "Never Will I Marry" as his anti-disco song, names the "ghosts of Disco" as an artistic apparition, and endorses California Proposition 14 (1976) in his "vote" callout (see Garcia 2012).[20] His greeting is a "lo-fi" intrusion that strings together diaristic, private, and political details, engendering another mail/male art salutation. Like an overture, it precedes the main event: Pursuits of the Penis.

With a poet's inclination to test the page and restructure the literary body, Carrillo crafts letters that are intentionally piecemeal, altering a chronological rhythm, rhyme, and type of writing. For instance, biblical verses, poems, diary entry duplications, and salacious teasers pervade the page. Postscripts are cinematic forecasts of "coming attractions," alluding to the next act in his tumultuous pursuits. All this, and yet Carrillo's missives are sent in nondescript mailers to Vargas's home. Carrillo is restrained in his attention to the envelope surface, sending an unassuming parcel. His subterfuge places more emphasis on the interior expression, on what his words are capable of showing on the inside in paper and ink.

Vargas exhibits no such discretion in his print productions. Responding to Pursuits of the Penis, Vargas's letters innovate the salutatory format, "outing" it from the trapped space of the letter enclosure. By dismantling private-public dichotomies governing postal carriage, he exteriorizes Carrillo's prompt on the envelope surface. In this way he confronts mail art's rebuke of institutional art gallery systems, using Carrillo's salutatory nomenclature to activate the mail/male room and make it his own. One such envelope lists "Worst Commercials,"

---

19 Ibid., 5.

20 Proposition 14 was a ballot initiative spearheaded by the United Farm Workers, guaranteeing labor union representatives access to workers. For a more detailed analysis, see Garcia (2012).

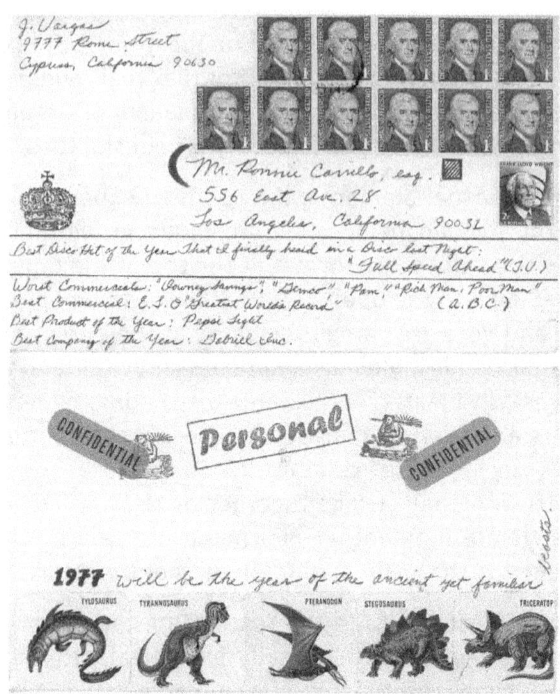

Figure 4

Jack A. Vargas, envelope addressed to Ronnie Carrillo, postmarked January 1977. Envelope, 7. x 4. inches. Image courtesy of Ronnie Carrillo.

"Best Commercial," "Best Product of the Year," and "Best Company of the Year" among his personal log entries, showing a Pop sensibility in his commercial attentions; this is also evident in his flamboyant sticker and rubberstamp embellishments of flora and fauna, dinosaur specimens, lunar motifs, and royal crowns affixed to the envelope (fig. 4).[21] His garish décor imitates an official notice dispatched from an Orange County monarch, perhaps from another queen competing for Rosa de la Montaña's royal subjects. Bold stickers marked "confidential" draw ironic attention to what's inside. Though his ornamented envelopes exteriorize what Carrillo keeps interior, both postal interlopers reconcile over a mutual attention to disco.

Responding to Carrillo's Anti-Disco Song category, Vargas nominates the "Best Disco Hit of the Year That I finally heard in a Disco last night: 'Full Speed Ahead' (T.V.)." His cryptic code (T.V.) is shorthand for Táta Vega, the Afro-Caribbean funk and disco queen, and "Full Speed Ahead" is the title track on her Motown album of the same name. The twenty-three year-old Vargas's own romantic quest may have influenced his

21 Jack A. Vargas to Ronnie Carrillo, December 30, 1976.

fondness for the anthem, in which Vega declares, "Full speed ahead 'til I find love for me (Come on, girls, say it like you mean it!)."[22] Sonic resonance pervades the envelope, showing not only the print material's literary and artistic utility in documentation but also its audible textures. Vargas's mail art technology *sounds*, expanding printed matter into a multisensory media platform that performs the intimate linkage between the boy and the disco, the body and the music, the sender and the receiver. As Ramón Rivera-Servera notes, "Dance, as an act of self-presentation and community building, becomes one of the mechanisms through which Latina and Latino queers negotiate their place and membership within and outside the club" (2011, 261). Queer affective relations blossom in the disco and thus structure Pursuits of the Penis and Judeo Christian Ethic Universal in a dance ordered by mail; their letters attune to a disco beat mediating the mailroom, urban sprawl, and suburban insularity.

Their physical distance remains painful, compromising contact and intensifying spatial isolation. Nonetheless, their feelings deepen, eliciting confessional moments. Vargas admits, "I wish I lived in closer proximity to where you live—I too think of you after—actually, being very honest, I do need you (I think you and I feel a need but we don't understand it yet enjoy it,) and miss you, Ronnie, and I don't know why but I do."[23] Carrillo is similarly confused, expressing elation over the letter correspondence. His body responds with excitement after receiving Vargas's package: "Jack. . . received your letter several days ago—what a joy! I was uplifted so much and pleased with your letter that I temporarily forgot about tricking. For you see I was going to the Park when your letter came and after experiencing it I felt too good to go assault myself."[24] The mail disrupts his carnal urges as he finds "joy" in Vargas's handwritten pages. The correspondence stands in for physical closeness, providing an emotional resource that enables Carrillo to reserve his body for Vargas's (literary) consumption, even if only temporarily. The corporeality represented by this epistolary exchange enhances the performative capabilities of paper as it acts on and acts through sender and receiver. As Alison Piepmeier notes,

22 "Tata Vega: Full Speed Ahead." YouTube video, posted April 4, 2013. https://www.youtube.com/watch?v=ELGVpNpR7Hk.

23 Jack A. Vargas to Ronnie Carrillo, December 30, 1976 (postmarked January 1977), 1.

24 Ronnie Carrillo to Jack A. Vargas, July 18, 1977 (postmarked August 6, 1977), 3.

"paper facilitates affection" (2008, 220), and for Carrillo and Vargas nothing could be truer. In their struggle to find a righteous path between God, trick, and disco, their correspondence catalyzes connection and provides a temporary refuge from "fleshy debris," the "ancient yet familiar beasts" baiting them.[25]

Performing alter personae, printing collective bodies, and leaving impressions of their complicated desires in epistolary expressions, these avant-gardists construct queer racialized subjectivities in the unlikely flows of self-publishing, mail art, flyers, and image-text letter correspondence. For queer Chicano avant-garde circles, paper closed distances, forged intimacies, and cultivated contact between bodies by impressing physical traces into printed matter's fleshy surface. Whether rubberstamping a self-portrait onto the page, citing phantom personae in text, or creating a transgender fiction of self, body and paper perform a powerful conjunction, a union that *Homeboy Beautiful* understood. Terrill's collaborative avant-garde art publication became a printed zone of contact rife with Chicano art school factions, party boy cadres, mail art networks, and transient art happenings. Though it was short-lived as a print enterprise, various queer Chicano avant-garde entities permeated, circulated around, and broke off within it and against it. This circuitous relation replayed itself even in the Maricón Collective's resuscitation of *Homeboy Beautiful* nearly forty years after its original publication. Clearly, these artists were and remain touched by paper. By innovating mail/male art forms, they reshaped their social circumstances and found each other between the folds.

---

25 "Fleshy debris" is Carrillo's euphemism for casual tricking with anonymous men in the "meat market." Ronnie Carrillo to Jack A. Vargas, September 16, 1977 (postmarked December 5, 1977), 3. "Ancient yet familiar beasts" is another Vargas textual insignia, shown on the envelope in figure 4.

Bibliography

Benavidez, Max. 2007. *Gronk*. A Ver: Revisioning Art History, vol. 1. Los Angeles: UCLA Chicano Studies Research Center Press.

Bourriaud, Nicolas. 2002. *Relational Aesthetics*. Paris: Les Presses du Reel.

Crane, Michael. 1984. "A Definition of Correspondence Art." In *Correspondence Art: Source Book for the Network of International Postal Art Activity*, edited by Michael Crane and Mary Stofflet, 3–36. San Francisco: Contemporary Arts.

Cvetkovich, Ann. 2003. *An Archive of Feelings: Trauma, Sexuality, and Lesbian Public Cultures*. Durham, NC: Duke University Press.

De Salvo, Donna. 1999. "Correspondences." In *Ray Johnson: Correspondences*, edited by Donna De Salvo and Catherine Gudis, 15–29. Columbus: Wexner Center for the Arts/Ohio State University Press.

Gamboa, Harry Jr. 1998. "In the City of Angels, Chameleons, and Phantoms: Asco, a Case Study of Chicano Art in Urban Tones (or, Asco Was a Four-Member Word)." In *Urban Exile: Collected Writings of Harry Gamboa Jr.*, edited by Chon A. Noriega, 71–87. Minneapolis: University of Minnesota Press.

Gangadharan, Seeta Peña. 2009. "Mail Art: Networking without Technology." *New Media and Society* 11, nos. 1–2: 279–98.

Garcia, Matt. 2012. *From the Jaws of Victory: The Triumph and Tragedy of Cesar Chavez and the Farm Worker Movement*. Berkeley: University of California Press.

Gerhard, Jane. 2011. "Judy Chicago and the Practice of 1970s Feminism." *Feminist Studies* 37, no. 3: 591–618.

Hayden, Dolores. 1997. *The Power of Place: Urban Landscapes as Public History*. Cambridge, MA: MIT Press.

Held, John Jr. 2005. "The Mail Art Exhibition: Personal Worlds to Cultural Strategies." In *At a Distance: Precursors to Art and Activism on the Internet*, edited by Annmarie Chandler and Norie Neumark, 88–115. Cambridge, MA: MIT Press.

Hernández, Robb. 2009. *The Fire of Life: The Robert Legorreta–Cyclona Collection*. Chicano Archives, vol. 2. Los Angeles: UCLA Chicano Studies Research Center Press.

———. 2014. "Drawing Offensive/Offensive Drawing: Toward a Theory of Mariconógraphy." MELUS 39, no. 2: 121–52.

Johnston, Tracy J. 1979. "La Vida Loca: Girls in the Gangs of East L.A." *New West*, January 29, 38–46.

Jones, Amelia. 1995. "'Clothes Make the Man': The Male Artist as a Performative Function." *Oxford Art Journal* 18, no. 2: 18–32.

———. 2011. "'Traitor Prophets': Asco's Art as a Politics of the In-Between." In *Asco: Elite of the Obscure: A Retrospective*, 1972–1987, edited by C. Ondine Chavoya and Rita Gonzalez, 18–27. Ostfildern, Germany: Hatje Cantz.

Knight, Christopher. 2011. "A Permanent Asco Mural Is Slated for City Terrace." *Culture Monster* (blog), *Los Angeles Times*, September 12. latimesblog.latimes.com/culturemoster/2011/09/a-permanent-asco-mural-is-slated-forcity-terrace.html.

Latorre, Guisela. 2009. *Walls of Empowerment: Chicana/o Indigenist Murals of California*. Austin: University of Texas Press.

Longstreth, Galen Goodwin. 2001. "Epistolary Follies: Identity, Conversation, and Performance in the Correspondence of Ellen Terry and Bernard Shaw." *Shaw* 21: 27–40.

Miranda, Carolina A. 2015. "Five Must-See Booths at the LA Art Book Fair." *Los Angeles Times*, January 29.

Muñoz, José Esteban. 1999. *Disidentifications: Queers of Color and the Performance of Politics*. Minneapolis: University of Minnesota Press.

Ontiveros, Randy J. 2014. *In the Spirit of a New People: The Cultural Politics of the Chicano Movement*. New York: New York University Press.

Piepmeier, Alison. 2008. "Why Zines Matter: Materiality and the Creation of Embodied Community." *American Periodicals* 18, no. 2: 213–38.

Puar, Jasbir K. 2007. *Terrorist Assemblages: Homonationalism in Queer Times*. Durham, NC: Duke University Press.

Rivera-Servera, Ramón H. 2011. "Choreographies of Resistance: Latino Queer Dance and the Utopian Performative." In *Gay Latino Studies: A Critical Reader*, edited by Michael Hames-García and Ernesto Javier Martínez, 259–80. Durham, NC: Duke University Press.

Rodríguez, Richard T. 2009. *Next of Kin: The Family in Chicano/a Cultural Politics*. Durham, NC: Duke University Press.

———. 2011. "Being and Belonging: Joey Terrill's Performance of Politics." *Biography* 34, no. 3: 467–91.

Smith, Cherise. 2011. *Enacting Others: Politics of Identity in Eleanor Antin, Nikki S. Lee, Adrian Piper, and Anna Deavere Smith*. Durham, NC: Duke University Press.

Terrill, Joey. 1978. *Homeboy Beautiful*, issue 1.

———. 1979. *Homeboy Beautiful*, issue 2.

———. 2007. Interview by author, Los Angeles, August 23.

———. 2010. Interview by author, Los Angeles, August 28.

———. 2015. Interview by author, Los Angeles, June 13.

Thomas, Susan E. 2009. "Value and Validity of Art Zines as an Art Form." *Art Documentation* 28, no. 2: 27–36, 38.

Villarreal, Yezmin. 2015. "Maricón Art and DJ Collective Celebrates Queer Chicano Culture." *LA Weekly*, January 20.

"Kitchen-Table Kinds of Things"[1]

Radical Women's Poetics as a Model for Small Press Collecting

Shannon Tharp, Katherine Crowe, and Peggy Keeran

> *The cool thing is that you can just make a magazine or a book. Kitchen-table kinds of things. Very hands-on. You just decide to do it. Take matters into your own hands. It's a women's thing in the sense that if you don't have money or anything, you just do with what you have there.*
>
> Maureen Owen

The exploration of library collections and archives as spaces of power has not yet fully incorporated a discussion of the small press mimeo revolution in the United States that spanned the 1950s-'80s and produced hundreds of little magazines. These little magazines were radical in different ways, but common to each was the foundational meaning of radical: "at the root." In some cases, radical meant "shocking or edgy," while in other cases it meant politically far left of center. For women editors of the time like Maureen Owen, the ability to make something fundamental, tangible, and vital—great art, period—was, in its own right, radical.

One of the standout magazines that emerged from this period is *Telephone*, edited by Owen, who lives in Denver, Colorado. The University of Denver (DU) Libraries recently acquired Owen's archive of correspondence, papers, and ephemera from 2000 onward. Owen's archive,

---

1 Maureen Owen, "Notes on Publishing: From a Telephone Interview with Marcella Durand," *Jacket* 11, April 2000. http://jacketmagazine.com/11/owen-durand.html.

alongside a nearly full run of *Telephone* held by DU Libraries, presents the opportunity to deeply engage with and center small press publishing, as well as the work of a woman whose " ... epiphany was to publish a magazine as big and as inclusive as Ma Bell's telephone directory."[2] And that she did.

Poetry, Little Magazines, and the Mimeo Revolution

In a 1964 *Times Literary Supplement* article, Kirby Congdon of Crank Press, refers to a new publishing trend in little magazines as the "mimeography revolution, the end of the competitive approach to poetry and waiting and pleading at the doors of big time publishing."[3] The little magazine mimeograph revolution, or mimeo revolution, spanned the years from the 1960s to the 1980s, making it possible for writers to publish writers,[4] and to print, assemble, and distribute new and experimental poetry quickly and economically, sometimes within a week of being written, thus avoiding the lengthy acceptance and publishing process of the traditional publishing houses. Poetry and even the titles of the magazines didn't have to conform to what were viewed as bourgeois standards of taste, but could be edgy and even shocking for the time period in terms of perceived obscene language and imagery. As cited in the *TLS* article, "Congdon attacks all encouragement of the writing of 'good poetry' ... 'Poetry is for now, not tomorrow. And what is exciting is a matter of the reader's own taste, his own convictions, and his own curiosity, rather than fashion.'"[5] The members of the poetry community controlled the process and content, not the establishment, which was revolutionary and in keeping with the other political and social upheavals of the 1960s.

Although *mimeograph* may not be the most accurate term—Fulton found in his analysis of little magazines published between 1965 and 1969 that the majority were letterpress, followed by offset, and then

---

2 Anna Zumbahlen, "Poetry cracked around me': Interview with Maureen Owen," *Denver Quarterly* 54, no.3 (2020): 109.

3 Eric Mottram, "The Mimeograph Revolution," *Times Literary Supplement*, August 6, 1964, 714.

4 Lisa Chinn, "How the Mimeo-MagazineSounds in 1960s Counterculture: *The Floating Bear* as Sonic Artifact," *Journal for Literary and Intermedial Crossings* 5, no.1 (2020): fl, https://clic.research.vub.be/sites/default/files/JLIC%205.1f%20CHINN.pdf.

5 Mottram, "The Mimeograph Revolution," 714.

by mimeo[6]—as Steven Clay and Rodney Phillips point out, the "formal means of production" itself isn't as important as the content.[7] To Linda Russo, the phrase mimeo revolution refers to the "machinic aspect of the period" overall, not to a specific type of machine.[8] With rapid advancements in printing technology, used presses became more readily available and affordable for individuals and groups to acquire.[9] The mimeograph machine, patented by Thomas Edison in 1876 and retailed later that century, allowed individuals and groups to quickly create and disseminate print information, making it possible for anyone to become a publisher. The mimeograph machine itself could be easily mastered, and was used by governments, organizations, and communities around the world to print everything from military documents to school and community newsletters to fanzines to underground political and alternative press materials. In 1970, Roy Loewinsohn wrote of the speed with which poetry was published, distributed, and responded to via mimeograph: "Having them, we could see what we were doing, as it came, hot off the griddle," instantaneous feedback to all poets, including for young experimental poets who, being neglected by established publishing houses, "could get exposure &, more importantly, encouragement &/or criticism."[10] Russo credits communal support for the achievements of poets such as Kathleen Fraser, Alice Notley, and Susan Howe, who, "partly because they experimented, but also because they were women, found receptive and critical communities in the small press."[11] James Elmborg reflects on how these magazines created connections nationally and locally, and connections between unknown poets who were published alongside "famous" poets.[12] Little magazines helped create a nationwide network of

6 Len Fulton, "Anima Rising: Little Magazines in the Sixties," *American Libraries* 2, no. 1 (January 1971): 26.

7 Steven Clay and Rodney Phillips, *A Secret Location on the Lower East Side: Adventures in Writing, 1960–1980* (New York: New York Public Library and Granary Books, 1998), 15.

8 Linda Russo, "The 'F' Word in the Age of Mechanical Reproduction: An Account of Women-Edited Small Presses and Journals," in *The World in Time and Space: Towards a History of Innovative American Poetry in Our Time*, eds. Edward Foster and Joseph Donahue (Jersey City, NJ: Talisman House, 2002), 249.

9 Fulton, "Anima Rising," 26.

10 Ron Loewinsohn, "After the (Mimeograph) Revolution," *TriQuarterly* 21 (Spring 1971): 222.

11 Russo, "The 'F' Word in the Age of Mechanical Reproduction," 247.

12 James Elmborg, "Toward Building a Digital Index of Little Magazines of the 1960s," *Serials Review* 44, no. 1 (2018): 20.

poets and poet-editors built upon smaller, local poet and poet-editor communities.

Little Magazines, Mimeo, Community, and the Lower East Side Poets

The New York School poets congregated in the Lower East Side of New York City during this era and created their own little magazine mimeo revolution and community. Ted Berrigan arrived in the Lower East Side from Tulsa from 1960 to 1961, and brought his skill using the mimeograph machine from his stint in the army.[13] "Mimeograph machines were often located in shared spaces, including bookstores, libraries, or print co-ops, where they might be used after hours, enabling a variety of people to come and go."[14] LeRoi Jones/Amiri Baraka and Diane di Prima produced *The Floating Bear* on the mimeograph in 1961 at Robert Wilson's Phoenix Bookstore in New York City, in return for copies of the magazine.[15] After its acquisition in 1967, many poet-editors used The Poetry Project's Gestetner mimeo machine at St. Mark's Church-in-the-Bowery (St. Mark's Church) to produce books and magazines, including Joel Sloman and Anne Waldman's *The World*, Anne Waldman and Lewis Warsh's Angel Hair press, Larry Fagin's *Adventures in Poetry*, and Maureen Owen's *Telephone*. As Clay and Phillips state, mimeographing put "the means of production in the hands of the poet. In a very real sense, almost anyone could become a publisher" for the "price of a few reams of paper and a handful of stencils."[16]

The poet-editors' memories of the mimeographing and collaborative collation processes provide insight into this community and its poetry production. Waldman reminisces about early attempts mimeographing *The World*, and the unexpected aesthetic pleasure resulting from what looked like a potential mess:

> A not-so-efficient brainstorm as it turned out, Joel Sloman and I sent out stencils to our desired contributors in mailing tubes that were to be returned with hot-from-the-muse in-progress works.

---

13 Clay and Phillips, *A Secret Location on the Lower East Side*, 40.

14 Rona Cran, "Space Occupied: Women Poet-Editors and the Mimeograph Revolution in Mid-century New York City," *Journal of American Studies*, 55, no. 2 (2021): 480.

15 Clay and Phillips, *A Secret Location on the Lower East Side*, 29.

16 Clay and Phillips, *A Secret Location on the Lower East Side*, 14.

> They came back mangled, or improperly typed. Banged out in creative fervor. Holes for "o's" from those with expressive macho typewriters. No, that sheet has to go under the blue part shiny side up, you dummies! Exasperation, but soon it started to look good *in the tradition*, as we in the Mimeo Revolution say. Long hours late at night in the office minding the machines. Then we'd have a collation party the next day with the heavy-duty stapler. The over-inked pages had a certain charm.[17]

Larry Fagin describes logistical aspects of the process to put together an issue of *Adventures in Poetry*:

> A typical issue was 300-350 copies, consuming thirty reams of 24# mimeograph paper, run through the Gestetner machine of The Poetry Project at St. Mark's Church. Most numbers were as thick as possible—as many as fifty double-sided pages. I purchased a state-of-the-art Novus ½" stapler from Germany that cut through an issue like it was butter, a very satisfying sensation. After the final editing, typing, proofing, correcting, and mimeographing, a bunch of us would set up long tables in the Parish Hall, often after a reading, and collate and staple late into the night.[18]

Maureen Owen reflects upon the support she received from Waldman, Fagin, and Tom Veitch, a graphic novelist. Waldman gave Owen permission to use the facilities of The Poetry Project to produce the little magazine *Telephone*, and provided "a first, frightening lesson in using the Gestetner mimeo," while Veitch gave her lessons by running off the entire first issue, thus setting her up to do the subsequent issues herself. Fagin instructed her where to buy stencils, how to type them, how to use stencil correction fluid and a stylus for visuals, and where to buy paper remnants cheaply.[19] Owen shares her enthrallment with the process:

> I loved mimeoing. I loved the hands-on mechanics of putting the stencil on the cylinder, adding the ink, stacking the clean white paper. The Gestetner made a roar of sound like a locomotive jolting forward—kachunck! The first sheet would drop down with a poem

17 Clay and Phillips, *A Secret Location on the Lower East Side*, 187.

18 Clay and Phillips, *A Secret Location on the Lower East Side*, 195.

19 Zumbahlen "Poetry cracked around me," 105-6.

> on it. That moment from raggedy stencil to the page always seemed a miracle of weird wonder to me. Mimeo is the most beautiful thing! The utter black of the ink, still wet, sits up on the white paper. One has such control over the whole process. So radical you can do it yourself, get it out on the street next day, so immediate. The machine and the ink and the paper.[20]

Community building is an important outcome of little magazine production in the Lower East Side during the mimeo revolution, from poet-editors discovering and publishing new poets who shared their work through readings to bringing together members of the community at a social event to compile and staple a magazine. As Russo says, "Ask any mimeo poet-editor and they'll tell you, it was an ethic, a way of life, a way of creating community for oneself and for giving back to one's community, of encouraging and locating poetic affinities, and of cultivating a scene."[21] Poetry as a communal effort, from creation to distribution, deviates from the traditionally understood narratives of literary authorship and production. "Most obvious, Ginsberg's naming of poets as 'community and family' underscores the tacit acceptance of poetry as a group phenomenon and threatens the prevailing romanticized conception of the author as a solitary inspired figure."[22]

The process of putting together a little magazine, "collating, stapling, and mailing parties helped speed up production, but, more significantly, they helped galvanize a literary group."[23] Chinn remarks that "communal space is created through the production of the little magazine on the mimeograph machine. Thus, the community of readers would have also known themselves to be a community of listeners, transporting themselves from the pages of the magazine to the coffeeshops where performances were held."[24] Owen remembers that communal experience a precious, for "after we ran off the pages we stacked them to dry, and some days later I gathered every friend I'd made and their friends and we collated. One of the beautiful things

---

20 Zumbahlen "Poetry cracked around me," 106.

21 Russo, "The 'F' Word in the Age of Mechanical Reproduction," 261.

22 Daniel Kane, *All Poets Welcome: The Lower East Side Poetry Scene in the 1960s* (Berkeley: University of California Press, 2003), xiv.

23 Clay and Phillips, *A Secret Location on the Lower East Side*, 14.

24 Chinn, "How the Mimeo-Magazine Sounds in 1960s Counterculture," 3-4.

about mimeo is the sense of community. People collated and stapled and took copies to hand around."[25] In addition to building community, we believe that Owen's relationships with other poets transcended the broader idea of community, and informed her little magazine and small press book publishing with what we characterize as her ethics of care philosophy. Women, geographically isolated from their poet colleagues and friends, started little magazines to keep in touch with far-flung communities.[26]

In Owen's case, she began editing and publishing *Telephone* magazine and Telephone Books not long after she moved to the Lower East Side in the summer of 1968. The magazine, published from 1969 to 1983, comprised 19 issues printed in runs of 750 copies apiece. Over the course of its publication, the magazine featured the work of 630 unique contributors.[27] In a brief history of *Telephone* in Clay and Phillips's *A Secret Location*, Owen writes:

> I came to the Lower East Side by way of San Francisco, Japan, and Branson, Missouri. I was with Lauren Owen at the time, and when we got to New York, we stayed at the apartment of his friends from Tulsa, Ron and Patty Padgett. Ron and another pal, Johnny Stanton, told me about The Poetry Project at St. Mark's. I immediately took myself over there and began going to readings and meeting other poets. Anne Waldman was bringing out *The World*, and it was very exciting. I started thinking about doing books and putting a magazine of my own together.[28]

As mentioned previously, Owen asked Waldman, who was director of The Poetry Project at St. Mark's Church at the time, if she could use the nine-hole Gestetner mimeo machine at The Poetry Project to launch Telephone Press. Fortunately for all of us, Waldman agreed, and Owen began by making the first two Telephone Books: Rebecca Brown's *Elusive Continent* (1972) and David Rosenberg's *Frontal Nudity* (1972). And, of course, the first issues of *Telephone*.

---

25 Clay and Phillips, *A Secret Location on the Lower East Side*, 227.

26 Russo, "The 'F' Word in the Age of Mechanical Reproduction," 260.

27 M.C. Kinniburgh, *About Telephone: An Introduction & Bibliography,* Among the Neighbors, 19.1 (Buffalo: The Poetry Collection of the University Libraries, University at Buffalo, The State University of New York, 2022), 3.

28 Clay and Phillips, *A Secret Location on the Lower East Side*, 227.

Through the Grapevine

To gain some context for what was happening around Owen and the community she was a part of on the Lower East Side in the late 1960s—a community sometimes referred to as the second and third generations of the New York School of poets—it's important to understand what was happening in and with the United States. In late January 1968, the U.S. launched the Tet Offensive, one of the largest campaigns of the Vietnam War. Less than two months later, the Mỹ Lai massacre occurred. The general public in the U.S. would not learn of the massacre until November 1969, when freelance journalist Seymour Hersch first reported its cover-up via the Associated Press wire service. This national and international context informed the mindset and orientation of many "mimeo revolution" poets working in New York at the time, as references to the Vietnam War and criticism of the U.S. escalation were frequent and fiery.

On April 4, 1968, Martin Luther King Jr. was assassinated in Memphis, Tennessee. One week later, as riots over King's assassination took place across the country, Lyndon Johnson signed the Civil Rights Act of 1968, which expanded the Civil Rights Act of 1964, and prohibited racial discrimination in the sale, rental, and financing of housing. Of the Act's expansion in *1968: A History in Verse*, Ed Sanders writes,

> Congress slid into the Act what they called the
> "Rap Brown amendment"
> making it a crime to cross state lines
> 'with the intent to incite, organize, promote,
> encourage, participate in and carry on a riot.'[29]

Sanders, a poet, publisher, historian, and co-founder of The Fugs, a band that was a lynchpin to 1960s counterculture, also ran Peace Eye Bookstore at 147 Avenue A in New York City. Peace Eye, the "secret location on the lower east side" that also served as a community print center and a refuge for people fleeing the war, was located across the street from Tompkins Square Park, where Owen took her two sons to play, and a few blocks' walk to The Poetry Project at St. Mark's Church, where Sanders and Owen were regulars. From 1962-1965, Sanders mimeographed 13 issues of *Fuck You/ A Magazine of the Arts*, attempting

29 Edward Sanders, *1968: A History in Verse* (Santa Rosa: Black Sparrow Press, 2000), 85.

to " ... reach out to the 'Best Minds' of my generation with a message of Gandhian pacifism, great sharing, social change, the expansion of personal freedom (including the legalization of marijuana), and the then-stirring messages of sexual liberation."[30] Peace Eye was raided by the New York Police Department on obscenity charges related to content in *Fuck You/* on New Year's Day 1966.[31] In the summer of 1967, Sanders stood trial and defeated the charges against him. Shortly thereafter, he re-opened Peace Eye on East 10th St. before moving the bookstore to Avenue A in the spring of 1968.

In late April 1968, students protesting the Vietnam War took over administration buildings at Columbia University and shut the school down for a week. In early June, Valerie Solanas shot Andy Warhol at his New York City studio, The Factory, less than a mile away from The Poetry Project at St. Mark's Church. Two days later, after winning the California and South Dakota primary elections, Democratic presidential candidate Robert Kennedy was assassinated while campaigning in Los Angeles.

On the first of July, The Band released its gorgeous first album, *Music from Big Pink*, having recorded several of the album's songs in Manhattan. In 1976, some of the most beautiful film footage we have would emerge from the album: The Staple Singers performing "The Weight" with The Band for Martin Scorsese's *The Last Waltz*.

In early October: the Tlatelolco massacre. Mexican armed forces opened fire on civilians who were protesting the upcoming Summer Olympics in Mexico City. At the Olympics, U.S. sprinter Tommie Smith set a world record in the 200 meters and won a gold medal, and his teammate John Carlos won bronze in the race. On the podium for the medal ceremony, Smith and Carlos, both Black, each raised a black-gloved fist during the U.S. national anthem. Both men were shoeless to protest Black poverty, while Smith wore a scarf to represent Black pride, and Carlos wore a necklace of beads for, in his words, " ... those individuals that were lynched or killed that no one said a prayer for, that were hung and tarred. It was for those thrown off the side of the

---

30 Clay and Phillips, *A Secret Location on the Lower East Side*, 167.

31 Kembrew McLeod, "The Police Raid Peace Eye Bookstore," Downtown Pop Underground. https://dsps.lib.uiowa.edu/downtownpopunderground/story/the-police-raid-peace-eye-bookstore/.

boats in the Middle Passage."[32] Smith and Carlos were kicked off the Olympic team. When they returned to the U.S., they received numerous death threats and had difficulty finding employment.

In November, Republican Richard Nixon was elected the 37th president of the U.S., and by year's end *2001: A Space Odyssey* and *Rosemary's Baby* were among the top-grossing movies of 1968, while Marvin Gaye's "I Heard It Through the Grapevine" was the number one song on the radio. Where poetry was concerned, the year saw the publication of Gwendolyn Brooks's *In the Mecca;* Robert Creeley's *Pieces;* Allen Ginsberg's *T.V. Baby Poem;* Etheridge Knight's *Poems From Prison;* Lorine Niedecker's *North Central*; George Oppen's *Of Being Numerous;* and Audre Lorde's first collection, *The First Cities*, on Diane Di Prima's Poets Press (to name only a few full-length collections published in 1968).

Meanwhile, telephone users, telephone system engineers, and information operators were debating the meaning of the term "information," telephone service in New York City was terrible at turns and unfairly priced, and telephone company workers in New York City were routinely striking for better pay and working conditions. Demand for telephone subscriptions and service had begun to outpace Bell Systems' capabilities, and major U.S. newspapers were publishing items about an upcoming name change to Bell Systems' information operator service.

In a *Chicago Daily News* brief from June 28, 1968, this passage about a name change to Bell Systems' information operator service appeared: "Illinois Bell Telephone Co. is changing the name of its information service to 'Directory Assistance' because too many persons take the name literally. A student recently called to ask the operator if he is a mammal, 'like a whale.' And one startled operator got a call from a frantic woman who wanted to know how to get a squirrel out of her house."[33] Three days later, on July 1, the name change took effect across the U.S. Communications scholar Emily Goodmann writes:

> The popularity of cybernetics post-World War II and the revolutions in computing and communication technologies encouraged expert

---

32 Dave Zirin, "The Living Legacy of Mexico City: An Interview with John Carlos," *Counterpunch*, Nov. 2, 2003, https://www.counterpunch.org/2003/11/01/an-interview-with-john-carlos.

33 Emily Goodmann, "A Tale of Two Networks: The Bell Telephone System and the Meaning of 'Information,' 1947-1968." *Information and Culture: A Journal of History* 54, no. 3 (2019): 281.

> telecommunication discourse communities to characterize information as meaningless, patterned, digital data. Nonexpert telephone subscribers, however, had nearly eighty years of experience with telephone system informational tools that encouraged a human-centered definition of 'information.'[34]

The first telephone informational tool that many users experienced was the telephone directory, the first of which was published in 1878. By 1968, then, telephone directories had been a fixture in people's lives for nearly 100 years. Throughout the turn of the two centuries that make up this timespan, telephone directories belonged to a class of print media that included dictionaries, encyclopedias, railway timetables, travel guides, and the newspaper, all of which "...gave more visibility to the slow and ad hoc emergence of information as a thing that existed in the world."[35] As media historian Craig Robertson notes, paper gave a material existence to information.[36]

And couldn't it be said that the aforementioned items—railway timetables, travel guides, the newspaper and the like—are ephemeral? These pieces of any one person's world that might only be of use to them for a short time, but which, when studied years, decades, centuries later become part of the story that the reader, the researcher, the curious one conjures. What was set to paper in 1968 and given life through text and image—the brutality of war, protests in which people demanded dignity and respect, layers of grief and feeling that can't be approximated here, the buzz of change ahead—led up to the making of one of the mimeo revolution's greatest little magazines.

Daring and Vision

When Owen was thinking about the look and feel of *Telephone*, Waldman mentioned to her that some paper companies in Lower Manhattan sold cheap paper leftovers. While visiting a paper company to buy a few reams of paper, Owen saw 8 1/2 by 14-inch sheets of paper and thought that they looked like a telephone booth. The magazine's size

---

34 Goodmann, "A Tale of Two Networks," 282-283.

35 Craig Robertson, "Learning to File: Reconfiguring Information and Information Work in the Early Twentieth Century." *Technology and Culture* 58, no. 4 (2017): 957.

36 Robertson, "Learning to File," 958.

was decided. Owen details her decision in a 2021 interview with poet, scholar, and bookseller M.C. Kinniburgh:

> ... the reason I went to that size—the 8 1/2 by 14 inches—was that I wanted to call the magazine *Telephone*, for a couple reasons. Briefly: I was from the West Coast—the Midwest and the West Coast—and in those environments socially you'd just drop in on people. But I found pretty fast that in New York, you called first in those days, because people were usually up all night writing or something and they were half asleep during the day or sleeping during the day. ...I started to learn that the telephone's important to do, to just make a call. Then also Ma Bell was a big issue right at that period of time. There was all this stuff going on about pricing and corruption.[37]

Owen, who was born in Minnesota and raised in Minnesota and California, wanted to publish a magazine as big and inclusive as Ma Bell's telephone directory.[38] She wanted to be inclusive because she recognized that some writers, many of them women, had few places to publish.

Talking with Doug Lang in a 1977 radio interview for WPFW, a Washington, D.C. radio station, Owen said, "...it seemed like there were a lot of unpublished women whose manuscripts I'd come across. It seemed like there were more opportunities for men to get published at the time I was starting. I don't feel tremendously feminist in my...there's so many men whose work I'm so enthusiastic about, but...I think I get more manuscripts from women because they don't have other outlets." [39]

Some of those women—Sandy Berrigan, Rebecca Brown, Fanny Howe, Susan Howe, Janine Pommy Bega, Patricia Spears Jones, and Rebecca Wright, for example—were writing terrific poetry. Many continue to do so to this day, and Brown now writes science fiction under the pseudonym Rebecca Ore. In fact, Brown's *The Bicycle Trip & Other Poems*, published on Telephone Books in 1974, notes on its title page: "none of these poems have appeared before, only one of them was sent out." And in Susan Howe's *Hinge Picture*, her first book, published

37 M.C. Kinniburgh, *About Telephone: An Interview with Maureen Owen*, Among the Neighbors, 19.2 (Buffalo: The Poetry Collection of the University Libraries, University at Buffalo, The State University of New York, 2022), 6.

38 Zumbahlen, "Poetry cracked around me," 109.

39 Maureen Owen, Interview, By Doug Lang, *Expressions*, WPFW, January 1977. https://archive.org/details/pacifica_radio_archives-WZ0052.

by Telephone Books in 1974, she notes, "This work has never appeared elsewhere, in whole or in part."[40] Howe's *The Liberties* was also published by Telephone Books in 1980, and she has emphasized that Owen was a great collaborator "...because she was open to any adventure. I showed her what I wanted and then we worked it out, though it was a mimeo edition and she had almost no money and naturally ran into trouble getting small-press grants. She has daring and vision, and Telephone Books, the magazine and the press, is where many people get into print for the first time."[41]

That daring and vision extended to the forthright way that that Owen initially approached contributors about publishing in *Telephone* magazine. She frequently attended poetry readings at The Poetry Project at St. Mark's Church, where she heard many writers who were just starting out, some of them giving their first poetry readings. When Owen heard someone whose work she liked, she'd walk up to them after their reading and ask if they'd be interested in submitting work to *Telephone*. In a 2016 interview with poet Pat Nolan, whose work was published in *Telephone* magazine, Owen said, "At readings I would be knocked off my chair by their [women's] stunning poems that were nowhere in print. It's so incredible to discover poems that take your breath away. I've always craved making things, hands on, making collages and such. So naturally I thought I could create a magazine."[42]

A Kind of Ongoing Thing

For *Telephone*'s first issue, Owen solicited submissions. In that issue, 24 unique contributors appear. On the cover, lower center, is George Schneeman's drawing of an inky black rotary telephone minus receiver and cord. On the cover's center left section is a black telephone booth with a white T on its front. Attached via a short cord is a small placard below the T that reads TELEPHONE. Above it all: space, which gives the illusion of the cover being divided into thirds. From its very beginning,

---

40 "The Telephone Books and Magazine Collection," Granary Books, Winter 2021: 1. https://www.granarybooks.com/images/upload/telephone-completeillustrated-final.pdf.

41 Lynn Keller, "An Interview with Susan Howe," *Contemporary Literature* 36, no. 1 (1995): 17-18.

42 Pat Nolan, "In Conversation with Maureen Owen," *The Black Bart Poetry Society*, Nov. 12, 2016. https://thenewblackbartpoetrysociety.wordpress.com/2016/11/12/in-conversation-with-maureen-owen/.

Telephone is playful, intriguing, humorous, even a little mysterious. It draws your attention and absolutely holds it.

Of the magazine's 8 1/2 x 14-inch scheme, Owen has noted how well this particular size functioned for space on the page and the presentation of poems. Space, she says, is crucial to her own poetry, as well as to *Telephone* magazine and Telephone Books. "I think the space is so important for the words. I just hate books where everything is crunched in. It was great, it was like having a landscape. You can make a painting, almost."[43]

The size and space of *Telephone* also lends a kind of columnar feel to some of the poems mimeoed in the magazine, situated down the center of the long page. Given a bird's eye view of the poems, a reader might well think of pillars, supports, the strength of stone. At other junctures, the landscape that Owen mentions is apparent, with poems expanding across and down the page, sometimes spiraling. One thinks here, too, of the rotary duplicator that's part of a mimeograph machine, an echo of the rotary dial common to telephones at the time, the circles one would spin to communicate.

After Veitch helped Owen with running off the first issue of *Telephone* on the Gestetner, Owen was set. She ran off everything by herself and would often work at night "...because I had the two boys, and so I'd go over [to the Poetry Project at St. Mark's Church] and had someone watch them."[44] The magazine picked up speed. For distribution, Owen used The Poetry Project's mailing list and other methods to put *Telephone* into the world. Answering a question about distribution specifics posed to her by Shannon Tharp, one of this chapter's authors, Owen responded:

> I would hand deliver copies to local bookstores and mail to a number of bookstores in other places. Some contributors were in England, and I would send them issues and to bookstores they knew of. I would also mail to contributors that were in other parts of the U.S. with extra copies for them to distribute in their areas. It was very much a hand-to-hand distribution, and copies went out quite fast. In those days book rate was about 13 cents as I recall, so it was possible to do a significant mailing without much cost. Different

43 Kinniburgh, *About Telephone: An Interview with Maureen Owen*, 7.

44 Kinniburgh, *About Telephone: An Interview with Maureen Owen*, 8.

> poets and folks in the community helped me with mailing, but I spent long hours on my own too.

In addition, friends and collaborators handed copies of *Telephone* out around New York City. When Owen delivered the magazine to bookstores around the city, she found that some bookstores were reticent about it, because the side-stapled magazine had no spine, and the size was unwieldy; they didn't know where they could put the magazine. One bookstore that Owen notes as having been welcoming about *Telephone* from the start was Eighth Street Bookshop in Greenwich Village, run by brothers Elias and Ted Wilentz. Per the Village Alliance's description of the bookshop, it "...gained fame as a literary gathering place with close ties to the nonconformist writers of the day."[45]

With subsequent issues of *Telephone*, Owen received so many submissions to her Chelsea Station mailbox that it was difficult for her to haul all the mail back to her apartment. "I would go to pick up my mail and the guys there would just start laughing, because it had gone way beyond the box. They would give me one of those big mail bags, and I literally would have to drag it, I couldn't pick it up, it was so full of submissions. I would drag it down the subway steps home."[46] The roster of 630 unique contributors to *Telephone*—writers, artists, children of some of those writers and artists—is astonishing, as is the pace at which new, always substantive issues of the magazine arrived. By Spring 1973, Owen ran a *Telephone* 8 "Special Giant Issue," its cover an orange Charles Plymell collage of telephones, a prodigious 64 unique contributors to that one issue alone. The magazine's cover art varies from an open letter from Joe Brainard dated Tues., Feb. 23, 1971 on the cover of *Telephone* 3: "I WOULD JUST LIKE TO TAKE THIS OPPORTUNITY TO SAY IN WRITING THAT THE TELEPHONE COMPANY IS FULL OF SHIT!" On the cover of *Telephone* 5, there's Emilio (Elio) Schneeman's drawing of Clark Kent emerging from a telephone booth as Superman. Further, Paula North's semi-risqué and mischievous animals, a smiling dinosaur in the middle of them talking on the phone, form the cover of *Telephone* 9. And then there's the cover of *Telephone* 17: a July 1981 photograph of a telephone booth that Owen snapped in Dumont,

---

45 "8th Street Bookshop," Village Alliance. https://greenwichvillage.nyc/places/8th-street-bookshop/.

46 Kinniburgh, *About Telephone: An Interview with Maureen Owen*, 9.

Minnesota, ten minutes north of Graceville, where she was born, not far from Traverse Gap and the Minnesota—South Dakota state line.

Talking with poet Anna Zumbahlen about her childhood and the role that the telephone played in it, Owen notes that for a while on the Minnesota prairie her family didn't have a telephone. Once lines made their way to the area, Owen's family telephone was on a party line.

> The phone made quite a social possibility in farms miles apart. When the phone rang and you picked it up, you heard a multitude of clicks and that was everyone on the party line picking up their phone too, to listen in. Everyone listening on the party line got all the latest local news firsthand and kept up to date on all the goings on. So that gave me a hot off the press and copies out to everyone passed from hand-to-hand idea.[47]

In issues 4-7 of *Telephone*, one sees an attribution for drawings by Texas Moon, which was Owen's pseudonym.[48] In *Telephone* 4 (1971), a Texas Moon backpage drawing depicts Goldilocks falling through a chair, *Telephone* 4 flying from her hands (See Figure 1). In *Telephone* 5 (1971), there's a small backpage drawing of a mouse tucked in bed asleep, a single candle sitting on a nightstand beside the sleeping mouse (See Figure 2). In *Telephone* 6 (Spring 1972), a drawing appears above the table of content: a pig seated at a table and eating, bib tied around its neck, END the WAR! written on its back, which is turned to the viewer/reader (See Figure 3). And in *Telephone* 7 (Fall 1972), there above the table of contents, are three bears: a little bear seated in between two big bears in their respective chairs, the bear on the left reading a newspaper open to a headline that reads TELEPHONE; the bear on the right reading a newspaper open to a headline that reads NUMBER; and the little one in the middle holding a page that reads 7 (See Figure 4).

Down to the smallest traces, Owen's presence and generosity are apparent throughout the entirety of *Telephone*. She rarely published her own poems in the magazine, leaving space for other people's writing and art. Given space and time, the writing, drawing, comics, and collages of *Telephone* talk between, across, among, and beyond its 19 issues. In a 1999 interview with Marcella Durand, Owen said, "It's all so

47 Zumbahlen, "Poetry cracked around me," 109.

48 Kinniburgh, *About Telephone: An Introduction & Bibliography*, 4.

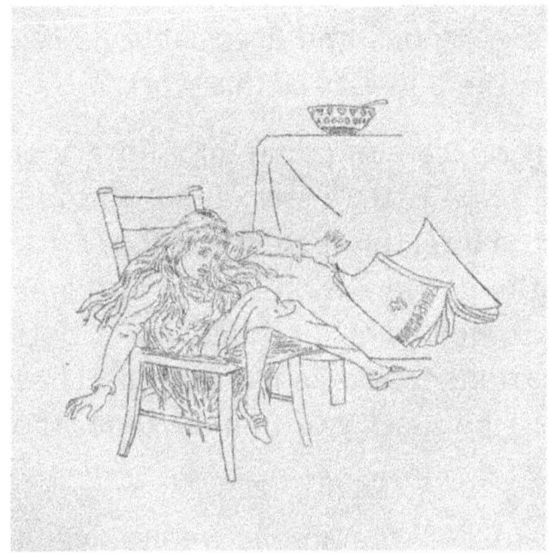

Figure 1

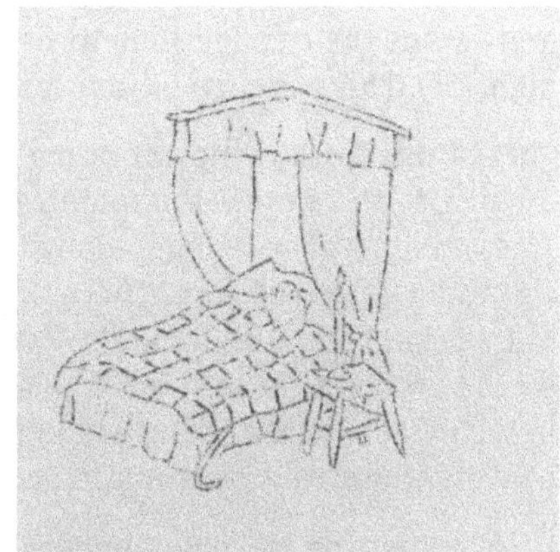

Figure 2

Figure 3

Figure 4

in-process. ... The purpose of a good little magazine is not the printed completion of work. It's a kind of ongoing thing. Here's what people are doing. What do you think? Much more of a community thing. ... It's alive in a way that a perfect-bound book isn't."[49]

The Logistics of This Work

A passage that corresponds to Owen's ethos and the purview of this chapter's authors can be found in Kinniburgh's *Messy Archivist*, in which Kinniburgh offers, "We no longer have to pretend that archives are 'neutral,' that the documents speak for themselves and are preserved uniformly. This conversation is a relief, because I'm not neutral either. I am full of compassion for poets and artists and their archives,

49 Owen, "Notes on Publishing."

and I want their collections to be as gorgeous and accessible as the night sky. There is such tenderness in the logistics of this work."[50]

Part of this work is the act of making space—on paper, in a library or archive, in the world—for something to be read, heard, seen, and felt. This work has everything to do with the interconnectedness that's crucial to an ethics of care. There are the conversations between some of this chapter's authors and Owen, as well as other poets and artists whose archives we care for, conversations that take place on porches, in backyards, just walking around our home city of Denver, Colorado, conversations that constellate entire seasons.

Through getting to know one another where we are, as we are, we insist that the act of collecting within libraries and archives is steeped in relational work. Through identifying, gathering, processing, describing, making accessible, and teaching with small press materials, we make space for poets and artists who've made space for poets and artists before them—a powerful, collective echo that's a stand against erasure. This relational work occurs alongside increasingly automated practices in collection development and reminds us as archivists and librarians that automation, as well as texts perceived to be "authoritative," often overlook great work that exists on the margins of mainstream publishing.

In fact, in our research for this chapter, we noted *Telephone*'s exclusion from the largest index of little magazines that originated during the mimeograph revolution, Christopher Harter's *An Author Index to Little Magazines of the Mimeograph Revolution*, published in 2008. Owen is cited in the index, but for her poems that appear in Larry Fagin's *Adventures in Poetry*, another little magazine that was part of the mimeograph revolution and printed on the same Gestetner that Owen used for *Telephone*. Fagin published Owen's first book, *Country Rush*, with cover and drawings by Yvonne Jacquette, on *Adventures in Poetry* in 1973.[51]

In addition to her visionary editorial work on *Telephone* magazine and Telephone Books, Owen was coordinator and co-director of The

---

50 M.C. Kinniburgh, *Messy Archivist* (TKS, 2020), 3.

51 Nick Sturm, "Crystal Set #17: Country Rush by Maureen Owen (Adventures in Poetry, 1973)." https://www.nicksturm.com/crystalset/2018/4/20/crystal-set-17-country-rush-by-maureen-owen-adventures-in-poetry-1973.

Poetry Project at St. Mark's Church from 1976–1980, during which time she received a fellowship grant from the National Endowment for the Arts that funded work on *Telephone*. Owen has taught creative writing courses at Edinboro University, Swarthmore College, St. Joseph's College, and Naropa University. Her publications include *Country Rush* (1973), *No Travels Journal* (1975), *A Brass Choir Approaches the Burial Ground* in *Big Deal 5* (1977), *Hearts in Space* (1980), *AE (Amelia Earhart)* (1984), *Zombie Notes* (1986), *Imaginary Income* (1992), *Untapped Maps* (1993), *American Rush: Selected Poems* (1998), *Erosion's Pull* (2006), *Edges of Water* (2013), *let the heart hold down the breakage Or the caregiver's log* (2022), *Everything Turns on a Delicate Measure* (2023), and with Barbara Henning *Poets on the Road* (2023).

Very fortunately and happily for this chapter's authors, we've come to know Maureen through our lives and work in Denver, where Maureen also lives. In our library and archival work at DU Libraries, we care for part of Maureen's papers, a run of *Telephone* magazine, and books that she published on Telephone Books. This chapter's writing is the result of many years of *Telephone*-related events and acquisitions that have unfolded in ways we couldn't have predicted, a trail to Maureen Owen.

Collecting Materials Must Mean Connecting to People

Understanding the social and cultural conditions of creation and production of any small press publication, particularly little magazines, is critical to thoughtful collecting of works produced during the mimeo revolution. As Kane notes, though poetry is often perceived to be a solitary practice, given the often deeply interconnected webs of people producing these mimeograph publications, community and collaboration are woven throughout.[52] The whole process of making little magazines was inherently relational. Poets, often also taking on roles as editors, typesetters, designers, and collators, worked together in a variety of permutations in different geographic locations, institutions, and the push-pull of friendships and more intimate relationships. These webs of relationships, as distinguished from the self-conscious "lineages" of anointers and anointees prevalent in the more male-dominated parts of the poetry world, are represented by title changes and endings, new publications, and sometimes idiosyncratic

---

52 Kane, *All Poets Welcome*, xiv.

volume and issue numbering. It matters that we understand current and past trends of distribution and artistic production in the poetry world as ways of acquiring and collecting little magazines contemporaneously at the time and now. It matters that we know that bookshops would get irritated because *Telephone* was 8 1/2 x 14", an odd size and no spine label, which made some reluctant to carry it. These relationships of people and organizations to publications are necessary to understand in some detail if we are to determine, as librarians and archivists, where our collections have gaps, if we've created accurate catalog records and finding aids, and how we teach with and exhibit these materials.

If we are to understand the origins of *Telephone* and similar publications, it helps that we know that Maureen Owen had access to a mimeograph machine because she developed a partnership with Anne Waldman, who was publishing the little magazine *The World*, and that Anne let Maureen borrow 'the Gestetner.' It matters that we know that the majority of mimeo publications edited by women were assembled in, to use Rona Cran's term, "embodied" domestic spaces.[53] It matters that we know that these publications were being produced coincident with massive social upheaval that found its way into a number of these publications. It matters that we know that, for Owen, this medium made her feel "completely in control" because she could "change anything up to the last minute," and "get it out a day later."[54] That, to Owen, and many others, "it's alive in a way that a perfect-bound book isn't"[55] and to di Prima, its communal nature was a kind of call back to an earlier, guild-based practice, rather than a radical break with tradition.[56]

Archivists, librarians, and catalogers who work with these kinds of short-lived niche materials can be particularly well placed to wrestle with the often ephemeral nature of little magazines. We are used to publications that, in Cran's words, flirt with ephemerality, that flout publication conventions and periodicity.[57] Catalogers, particularly

53 Cran, "Space Occupied," 490.

54 Owen, "Notes on Publishing."

55 Ibid.

56 Cran, "Space Occupied," 490.

57 Cran, "Space Occupied," 476.

those with a critical bent, can find creative ways to address some of the issues noted by Fulton about the difficulty of finding and acquiring, let alone classifying or collocating little magazines, so that they are more discoverable to library users. As Crowe and Elzi note in their discussion of feminist pedagogy and the critical catalog, the "historically contingent" and "discursively produced" nature of language—the genre term 'little magazines' does not appear in the Library of Congress Genre/Form Thesaurus—is often at odds with the limitations of Library of Congress thesauri, subject headings, and classification. It makes sense, then, to use these limitations as learning opportunities in classroom settings, while pushing the limits on alternative and expanded vocabularies when possible.[58]

The Ties That Bind Can Also Blind

For libraries interested in this kind of deep, specialized collecting, one theme clearly emerged from the literature and from our own experience: if you are new to the field or discipline, find your experts or, ideally, several. In this respect, our work developing collections at DU has evolved over several decades, through a series of changing relationships. In the early 2000s, faculty in our English and Literary Arts program like Bin Ramke, an internationally recognized poet, worked directly with poets and editors like Maureen to collaborate with the humanities librarian, Peggy Keeran, to acquire or accept donations of little magazines. To assure a more systematic approach to collecting small presses, Peggy sought out experts at DU for advice and input in small press poetry and creative writing, including Bin Ramke and later Graham Foust and others. As Kate Crowe and then Shannon Tharp, who, in addition to being our Collections Librarian, is a published poet with a deep personal knowledge of the contemporary poetry world, were hired, they worked with Peggy, Bin, and then-Dean Michael Levine-Clark, who had begun to buy fine press and artists' books in the early 2000s, to deepen and expand our collecting practices into further small press poetry and literature. A critical part of this expansion was working more closely with Steve Clay of Granary Books to acquire not only Granary's publications, but also more comprehensive collections of small press and little magazine titles, as well as archives of poets

58 Katherine Crowe and Erin Elzi, "Feminist Pedagogy and the Critical Catalog," in *The Feminist Reference Desk: Concepts, Critiques, and Conversations*, ed. Maria T. Accardi. (Sacramento, CA: Litwin Books, 2017), 274.

and artists like Maureen Owen and Bobbie Louise Hawkins. More recently, as M.C. Kinniburgh has taken a leadership role in Granary, we've partnered on more archives acquisitions and have drawn heavily on the recent scholarly work that M.C. has created, which brings both a poet's and an archivist's perspective to this era of small press poetry and literary studies.

Our particular example illustrates some benefits and challenges to building a collection based on relationships to experts in the field where there is an institutional, professional, or personal connection, and it can lead to some of the patterns we've critiqued throughout this chapter, which publications like *Telephone* were created to push against: these ties can bind, but they can also blind.

Owen's goal, of a publication that was as expansive as a literal telephone book, came out of a desire to see great writers, many of whom were women, in publication, often seeking them out and soliciting submissions. This ethos of seeking out great work beyond existing close relationships and connections must also be central to collection development, and it requires us and others doing this work to continue to learn and seek out and build, just as Owen was and is constantly learning, seeking, and building.

We've begun to look at expanding our scope to professional associations and conferences like AWP (Association of Writers and Writing Programs) and the Louisville Conference on Literature and Culture Since 1900, as well as sharing what we are doing in publications like *Jacket2* and *Post45*. As many in the library literature have noted, wide-ranging bibliographies don't exist and aren't created the same way as they were even into the very end of the 20th century. This is, in some senses, a loss, but as we discovered when we looked into the existing bibliographies of little magazines, *Telephone* was often not there, echoing issues present in the anthologies of mid-century poets. Thankfully, *Telephone* and related publications by poets and editors who may not have been anthologized have been digitized as part of Reveal Digital's Independent Voices collection and are openly available to all.

It's incumbent upon us as librarians and archivists to be part of envisioning the possibilities of a 'new bibliography,' and to acknowledge and build upon our relational work while not allowing it to be fully determinative of our collecting. Small press poetry and libraries are also both communities that can make wonderful use of our limited resources and can make "kitchen -table kinds" of collaborations if we choose, by building and sustaining relationships between and among institutions that collect, as not everyone has, can, or should try to collect everything. As Kinniburgh notes:

> ...it is significant that around the same time as creative writing programs were putting down roots, the Lower East Side and West Coast countercultures were in full swing with mimeographs, mail art, assemblages, poets' theaters, and experimental dance: permeable practices in which art and poetry imbued every aspect of life, spilling from classrooms and galleries into the street, bars, and cafes. Yet, too often, this history is not animated as the boundary-crossing crucible that it was; instead, it remains contained in distinct boxes —of individual memory, poets' archives that are spread across institutions and geographies, and libraries that have been dispersed. Politically speaking, this is convenient for the power structures that have made this inevitable in the United States. But ethically, for those of us who study literature, we are obligated to search across these containers for narratives that may be hidden by material circumstance.[59]

Our goal is to make this kind of discovery and collecting less onerous, as our collections of small press poetry become, like *Telephone*, as lovingly cataloged and comprehensive as "Ma Bell's directory."

---

59 M.C. Kinniburgh, *Wild Intelligence: Poets' Libraries and the Politics of Knowledge in Postwar America* (Amherst: University of Massachusetts Press), 20.

Bibliography

"8th Street Bookshop." Village Alliance. Accessed July 2, 2022. https://greenwichvillage.nyc/places/8th-street-bookshop.

Chinn, Lisa. "How the Mimeo-Magazine Sounds in 1960s Counterculture: The Floating Bear as Sonic Artifact." *Journal for Literary and Intermedial Crossings* 5, no. 1 (2020): https://clic.research.vub.be/sites/default/files/atoms/files/JLIC%205.1f%20CHINN.pdf.

Clay, Steven and Rodney Phillips. *A Secret Location on the Lower East Side: Adventures in Writing, 1960-1980*. New York Public Library and Granary Books, 1998.

Cran, Rona. "Space Occupied: Women Poet-Editors and the Mimeograph Revolution in Mid-century New York City." *Journal of American Studies* 55, no. 2 (2021): 474-501.

Crowe, Katherine, and Erin Elzi. "Feminist Pedagogy and the Critical Catalog." In *The Feminist Reference Desk: Concepts, Critiques, and Conversations*, edited by Maria T. Accardi. Litwin Books, 2017.

Elmborg, James. "Toward Building a Digital Index of Little Magazines of the 1960s." *Serials Review* 44, no. 1 (2018): 16-23.

Fulton, Len. "Anima Rising: Little Magazines in the Sixties." *American Libraries* 2, no. 1 (January 1971): 25-47.

Goodmann, Emily. "A Tale of Two Networks: The Bell Telephone System and the Meaning of 'Information,' 1947–1968." *Information & Culture: A Journal of History* 54, no. 3 (2019): 281 310.

Kane, Daniel. *All Poets Welcome: The Lower East Side Poetry Scene in the 1960s*. Berkeley: University of California Press, 2003.

Keller, Lynn. "An Interview with Susan Howe." *Contemporary Literature* 36, no. 1 (1995): 1-34.

Kinniburgh, M.C. 2022a. *About Telephone: An Interview with Maureen Owen*. Among the Neighbors, 19.2. Buffalo: The Poetry Collection of the University Libraries, University at Buffalo, The State University of New York.

Kinniburgh, M.C. 2022b. *About Telephone: An Introduction & Bibliography*. Among the Neighbors, 19.1. Buffalo: The Poetry Collection of the University Libraries, University at Buffalo, The State University of New York.

Kinniburgh, M.C. *Messy Archivist*. New York: TKS, 2020.

Kinniburgh, M.C. 2022c. *Wild Intelligence: Poets' Libraries and the Politics of Knowledge in Postwar America*. Amherst: University of Massachusetts Press.

Loewinsohn, Ron. "After the (Mimeograph) Revolution." *TriQuarterly* 21 (Spring 1971): 221-236.

McLeod, Kembrew. "The Police Raid Peace Eye Bookstore." *Downtown Pop Underground*. Accessed July 23, 2022. https://dsps.lib.uiowa.edu/downtownpopunderground/story/the-police-raid-peace-eye-bookstore.

Mottram, Eric. "The Mimeograph Revolution." *Times Literary Supplement* no. 3258 (August 6, 1964): 714. https://link-gale- com.du.idm.oclc.org/apps/doc/EX1200333984/TLSH? u=udenver&sid=bookmark–TLSH&xid=b6d2233b.

Nolan, Pat. "In Conversation with Maureen Owen." The New Black Bart Poetry Society, November 12, 2016. https://thenewblackbartpoetrysociety.wordpress.com/2016/11/12/in-conversation- with-maureen-owen.

Owen, Maureen. Interview by Doug Lang. Expressions, WPFW. January 1977. https://archive.org/details/pacifica_radio_archives-WZ0052.

Owen, Maureen. "Notes on Publishing: From a Telephone Interview with Marcella Durand." *Jacket* 11, April 2000. http://jacketmagazine.com/11/owen-durand.html.

Robertson, Craig. "Learning to File: Reconfiguring Information and Information Work in the Early Twentieth Century." *Technology and Culture* 58, no. 4 (2017): 955-981.

Russo, Linda. "The 'F' Word in the Age of Mechanical Reproduction: An Account of Women -Edited Small Presses and Journals." In *The World in Time and Space: Towards a History of Innovative American Poetry in Our Time*, edited by Edward Foster and Joseph Donahue. Talisman House, 2002.

Sanders, Edward. *1968: A History in Verse*. Black Sparrow Press, 2000.

Sturm, Nick. "Crystal Set #17: Country Rush by Maureen Owen (Adventures in Poetry, 1973)." https://www.nicksturm.com/crystalset/2018/4/20/crystal-set-17-country-rush-by-maureen-owen-adventures-in-poetry-1973.

"The Telephone Books and Magazine Collection." Granary Books, Winter 2021. https://www.granarybooks.com/images/upload/telephone-completeillustrated-final.pdf.

Zirin, Dave. "The Living Legacy of Mexico City: An Interview with John Carlos," *Counterpunch*, November 2, 2003. https://www.counterpunch.org/2003/11/01/an-interview-with-john-carlos.

Zumbahlen, Anna. "'Poetry cracked around me': Interview with Maureen Owen." *Denver Quarterly* 54, no. 3 (2020): 103.

Exclusion Zone

Observations on "Wikability" as a Measure of Notability in the Digital Age, inspired by Gregor Weichbrodt's *Dictionary of* non-notable *Artists* (2016)

Annette Gilbert

Translated and edited by Cadenza Academic Translations

What Do We Know About Wikipedia? Surface Observations

Wikipedia, which launched in 2001 with the mission of gathering all the knowledge in the world through a collective effort and making it freely available to humankind, claims to be continuing the Enlightenment project begun in 1751 by Diderot's universal encyclopedia. Although initially mocked, many now regard it as "the last best place on the internet" and as one of the last refuges of the vision of an "open web" and "knowledge as a commons": "It is the only not-for-profit site in the top 10, and one of only a handful in the top 100. [...] More than an encyclopedia, Wikipedia has become a community, a library, a constitution, an experiment, a political manifesto."[1] In terms of the reliability of knowledge, it has long been on equal footing with the large-scale projects of the past, such as the *Encyclopaedia Britannica*, and when it comes to topicality, comprehensiveness, and scope, it has been far ahead of the pack for some time. All this, despite the fact that we have only a hazy idea of the actual dimensions of this collective writing experiment, since information such as the following ultimately

1 Richard Cooke, "Wikipedia Is the Last Best Place on the Internet," *Wired* (Feb. 17, 2020): https://www.wired.com/story/wikipedia-online-encyclopedia-best-place-internet/.

remains completely abstract: "There are currently 6,532,805 articles, which means 4.0767316322×10^9 words, which means $2.44603897932 \times 10^{10}$ characters."[2]

This is precisely what the US artist Michael Mandiberg was addressing when he squeezed the online encyclopedia back into printed book form in his project *Print Wikipedia* (2015): "*Print Wikipedia* is a both a utilitarian visualization of the largest accumulation of human knowledge and a poetic gesture towards the futility of the scale of big data."[3] He chose the familiar book format as a yardstick because books, unlike abstract quantities of data, are concrete and comprehensible units of measure. He used special software to capture every article on Wikipedia, created 700-page PDFs from them, and sent them to the print-on-demand provider Lulu in preparation for printing in hardcover format. The resulting 7,473 volumes were uploaded in a live performance that took two weeks. There are also ninety-one volumes containing the table of contents and thirty-six volumes that list the names of all 7.5 million Wikipedia authors, a kind of monument raised to those who collaborated on the knowledge that the project visibly materializes.

This transformation into printed medium also reinstates the alphabetization of the entries, which, in combination with the highly variable length of the articles, reveals the idiosyncratic emphases and hidden preferences of Wikipedians. Even the volume numbers and letter sequences on the book spines give rise to telling observations: "Turning a database of knowledge into books reveals the patterns of history. The 28 volumes of BAT are not about flying bats or baseball bats, instead, they are a compendium of battles, from the 'Battle of Aachen' to the 'Battle of Żyrzyn.' Likewise the 27 volumes that start with NEW represent a structural history of European colonialism and empire."[4] In just a few years, *Print Wikipedia* will be an invaluable historical document of collective knowledge production—a snapshot of the state of knowledge at a precise point in time.

---

2 "Wikipedia:Size in volumes," Wikipedia, The Free Encyclopedia, updated July 1, 2022, https://en.wikipedia.org/w/index.php?title=Wikipedia:Size_in_volumes&oldid=1065930409.

3 Michael Mandiberg, *Print Wikipedia. About*, https://printwikipedia.com/#/about.

4 Michael Mandiberg, "Making *Print Wikipedia*," in *Library of Artistic Print-on-Demand. Post-Digital Publishing in Times of Platform Capitalism*, ed. Annette Gilbert and Andreas Bülhoff (Leipzig: Spector, 2025, 512–521).

Wikipedia's "Engine Room"

Wikipedia as a Living Document

While Mandiberg may have been the first to truly convey the immense volume of collected knowledge and the collective effort behind it, he still showed us only a tiny fraction of the Wikipedia universe. Concealed behind the surface view of articles are thousands of miles of text, including previous versions of each article (history pages)[5] and discussion pages (also known as talk pages), the length of which varies depending on the article. There are also countless pages that set out Wikipedia's principles and rules—about which there is also an absurd number of discussion pages, historical versions, opinions, surveys, and polls—not to mention the portal pages, user profile pages, community pages, statistics pages, template pages, tutorial pages, help pages, and so on.

Thanks to this exhaustive documenting and archiving, the entire process of the collective production and negotiation of knowledge is, for the first time in the history of the encyclopedia, open and transparent, and can thus be observed live or reconstructed in retrospect. This unimpeded view of the "engine room" allows conclusions to be drawn about the implicit assumptions, beliefs, logic, and value standards of those involved, who are obliged to explicitly state and justify them in their written communication with one another. With a constantly changing group of geographically scattered authors, this is the only way to create the conditions needed for longer-term collaborative work. The archive also makes it possible to understand how the taxonomy, quality, and quantity of knowledge has developed over the years, and how editorial principles, rules, organizational structures, and problem-solving strategies have been developed collectively and ensured through consensus, all in the course of ongoing operation rather than in advance, as with classic encyclopedias. In principle, the process has no end: Wikipedia is an emergent social phenomenon, the living document par excellence.

5 The potential scope of the history of just a single article is illustrated by James Bridle in his 12-volume series *The Iraq War. A History of Wikipedia Changelogs* (2010), which, over the course of 7,000 pages, documents all 12,000 changes made between 2004 and 2009 to the article on the Iraq War.

The Political Implications of the Interface

Nevertheless, little of this filters through to the general public; in fact, few even know that this engine room exists and can be accessed and examined. This is probably due in large part to the fact that significant portions of these backstage pages are not indexed by search engines, so a user will not come across them when running a related Google search. In addition, the default Wikipedia view only shows the most current version of an article, hiding the way into the backstage area behind inconspicuous tabs. Of course, this prioritization of the encyclopedia section on the Wikipedia interface makes sense in light of the website's mission, but it dramatically restricts the visibility and thus the accessibility of other Wikipedia spaces. Relegating them to the backstage masks the fact that the knowledge presented is essentially dependent on social interaction and, as social knowledge, is necessarily contested and disputed, contingent and inconsistent, dynamic and living, polyphonic and biased. There is no hint in Wikipedia's public appearance of competing bodies of knowledge, collective authorship, or potentially adversarial interactions: "In what could be called objectivism translated into design, the contributions of the single editors are unified into one anonymous, pseudo-univocal whole."[6] The simple, generically functional layout—stripped as it is to the bare essentials—with its dazzlingly pure white also gives the impression of neutrality, homogeneity, consensus, and authority.

These design and interface decisions are not simply superficial. There are political implications in the privileging of one thing and the relegation of others: "The blindness of today's arguably most advanced collaborative-hypertext-collective intelligence-open source-creative commons-Web 2.0-community media project to critical issues of internet media design is, give or take objectivism, astonishing."[7] It would arguably be more appropriate and more honest to bring this social interaction, with all its multivocality, disagreement, dynamics, and diversity, out of the backstage and into the light, and to recognize the specificities of Wikipedia's collected knowledge "as assets, rather than

---

6 Florian Cramer, "A Brechtian Media Design: Annemieke van der Hoek's Epicpedia," in *Critical Point of View. A Wikipedia Reader*, ed. Geert Lovink and Nathaniel Tkacz (Amsterdam: Institute of Network Cultures, 2011), 221–225, 222.

7 Ibid., 226.

liabilities to conceal."[8] If the countless warning text blocks indicating possible shortcomings or problems that now plaster many articles are anything to go by, this would presumably not damage Wikipedia's authority. What would have been unthinkable in earlier encyclopedias and newspapers has even worked to Wikipedia's advantage, as observed by David Weinberger: "These labels, oddly enough, add to Wikipedia's credibility. We can see for ourselves that Wikipedia isn't so interested in pretending it's perfect that it will cover up its weaknesses. [...] Wikipedia [...] only progresses by being up-front about errors and omissions. It Socratically revels in being corrected."[9]

Gazing into Wikipedia's "Deletion Hell"

Until now, expeditions into the backstage depths have been encouraged largely by external impulses such as Gregor Weichbrodt's *Dictionary of* non-notable *Artists* (2016). The German digital and experimental poet singled out one aspect of Wikipedia's engine room and turned it into the object of an enlightening project. Using a Python script, he filtered the unwieldy archive of English-language Wikipedia for the names of all authors and artists whose Wikipedia article had been nominated for deletion over the previous decade. In principle, any registered Wikipedian can initiate such a request when logged in.[10] In the German-language Wikipedia, users are even entitled to do so when not logged in, which considerably increases the number of nominations, and may be the reason for the deletion policy being considerably stricter in comparison to other language versions. A nomimation remains open to debate for at least seven days before an administrator makes a decision. Ultimately, it is not the number of votes that counts but the persuasiveness of the arguments introduced.

Weichbrodt put the resulting candidates for deletion in alphabetical order and sorted them into nineteen art disciplines, from music and

---

8 Ibid. The first experiments have already been run, such as colorcoding different authors or particularly contentious passages, visualizations of version history, and tools for data analysis and statistics, for example on the number of edits or authors per article.

9 David Weinberger, *Everything is Miscellaneous: The Power of the New Digital Disorder* (New York: Holt Paperbacks, 2007), 141.

10 As the number of articles for deletion shows, it is one of Wikipedia's most used tools. For a list on a daily basis, see: Wikipedia, https://en.wikipedia.org/wiki/Wikipedia:Articles_for_deletion/Log/Today; cf. the archive: https://en.wikipedia.org/wiki/Wikipedia:Archived_articles_for_deletion_discussions.

fashion design to dance and painting or illustration and literature. Alongside every name, he also included the short reason that Wikipedia stipulates must accompany each deletion nomination. The most frequent criticism is that those concerned do not meet the encyclopedia's "notability" requirements—a phrase that Weichbrodt took up in the title of his work, *Dictionary of* non-notable *Artists*.

Of course, this slender volume—like Mandiberg's *Print Wikipedia*—also captures only a small fraction of the Wikipedia universe. Nevertheless, deletion nominations represent a particularly sensitive site of power in the production and negotiation of knowledge, constituting one of the most repressive mechanisms of control available to Wikipedians, and one that has a major impact on the collectively produced article corpus; this is why the space is often referred to as a "deletion hell" populated by "deletion nazis." The deletion policy therefore offers us a window into the principles, rules, methods, and encyclopedic self-image of Wikipedians.

Furthermore, it is precisely missing, deleted, and newly added lemmata that have always been used as particularly telling indicators in the evaluation of encyclopedias and reference works: they play "a more important and revealing role than the form and content of the entries. Thus, [in every reference work,] the selection of articles alone [...] provides information about the mentality and hegemonial discourse of an epoch."[11] By pointedly focusing on articles for deletion, Weichbrodt thus implicitly exposes typical patterns of evaluation in the post-digital age, which only become discernible and observable as such when compiled as a corpus. In the following, Weichbrodt's *Dictionary of* non-notable *Artists* will be used as a starting point to discuss the conflict raging in Wikipedia between exclusion and inclusion, homogeneity and diversity, bias and balance, as evidenced by the disputes over the "Wikability" of artists and authors.

To Fail on Wikipedia

Personal experience was the catalyst for the *Dictionary*: Gregor Weichbrodt's own (German-language) Wikipedia entry was nominated for deletion in September 2016, as is still documented today in the

11 Oliver Jungen, "Der Wille zum Wissen. Die Kapitulation des Brockhaus," *Zeitschrift für Ideengeschichte* X, no. 2 (Summer 2016): 5-16, 14.

article's version history and in the archive of deletion discussions. The justification was succinct: "Apart from brief media attention, absolutely no perceivable influence on any field. Completely misses notability criteria for 'authors.' Unsatisfying notability criteria for artists too."[12]

As Weichbrodt quickly discovered, he was not alone in his fate; he accordingly dedicated his book to all artists and authors threatened with deletion. But what was intended as a gesture of brotherhood in a community of "rejected" artists was experienced by some of those concerned as yet more defamation. One blogger branded Weichbrodt's actions as a "violation of personal rights" and accused him of "character assassination + harassment" on the basis that those on the list, whose real names Weichbrodt used without permission, would be "publicly discredited once again."[13] In a public Facebook post, the Philippine poet Edwin Cordevilla also protested vehemently against being named in Weichbrodt's anthology because the request to delete his Wikipedia entry had ultimately been dismissed—for the sake of probity, he said, Weichbrodt should have checked this again before publishing his book.[14]

But this does not necessarily represent "a weakness in the overall artistic concept."[15] First, it could be argued that the *Dictionary* somehow reflects Wikipedia's typical distorted image in the public consciousness, which is all too often based on superficial knowledge about what goes on in the engine room. Second, whether the candidates for deletion were ultimately "rehabilitated" or whether the deletion nomination was justified was beside the point for Weichbrodt, as he said himself. Rather than "making truthful statements about who is actually notable and who is not," he wanted his book to "question why that

---

12 User 84.118.96.92, "Wikipedia:Löschkandidaten/18. September 2016," September 18, 2016, https://de.wikipedia.org/w/index.php?title=Wikipedia:L%C3%B6schkandidaten/18._September_2016#Gregor_Weichbrodt_(LAE).

13 In order to avoid perpetuating the accusations and triggering new hate speech on the internet, we will refrain from providing a URL at this point. This accusation is untenable if only because Weichbrodt used freely accessible data from the Wikipedia universe. However, the names were in fact transferred from Wikipedia's half-public, non-search-engine-indexed backstage to the wider public of the internet, where the *Dictionary* first circulated for free.

14 "Weichbrodt could have not missed it if he only bothered to check. If he's responsible enough, he should have been more careful. He may have made a name for himself now because of this book." Edwin M. Cordevilla, Facebook, November 30, 2016, https://www.facebook.com/emcordevilla/posts/1308824182490620.

15 Gregor Weichbrodt, email message to author, July 6, 2018.

even matters."[16] The focus is thus on the performative power that an entry or even a non-entry in Wikipedia has in real life, irrespective of its substance. The strong reactions to his book testify to the reality of this power. A personal article on one of the most-visited websites in the world evidently now confers such distinction that its absence can seem stigmatizing.

It is in this sense that the US poet Kenneth Goldsmith interprets Weichbrodt's *Dictionary* as a document of public failure. He promoted it on Facebook by saying, "If you're on this list, you're a failed artist."[17] But not everyone sees this as a disaster. In certain literary-artistic circles, to which Goldsmith and Weichbrodt undoubtedly belong, not having a Wikipedia entry is in no way perceived as a lack but rather as a seal of approval and distinction, as revealed by the Greek artist Miltos Manetas' proud comment on Goldsmith's post: "I am on the list! :)"[18] In the experimental, avant-garde literary and art scenes, failure in the traditional spheres of literature and art and their institutions of legitimation and consecration has always been regarded as a mark of belonging and an accolade. This field of restricted production, to nod to Pierre Bourdieu, has its own laws of consecration: here, recognition by one's own peers counts for much more than the Wikipedia pages, high circulation, or quick commercial success that represent the most important currency in the subfield of mass production: "Therefore, having a page on Wikipedia has more gravity in the world of mass self-communication than having a profile on Facebook."[19]

Even if Wikipedia was originally set up as an anti-elitist, direct democratic project, many have since come to regard it as an expression of the "establishment." It has blossomed into a serious institution of consecration in the literary-artistic field, not only representing the public standing of an artist but instrumentally contributing to it; its share in the intensification of media attention and the consecration spiral that builds upon it should not be underestimated. This also corresponds to the perception of those concerned, as shown by another

---

16 Ibid.

17 Kenneth Goldsmith, Facebook, September 29, 2016, https://www.facebook.com/kenneth.goldsmith.739/posts/538599506325863 (no longer available).

18 Miltos Manetas, comment on ibid.

19 José van Dijck, *The Culture of Connectivity: A Critical History of Social Media* (New York: Oxford UP, 2013), 150.

comment on Goldsmith's Facebook post by the Norwegian poet Olav Gisle Øvrebø: "Everyone can be a poet but only one page gets to amalgamate all that poetry and present it to the larger world wide web of art, endowing it with value. This time, that page is Wikipedia."[20]

Encyclopedic Self-Image: Inclusion vs. Exclusion

Nevertheless, because Wikipedia first entered the history of the universal encyclopedia in the digital age, it was in the luxurious position of having no limits to its scope. It was, in principle, able to pursue the ideal of completeness. Paradoxically, however, rather than working to its advantage, this has caused of a longstanding, unresolvable argument amongst Wikipedians concerning the encyclopedia's self-image. The frontline runs between those for whom Wikipedia is the domain of "everything that is *correct*" and those for whom it should contain "only what is *important*."[21] It has become common in the German-speaking world to refer to "inclusionists" and "exclusionists," although among English speakers the latter go by the name of "deletionists," which shows their strong association with the rigid deletion policies in which the underlying exclusionist attitude manifests itself particularly clearly.

The fact that this debate could have arisen at all is a novelty. Previously, traditional print editions were necessarily exclusionist due to their finite volume. An online encyclopedia that is in principle infinitely expandable, on the other hand, is "*a priori* inclusionist."[22] Accordingly, the maxim of the inclusionists is "Wikipedia is not paper." The only limitations they accept are derived from the basic principles of Wikipedia, according to which copyright must be respected and content must refer to knowledge that has already been published elsewhere and can be verified through reliable sources. These stringent policies on verifiability and "No Original Research" are supplemented by the "Neutral Point of View" policy, which requires the representation of "significant

---

20 Olav Gisle Øvrebø, comment on Goldsmith, Facebook, September 29, 2016, https://www.facebook.com/kenneth.goldsmith.739/posts/538599506325863?comment_id=538608692991611&comment_tracking=%7B%22tn%22%3A%22R9%22%7D (no longer available).

21 Tobias Lutzi, "Exklusionisten gegen Inklusionisten – ein enzyklopädischer Bruderkrieg," in *Alles über Wikipedia und die Menschen hinter der größten Enzyklopädie der Welt*, ed. Wikimedia Deutschland e.V. (Hamburg: Hoffmann und Campe, 2011), 164–172, 166 (emphasis in original).

22 Ibid., 167.

views fairly, proportionately and without bias." From an inclusionist perspective, the Wikability of an entry is only limited by these three "core content policies."[23]

The exclusionists, on the other hand, argue that "the basic fact that it is possible to create an inclusionist encyclopedia with unlimited contents" by no means leads to a "logical imperative."[24] Simply put, not every subject is relevant for Wikipedia. This is spelled out in the policy "What Wikipedia is not," which stipulates that, to live up to its name, an encyclopedia must clearly differentiate itself from an advertising or propaganda platform, a news portal, repository, dictionary, industry telephone book, or similar register of people, associations, or companies.[25] The slogan of the exclusionists is, therefore "Wikipedia is not a junkyard." But this necessitates strict "intake control" whereby the subject of an article must first be checked for notability, in the sense of the likelihood it will be of enduring significance, before the content of the article can be discussed with regard to the core content policies: "Notability is a property of a *subject* and not of a Wikipedia article."[26] The fact that the exclusionists draw the boundaries of encyclopedic knowledge considerably more narrowly and pursue such a rigid policy of elimination is, however, ultimately a crucial reason for why a Wikipedia entry confers distinction on its subject at all, and thus also takes on greater significance for marginalized groups in their fight for equal representation.

Misuse of Wikipedia as an Advertising Platform

In some cases, the exclusionists' restrictive selection of articles does seem to be completely justified. At the very least, several of the deletion nominations documented by Weichbrodt insinuate that the article in question seemed to be an act of self-promotion. More than once, the reasons for deletion criticize e.g. language typical of advertising that would be more appropriate for a blurb than an encyclopedia entry:

---

23 See "Wikipedia:Core content policies," Wikimedia, May 3, 2022, https://en.wikipedia.org/w/index.php?title=Wikipedia:Core_content_policies&oldid=1085939107

24 Lutzi, "Exklusionisten gegen Inklusionisten," 167.

25 See "Wikipedia:What Wikipedia is not," Wikimedia, July 1, 2022, https://en.wikipedia.org/w/index.php?title=Wikipedia:What_Wikipedia_is_not&oldid=1096046659.

26 "Wikipedia:Notability," Wikimedia, June 3, 2022, https://en.wikipedia.org/w/index.php?title=Wikipedia:Notability&oldid=1091359595 (emphasis in original).

"Poet who has garnered almost no media attention, yet is 'superior to Shakespeare,' 'better than Ted Hughes,' and 'a much bigger thing than Sylvia Plath.'"[27] Other articles were also branded as insubstantial: "He may be the son, grandson, and great-grandson of notable writers, but is there any indication that he himself is notable in any way?" (p. 54)

These examples prove that Wikipedia's potential as a marketing tool has been discovered: thanks to its direct influence on page ranking in Google searches and its ability to stimulate web traffic to a home page, it now forms part of PR strategy in the fight for visibility being waged in the attention marketplaces of the internet. Even if the exact effects are hard to quantify and "the entrepreneurial self"[28] usually also takes further mutually reinforcing measures to shape its performance and intensify media attention, the misuse of Wikipedia for advertising and PR purposes has sharply increased in recent years. This development reflects the changes undergone by the Internet more generally: the old participatory culture of the Web 2.0 has been superseded by the world of social media, in which "it is not the furthering of collective knowledge or altruistic collaboration [...] that [is] in the foreground, but rather image building and self-representation."[29]

Bias and Marginalization

Weichbrodt's *Dictionary* does not, however, merely showcase the peculiar behavior of some authors under the conditions of the attention economy. Several reasons given for the deletion nominations raise doubts about the adequacy and robustness of their underlying value standards and selection criteria, which in turn poses the question of what justifies and legitimizes the Wikipedians to sit in judgment over artists day after day and make decisions about their inclusion or exclusion.

---

27 This and all following quotations from Gregor Weichbrodt, *Dictionary of* non-notable *Artists* (Berlin: Frohmann, 2016), 57. The artists concerned have not been named in this article so as not subject them once again to a public discussion of their notability.

28 See Ulrich Bröckling, *The Entrepreneurial Self: Fabricating a New Type of Subject* (Los Angeles, CA: Sage, 2016). See also William Beutler, "Paid with Interest: COI Editing and Its Discontent," in *Wikipedia @ 20: Stories of an Incomplete Revolution*, ed. Joseph Reagle and Jackie Koerner (Cambridge, Mass.: MIT Press, 2020), 71–85.

29 Karin Janker and Thomas Urban, "Die Besserwisserei," *Süddeutsche Zeitung*, October 5/6, 2019, 11.

According to one reviewer, Weichbrodt's selection "sculpts a dictionary of the different ways an artist's work can be marginalized."[30] In the field of literature, for example, there seem to be clear reservations about certain genres and media. The encyclopedic relevance of authors of children's and young adult literature is thus repudiated more often than average, which is indicative of an implicit genre hierarchy in the value system of those casting judgment:

> Non-notable children's book author.
> Non-notable author of a single fiction book for teens.
> Subject appears to be a barely notable author of children's fiction.
> Unnotable author of a single series of teen books.
> Unremarkable children's and mystery author (pp. 44, 52, 56).

The same is true for blogs, e-books, and other digital media, which seem to be *per se* suspected of not being serious and therefore not "encyclopedia-worthy" literature:

> Non-notable rabbi and author and blogger.
> Not notable poet blogger.
> Webcomic author of dubious notability.
> Unremarkable e-book author.
> eBook author (possibly selfpublished) of questionable notability (pp. 49, 50, 55, 59, 57).

This clearly shows that the printed book is still the "hard currency" of the literature industry, and thus also represents a ticket into Wikipedia—not including self-published books, of course, as the final quotation above suggests. Very often, the reason simply says: "Non notable author, has 3 books published by vanity presses" (p. 45).

Just as striking is the mention of nationalities, which seems to primarily happen with authors from smaller literatures and cultures, and thus easily takes on a discriminatory tone that flies in the face of the intended neutral point of view:

> Indian TV actress.
> Appears to be non-notable Pakistani architect and writer.

---

30 James Ardis, "*Dictionary of non-notable Artists* by Gregor Weichbrodt," review, *The Rumpus*, January 3, 2017, https://therumpus.net/2017/01/dictionary-of-non-notable-artists-by-gregor-weichbrodt/. Because the underrepresentation of women on Wikipedia has been sufficiently documented, the following section focuses on other forms of marginalization.

Non-notable Scandinavian architect.
A 17-year old Nepali poet and social worker.
Non-notable Polish author.
A Burmese author of questionable notability.
Not a notable Danish author.
Non-notable Algerian writer.
Non-notable Cambodian writer.
A non-notable writer from Slovenia (pp. 38, 43, 48, 53–56, 59, 66).

'Self-focus' vs. Universal World Knowledge

This marginalizing, occasionally biased handling of the requirement for other languages and cultures to be represented on English-language Wikipedia is dismaying. But studies show that this restriction to the perspective of one's own region, language, culture, etc., is inherent in all Wikipedia language versions, because each one addresses a specific public with its own interests, and so necessarily breeds "a high degree of 'self-focus.'"[31] It is therefore entirely "natural that Wikipedians' [...] values are influenced by their dominant culture and that they want to include events [and subjects] that are 'close to home.'"[32]

Nevertheless, this bias is more serious in the case of the English-language Wikipedia —it was no accident that Gregor Weichbrodt chose it as his object of study, even though the German-language version pursues an even stricter deletion policy—because it occupies a special position among all other Wikipedia versions. First, because English is also spoken in countries such as South Africa, Nigeria, Uganda, Kenya, and Jamaica, the English-speaking Wiki-community must itself already allow for several strongly divergent "self-foci," although experience

31 Brent Hecht and Darren Gergle, "Measuring Self-focus Bias in Community—maintained Knowledge Repositories," in *Proceedings of the Fourth International Conference on Communities and Technologies* (New York: ACM Press, 2009), 11–20. Similarly, Ewa S. Callahan and Susan C. Herring, "Cultural Bias in Wikipedia Content on Famous Persons," *Journal of the American Society for Information Science and Technology* 62, no. 10 (2011): 1899–1915.

32 Jahna Ottenbacher, "Our News, Their Events: A Comparison of Archived Current Events on English and Greek Wikipedia," in *Global Wikipedia. International and Cross-cultural Issues in Online-Collaboration*, ed. Pnina Fichman and Noriko Hara (Lanham et al.: Rowman & Littlefield, 2014), 49–67, 63.

shows that is actually dominated by the Western perspective.[33] Second, as the original version of Wikipedia, the English version has an exemplary function; many of its principles, rules, and features, as well as its article contents, have been adopted by other versions.

Moreover, the English language's dominant position as a global lingua franca sets the bar for inclusion, coverage, diversity, and openness especially high, since it has a much greater reach than its sister encylopedias. For this reason, it is burdened with the expectation that it might finally realize the centuries-old vision of a truly universal encyclopedia, representing all the knowledge in the world. So, while the sister encyclopedias in other languages are allowed "to enshrine landmarks of shared historical and cultural importance to people who share a language,"[34] the English-language edition, as a supposedly universal platform that serves as a global repository, is thus required to also represent figures who are "only" important in one specific culture and language.[35] The strong rejection of this imposed role that can be discerned in the quotations above does not, therefore, necessarily reflect implicit prejudices; it may also be the expression of differing opinions on the function and status of the English-language version within the Wikipedia universe and the result of a clash between the "language point of view," as Massa and Scrinzi call it in reference to Wikipedia's neutral point of view (NPOV), and that of a more globalized, universal POV.[36]

Regardless, there is indisputably some systemic bias, as self-critically acknowledged by the WikiProject "Countering systemic bias," which seeks to strengthen the community's efforts to diversify both the content and authorship of its collected knowledge.[37] Wikipedia's architecture is actually conducive to this: "There is enormous potential for

---

33 See Mark Graham and Martin Dittus, *Geographies of Digital Exclusion. Data and Inequalities* (London: Pluto Press, 2022). On the issue of "different Wikipedias in countries where English dominates as the written language [and] [...] Wikipedians on the edges of the Wikipedia network," see also the case study of an article about a viral meme from Kenya that was deleted several times: Heather Ford, "The Missing Wikipedians," in *Critical Point of View*, 258–268, 260.

34 Ibid.

35 Ewa Callahan, "Crosslinguistic Neutrality. Wikipedia's Neutral Points of View from a Global Perspective," in *Global Wikipedia*, 69–84, 73.

36 Paolo Massa and Fiederico Scrinzi, "Manypedia. Comparing language points of view of Wikipedia Communities," *First Monday* 18 (2013): 1–7.

37 "Wikipedia:WikiProject Countering systemic bias," Wikipedia, May 2, 2022, https://en.wikipedia.org/w/index.php?title=Wikipedia:WikiProject_Countering_systemic_bias&oldid=1085856665.

Wikipedia to open participation in knowledge construction and loosen the West's entrenched grip on globally accessible representations. The platform, available in 271 [June 2022: 316] languages, in theory allows marginalized groups to be heard around the world."[38]

"Imagine a world [...]"

But is English-language Wikipedia really the best place to realize this utopia of a truly global knowledge resource? Perhaps this demand should instead be directed at the entire Wikipedia universe, which currently has 316 active language versions. Every single version, with its specific perspective and its specific set of authors, would then contribute to this universal repository, so that as the number and size of the versions increased, the "self-foci" and knowledge bases would also increase and mutually complement each other, leading to the gradual rectification problems: blank areas on the map would remain even then, because Wikipedia is nowhere near being used and established in every country in the world. It would also fail to remedy the demographic preponderance of any imbalances. This would not solve all of younger, well-educated, male Wikipedians from Western, highly developed countries.

But perhaps it would still get us one step closer to Wikipedia's initial vision, which its founder Jimmy Wales once captured in these words: "Imagine a world in which every single person on the planet is given free access to the sum of all human knowledge." This vision is still affirmed by the current English-language community as the "prime objective": "And that is the world that we [...] are working toward."[39] In this world, though, "every single person"—irrespective of the language they speak or the culture they feel they belong to—would actually have to be able to access all Wikipedia versions, and so a necessarily diversified world knowledge, for any query. This might be hard to imagine, but the first attempts and tools that prove the feasibility and potential

38 Mark Graham, "Wiki Space: Palimpsests and the Politics of Exclusion," in *Critical Point of View*, 269–282, 280.

39 "Wikipedia:Prime objective," Wikipedia, February 10, 2022, https://en.wikipedia.org/w/index.php?title=Wikipedia:Prime_objective&oldid=1070972014.

of such cross-version and cross-language access already exist.[40] Anyway, when has the idea of a universal encyclopedia not been utopian? And no one could have predicted the success of Wikipedia twenty years ago, either.

Community as Corrective

There is hope to be found in the fact that Wikipedia has, on more than one occasion, already demonstrated its capacity for constant self-monitoring and self-correction, as well as for continued development. Even on the level of a single language version, therefore, the situation is not as awful as is implied by Weichbrodt's *Dictionary*, which deliberately confines itself to what triggers deletion discussions while ignoring their progression and outcomes. It is worth advancing deeper into the backstage of Wikipedia and following up on some of the deletion nominations that Weichbrodt documented. It then becomes clear that such nominations are by no means guaranteed success, and that dubious arguments and biased statements usually do not remain unchallenged for long. These processes of community review thoroughly vindicate a belief in the corrective power of the swarm intelligence.

To single out just one example: the erroneous description of the *Romanian* folk singer Ștefan Hrușcă as a "not notable seasonal Hungarian folk singer" in a deletion nomination was immediately and indignantly noted by other Wikipedians: "Keep. Hungarian singer?! Are you kidding? He is an iconic Romanian Christmas carols singer, very famous in Romania. Basically Romanians can't imagine a Christmas without his songs. Ridiculous request."[41] A different user introduced evidence

---

40 Cf. automatic translation services, interwiki and interlanguage links, which connect related entries in the sister encyclopedias, tools such as Wikipedia Cross-lingual Image Analysis, and Wikidata as multilingual secondary database. There are also ambitious future projects such as the Wikimedia 2030, envisioning "free knowledge as truly representative of human diversity," and the Abstract Wikipedia "in which the actual textual content is being represented in a language-independent manner." Jackie Koerner, "Wikipedia Has a Bias Problem," in *Wikipedia @ 20*, 311–321, 312, and Denny Vrandečić, "Collaborating on the Sum of All Knowledge Across Languages," in ibid., 175–188, 180.

41 Codrin.B, comment on "Wikipedia:Articles for deletion/Ștefan Hrușcă," Wikipedia, December 27, 2013, 15:22 (UTC), https://en.wikipedia.org/wiki/Wikipedia:Articles_for_deletion/%C8%98tefan_Hru%C8%99c%C4%83.

from Romanian newspapers of record as proof of media resonance,[42] and cautioned: "before making this kind of nomination, it helps not only to search for the subject, but also to get the basic facts right. Romania, Hungary. Romania, Hungary. Romania, Hungary. Learn the difference. Hrușcă is from Romania. He is not from Hungary."[43]

When Gregor Weichbrodt's article was nominated for deletion, several Wikipedians also came running to his defense, bringing evidence of media and public resonance. The result was that Weichbrodt's Wikability was proven unequivocally within just a few hours, and an administrator closed the deletion nomination. Weichbrodt's Wikipedia page survived—at least this time: in principle, deletion nominations, and with them doubt over notability, can always be raised again.

Guidelines: Solution or Problem?

In order to place the increasingly fierce dispute over how to determine Wikability on a consistent, consensually established basis, notability criteria have been defined, and indeed were referred to when Weichbrodt's article was nominated for deletion: "Completely misses notability criteria for 'authors.' Unsatisfying notability criteria for artists too."[44] The German-language Wikipedia was a trailblazer in introducing notability criteria, which it did on April 27, 2004.[45] Just one year later, they were extended, with specific criteria for different groups of people like academics, religious and political officials, artists, sportspeople, soldiers, and adult-film actors.[46] Over the years, an extravagant consensus-building process developed them still further, differentiating

42 English-language Wikipedia mentions the higher burden of proof for demonstrating the notability of people from the non-Anglophone and non-Western world as a reason for systemic bias: "because of a lack of English sources and little incentive among anglophone participants to find sources in the native language of the topic. A lack of native language editors of the topic only compounds the problems." "Wikipedia:Systemic bias, "Wikipedia, June 19, 2022, https://en.wikipedia.org/w/index.php?title=Wikipedia:Systemic_bias&oldid=1093861193. Moreover, the privileging of printed text sources, regardless of language, necessarily leads to discrimination against e.g. oral history and related types of knowledge.

43 Biruitorul, comment on "Wikipedia:Articles for deletion/Ștefan Hrușcă," Wikipedia, December 27, 2013, 03:05 (UTC).

44 User 84.118.96.92, "Wikipedia:Löschkandidaten/18. September 2016."

45 English-language notability guidelines were first introduced in 2006, see "Wikipedia:Notability in the English Wikipedia," Wikipedia, April 14, 2022, https://en.wikipedia.org/w/index.php?title=Notability_in_the_English_Wikipedia&oldid=1082657701.

46 "Wikipedia:Relevanzkriterien," Wikipedia, April 27, 2004, https://de.wikipedia.org/w/index.php?title=Wikipedia:Relevanzkriterien&oldid=1169003.

an impressive number of objects, events, living organisms, institutions, places, fictional objects, and groups of people in a comprehensive set of guidelines that is one of the most elaborate among all the Wikipedia versions, which vary in terms of their scope, contents, taxonomic division, and policies.

All notability guidelines are subject to constant modification, and many criteria are still notoriously controversial today. The fact that discussions keep flaring up and that they are often repetitive and inefficient is not least due to high turnover among Wikipedians themselves, which prevents the formation of an institutional memory. Moreover, seeking "clear democratic legitimation [is] futile," because ultimately most of the criteria have "never been subject to a vote." The fact that they "have been strengthened in the meantime to a kind of common law is primarily due to their strict and constant use in deletion discussions," where they are applied with increasing rigidity. "This is already problematic because, by and large, the authors active there are advocates of a restrictive notability policy,", i.e., they belong to the exclusionist wing.[47]

Furthermore, in these often heated debates, little attention is paid to the fact that they are "sufficient, but not necessary, conditions for notability." They are thus certainly not expected to "cover all conceivable individual cases,"[48] and other cogent arguments can be used on a case-by-case basis. All this means it is becoming increasingly difficult to create new articles—especially for Wikipedia newbies and unregistered users, who are only recorded by their IP address and whom Wikipedians treat with particular mistrust.

Case Study: Notability of Authors

1. *Canonization and media resonance*

We will now illustrate the problem that confronts Wikipedians using the example of the notability criteria for authors on German-language Wikipedia: the criteria which, according to his deletion nomination, Gregor Weichbrodt did not fulfil. The first section runs as follows:

---

47 All quotes Lutzi, "Exklusionisten gegen Inklusionisten," 168 and 169.

48 Both quotes "Wikipedia:Relevanzkriterien," May 3, 2022, https://de.wikipedia.org/w/index.php?title=Wikipedia:Relevanzkriterien&oldid=222583335 (emphasis deleted).

> Writers and authors are deemed to be notable
>
> - when special significance or prominence can be proved by inclusion in a recognized, editorially supervised reference work (encyclopedias, etc.) or a comparable renowned source such as *Perlentaucher* magazine [...].[49]

This recourse to reference works as established instances of literary canon-building shows that institutionally safeguarded, expert knowledge is as in demand as it has ever been. Encyclopedias, the evidence suggests, reliably capture "the intersection of the institutional reading canon used in schools and universities with the social canon."[50] Because of their long lead time and the fact that they cannot be altered after publication, however, they are of less help precisely when it comes to contemporary authors, who are the target of most deletion nominations.[51]

Using the online magazine *Perlentaucher*—in its own words, "the internet's leading independent German-language magazine for culture and literature"[52]—as an example of a "comparable renowned source" ensures greater topicality than print references, but also causes a great deal of contention. This is because *Perlentaucher* derives its "renown" and authority less from its own content than from the culture sections of the major daily and weekly newspapers, whose book reviews it agglomerates and edits in its daily press reviews. The established institutions of consecration and the typical value standards of the educated, middle-class spheres of literary criticism and book culture are thus reinscribed into Wikipedia. Pragmatic reasons are usually cited to justify using *Perlentaucher* as an indicator of notability: "*Perlentaucher* [is] helpful because it compiles reviews, so they're easy to find."[53] Ease of verifiability and practicality are thus the trump cards.

---

49 "Wikipedia:Relevanzkriterien, 8.4 Autoren," Wikipedia, May 3, 2022, https://de.wikipedia.org/w/index.php?title=Wikipedia:Relevanzkriterien&oldid=222583335#Autoren.

50 Heinz Ludwig Arnold, "Arbeit am Mythos Kindler," in *Wertung und Kanon*, ed. Matthias Freise and Claudia Stockinger (Heidelberg: Winter, 2010), 125–139, 133f.

51 The same is true of the English-language version of Wikipedia: in its guidelines for books, it says: "The vast majority of books whose Wikipedia articles are nominated for deletion, and whose notability could reasonably be called into question, are contemporary." "Wikipedia:Notability (books)."

52 Perlentaucher, "Wer wir sind," https://www.perlentaucher.de/wer-wir-sind/wer-wir-sind.html.

53 Sarkana, comment on "RK Autoren," December 31, 2016, 18:38 (CET), https://de.wikipedia.org/w/index.php?title=Wikipedia_Diskussion:Relevanzkriterien/Archiv/2016/Dez&oldid=163562475#RK_Autoren.

What else can be deemed "a comparable renowned source" is disputed. The idea of treating the existence of an article in another Wikipedia language version as proof of notability has been rejected, since this raises the thorny question of whether "Wikipedia is notable enough for itself."[54] The principle thus established is: "Wikipedia is not a source."[55] Moreover, there is a fear that treating it as a source would soften German-language Wikipedia's strict rules; after all, other language versions have very different ideas about the nature of the encyclopedia as well as varying editorial and deletion policy standards. As understandable as both these arguments are, they prevent the expansion of one's own "language POV" through other cultures and languages.

2. <u>*Circular criteria*</u>

The next two bullet points in the notability criteria on German Wikipedia state that authors must have "written a standard work" or "won a renowned literary prize"[56] in order to be considered notable. These hardly play a role in deletion discussions, however, because as mentioned above, most deletion nominations target newcomers who do not yet have any prizes or standard works to their name. That being said, it is beyond question that literary prizes have an important consecration function. However, in view of the vast prize landscape, it must first be established which prizes are themselves considered "renowned." As a result, notability criteria have also been established for literary prizes: among other requirements, a prize is deemed relevant if it has been "conferred upon several particularly renowned writers and accepted by them."[57] The problem here is obvious: what we have is mutually reinforcing acts of consecration and legitimation between awarding institutions and authors. This circularity is not atypical, both

---

54 Ruiin, comment on "Globales Relevanzkriterium en.Wikipedia.org," March 24, 2010, 10:43 (CET), https://de.wikipedia.org/w/index.php?title=Wikipedia_Diskussion:Relevanzkriterien/Archiv/2010/Mrz&oldid=77531028#Globales_Relevanzkriterium_en.Wikipedia.org. Cf. also "Artikel in anderssprachigen Wikipedias als Relevanzkriterium," October 2007, https://de.wikipedia.org/w/index.php?title=Wikipedia_Diskussion:Relevanzkriterien/Archiv/2007/Okt&oldid=128234063#Artikel_in_anderssprachigen_Wikipedias_als_Relevanzkriterium.

55 "Wikipedia:Belege," Wikipedia, June 7, 2022, https://de.wikipedia.org/w/index.php?title=Wikipedia:Belege&oldid=223508411.

56 "Wikipedia:Relevanzkriterien, 8.4 Autoren." Similarly in the English-language Wikipedia.

57 "Wikipedia:Relevanzkriterien, 3.8 Literaturpreise," Wikipedia, May 3, 2022, https://de.wikipedia.org/w/index.php?title=Wikipedia:Relevanzkriterien&oldid=222583335#Literaturpreise

for consecration authorities themselves and for Wikipedia's notability criteria.

3. Arbitrariness vs. practicality

The next criterion is used most on a daily basis, but is also the most contested:

> Writers or authors are considered notable, [...]
>
> - if they have published at least two monographs (in the formal sense used in library science) of fiction/belles lettres or four non-literary monographs (for example nonfiction) as the lead author with a conventional publisher.[58]

Practically every word of this provision has ignited debate: Why must they be monographs? Is this specification not based on an antiquated and one-dimensional understanding of literature and its media and genres? Does it not disadvantage representatives of oral, performative, or digital language arts, playwrights—whose pieces are often staged but not published—, and poets—whose careers usually begin with the publication of individual poems in anthologies or magazines? According to one Wikipedian, this criterion reflects "not the judgment of experts but the plight of the scene and the hostility towards poetry in a field that is still largely commercially oriented."[59]

The specification that two or four monographs form a critical mass has created just as much debate. It corresponds to the old practice in culture pages and the book trade of having particularly high expectations for sophomore publications. At the same time, it sets the bar higher than in the field of music, where one-hit-wonders are given their own Wikipedia article as a matter of course. Furthermore, many people also vehemently oppose this kind of "measuring" of literature on the basis that every "quantitative criterion is inherently arbitrary" and "no objective criterion exists that would objectively justify a concrete threshold." The user sambalolec notes: "the significance of a writer or

58 "Wikipedia:Relevanzkriterien, 8.4 Autoren."

59 Mario Scheuermann, comment on "Schriftsteller," Wikipedia, January 15, 2007, 8:20 (CET), https://de.wikipedia.org/wiki/Wikipedia_Diskussion:Relevanzkriterien/Archiv/2007/Jan#Schriftsteller.

author cannot be gauged based on output alone, because there is no causal connection between a person's output and significance."[60]

This discussion echoes a paradigm shift affecting the way scientific theories are formed: in the age of Big Data, statistically determined correlation is threatening to replace the old style of scientific modeling based on causality, as Chris Anderson diagnosed back in 2008: "The new availability of huge amounts of data, along with the statistical tools to crunch these numbers, offers a whole new way of understanding the world. Correlation supersedes causation, and science can advance even without coherent models, unified theories, or really any mechanistic explanation at all."[61] This phenomenon can be seen in Computational Literary Studies, where methods such as John Burrows's Delta, n-grams, and lists of word frequency have proved to be remarkably powerful tools for stylometry and authorship attribution, even though it is impossible to give more than a rough explanation of why they work. The underlying causal connections are still completely opaque.[62]

In a way that is similarly difficult to explain, the specification of two or four publications has apparently proved to be a meaningful indicator of an author's notability: "This 'output alone' simply *has* worked for quite a long time."[63] As with the use of *Perlentaucher,* the practical utility of this specification is often invoked in the absence of evidence of a causal connection between output and significance: "That's why x books are so convenient: You just have to count."[64] It also helpfully reduces the "discussion overhead"[65] in Wikipedia, which is tiring for everyone involved.

---

60 All quotes from Sambalolec, comment on "Autoren," Wikipedia, September 16, 2008, 02:06 and 03:26 (CEST), https://de.wikipedia.org/w/index.php?title=Wikipedia_Diskussion:Relevanzkriterien/Archiv/2008/Sep&oldid=178323078#Autoren.

61 Chris Anderson, "The End of Theory: The Data Deluge Makes the Scientific Method Obsolete," *Wired*, June 23, 2008, https://www.wired.com/2008/06/pb-theory/.

62 Fotis Jannidis, "Der Autor ganz nah. Autorstil in Stilistik und Stilometrie," in *Theorien und Praktiken der Autorschaft*, ed. Matthias Schaffrick and Marcus Willand (Berlin et al.: de Gruyter, 2014), 169–195, 187ff.

63 Sambalolec, comment on "Autoren," September 16, 2008, 02:06 (CEST).

64 Perrak, comment on "Autoren," September 11, 2008, 01:23 (CEST).

65 Sambalolec, comment on "Autoren," September 17, 2008, 03:29 (CEST).

4. Recourse to external criteria

The number of publications criterion has since been tightened further by adding "with a conventional publisher." Apart from the fact that this just shifts the discussion to the definition of what constitutes a "conventional" publisher, it speaks of great mistrust toward a large part of contemporary literary production, which is often hastily and broadly pegged with the label "vanity press." In this respect, the German-language version of Wikipedia is barely distinguishable from the English-language, which is similarly decisive:

> Self-publication and/or publication by a vanity press do not correlate with notability. [...] Many vanity press books are assigned ISBN numbers, may be listed in a national library, may be found through a Google Books search, and may be sold at large online book retailers. None of these things is evidence of notability.[66]

But because the profound change in contemporary publishing practices cannot be completely ignored, after long discussion self-publishing was eventually accepted in German-language Wikipedia in 2012—albeit it under strict conditions:

> In exceptional circumstances, books that are released through self-publishing, "pseudo" publishing or subsidy publishing are counted if
>
> - appropriate distribution in research libraries can be proved ("appropriate distribution" means having the work in five locations in at least two regional networks—legal deposit in national and state libraries does not count),
> - they have received particular public attention (for example, reviews in renowned national newspapers) or
> - they are published by a recognized academic publisher with editorial selection.[67]

Thus, literary critics, newspaper culture pages, and academic publishing again assume the gatekeeper role as established institutions of value and consecration; libraries are another equally powerful institution. The criterion of "appropriate distribution" was introduced in 2008 because it can be easily checked using the Karlsruher Virtueller

66 "Wikipedia:Notability (books)."

67 "Wikipedia:Relevanzkriterien, 8.4 Autoren."

Katalog (KVK)—a meta search machine of library and bookselling catalogues worldwide—and because it has proved its worth, including outside Wikipedia: "The term and definition come from VG Wort—they do the work for us."[68] VG Wort (a German copyright collective) manages the secondary publication rights of authors and publishers and distributes the renumeration received—e.g. through photocopying levies and library royalties—to the beneficiaries. This distribution is regulated according to a scheme in which "appropriate distribution" of works is a prerequisite of royalty payments. This helps to ensure distributive justice.

It is surprising that Wikipedians have taken this criterion, which is based on economic exploitation, and elevated it to the yardstick of notability in the sense of cultural significance, even if it could be argued that copyright collectives are obliged by law to promote "culturally significant works and performances" (§ 32 (1) VGG). The provision is also problematic in that it only covers books in research libraries, which naturally excludes large parts of the book market, from light fiction through to popular nonfiction. Checking distribution or lending through *public* libraries would be more effective. The fact that this is not considered on Wikipedia is probably solely because—at least in Germany—there is no meta search engine like the KVK (which primarily covers research libraries) that would make it feasible to check.

Nevertheless, Wikipedia user Sarkana, who was largely responsible for the addition of the VG Wort provision to the notability criteria in 2008, still asserted in 2019 that "reliance on external criteria is the best way to develop notability criteria" because they have already been put to the test outside Wikipedia and proved to be practicable. Furthermore, they have the advantage that, for once, any criticism cannot be directed at Wikipedians: "We didn't create the standard, it was VG Wort—please direct complaints about its arbitrariness to them."[69]

---

68 Sarkana, comment on "Relevanzkriterien für Autoren von Fachbüchern (erl., umgesetzt)," Wikipedia, April 22, 2008, 03:47 (CEST), https://de.wikipedia.org/wiki/Wikipedia_Diskussion:Relevanzkriterien/Archiv/2008/Mrz#Relevanzkriterien_f%C3%BCr_Autoren_von_Fachb%C3%BCchern_(erl.,_umgesetzt).

69 Both quotes from Sarkana, comment on "Relevanz Sachbuchautoren jeglicher Art," March 20, 2019, 17:46 (CEST) and April 1, 2019, 20:01 (CEST), https://de.wikipedia.org/wiki/Wikipedia_Diskussion:Relevanzkriterien/Archiv/2019/Feb#Relevanz_Sachbuchautoren_jeglicher_Art.

Old Wine in New Bottles?

It appears that notability guidelines for authors are still profoundly marked by the traditional institutions of legitimation, value, and consecration that preside over book culture and the academic and literary worlds: thanks to the notability criteria, it is still printed reference works, newspaper culture pages, literary critics, literary prizes, publishers, libraries, and even copyright collectives that have the power to determine the "acute canon"[70] of contemporary literature on Wikipedia—and this in an online encyclopedia that claims to rely not on expert culture but on "every single person" and the promise of grassroots democracy and the swarm intelligence; to have declared war on the established institutions of knowledge and cultural value production; and to have become the most up-to-the-minute and flexible encylcopedia of all time.

Yet its notability criteria do not support that claim. The definition of what is worth knowing and including in an encyclopedia is too oriented towards well-established, longstanding standards, but it is apparently not (yet) possible to reach a consensus on alternative ones: "Wikipedia risks mimicking the same system it was built to disrupt."[71] This is particularly true for contemporary, experimental, avant-garde, and popular literature, literature not published in a traditional book format, and various forms of literature that are marginalized for other reasons. This has led some Wikipedians to the bitter realization that "in its fussy way, Wikipedia is once again unable to keep up with changing technological and social conditions."[72] Ultimately, however, everyone is aware that further notability criteria will be needed sooner rather than later:

> Classical (print) books, classical publishers, classical bookstores, classical newspapers with culture pages and reviews—all that is being becoming less and less important. A book that has [...] traveled along this classical path will, unless there is an about-face, soon be

70 The "acute canon" reacts to the "needs of the particular hour" and is subject to constant adjustment, updating, and negotiation. It is thus "less stable." All quotes from Renate von Heydebrand, "Probleme des 'Kanons' – Probleme der Kultur- und Bildungspolitik," in *Germanistik, Deutschunterricht und Kulturpolitik*, ed. Johannes Janota (Tübingen: Niemeyer, 1993), 3–22, 5.

71 Jina Valentine, Eliza Myrie, and Heather Hart, "The Myth of the Comprehensive Historical Archive," in *Wikipedia @ 20*, 259–272, 265.

72 Artmax, comment on "Relevanz Sachbuchautoren jeglicher Art," March 9, 2019, 14:16 (CET).

> the exotic exception. Forms of production, distribution, and reception are changing dramatically. [...] We will have to adapt the author notability criteria to the new reality, but they will have to go in a completely different direction from what is being suggested here.[73]

Perspectives

The question is, how could they be changed? There is no simple solution in sight, and none of the alternatives suggested so far have been entirely convincing. Because of the legal deposit requirement, the German National Library indiscriminately collects all publications with an ISBN released in the country. There is also no critical assessment of quality in directories such as *Kürschners deutscher Literatur-Kalender*, which for more than 130 years has recorded all living German-language authors, and in which it is possible to even enter oneself for a fee. It is usually impossible to determine and document sales and circulation figures, and independent research would run contrary to the "no original research" dictate. Quantitative parameters that are easy to ascertain from the internet—such as number of followers, likes, stars, downloads, reviews on social media or on platforms such as lovelybooks, wattpad, Archive of Our Own, and Amazon—are also easy to manipulate and unsuitable for judging notability because they tend to reveal more about the current resonance, attention, and popularity of an author than about their longer-term cultural significance. The same is true of the number of Google hits, especially as Google captures only part of the internet and search results are not reproducible, so they cannot be used as evidence. Absolute sales figures cannot be derived from Amazon sales rankings, either, because they merely show how often a title is being sold on Amazon in comparison to all other titles *at the time*.

Rather than resorting to the kind of numerical rating systems being mass-produced by the global players in today's platform and surveillance capitalism, it might be more expedient to consult other authorities and actors outside the established book and literary industry as "reputable" sources for determining the notability of previously marginalized groups of people and forms of literature: "we should not only

---

73 Amberg, comment on "Autoren," September 5, 2019, 20:45 (CEST), https://de.wikipedia.org/w/index.php?title=Wikipedia_Diskussion:Relevanzkriterien&oldid=192308598#Autoren.

look to 'mainstream' sources for proof; we also need to look to the reliable sources *in these communities* from which these figures emerge to establish their notability." This would take into account the fact that the systemic bias inherent in the notability criteria is often additionally reinforced by the verifiability policy. In the field of literature, for example, this kind of "'community standard' of notability"[74] would enable scene-specific entities such as Electronic Literature Collection, PennSound, UbuWeb, Versopolis, Rhizome, and Lyrikline to be considered as institutions of memory and collection, while festivals, competitions, and residencies could serve as "scouts" with their finger on the pulse. In principle, this could also be worked out for other areas currently underrepresented on Wikipedia, like popular literature, which is often not mentioned in precisely those sources that Wikipedia considers reliable and reputable: "Marginalized groups are often best studied and reported on in sources Wikipedia deems 'unreliable.'"[75]

What is needed more than anything, though, is to bring all these debates, waged on Wikipedia for such a long time, out of the semi-public sphere of the backstage so that they can be opened up, invigorated, diversified, reshaped, and advanced. One of Wikipedia's many guidelines, which claims that Wikipedia is ultimately "not a place where things should stay the same just because they have been the status quo for a long time," might serve as a motto: "Wikis only work when people are bold. Go for it [...] Be bold"![76]

74 The corresponding notability criterion could thus be: "a person who had a noticeable impact on a community as recognized in *that community's* most reputable sources." All quotes from Jake Orlowitz, "How Wikipedia Drove Professors Crazy, Made Me Sane, and Almost Saved the Internet," in *Wikipedia @20*, 125–139, 137 (emphasis in original).

75 Ibid.

76 "Wikipedia:Sei mutig," Wikipedia, May 13, 2022, https://de.wikipedia.org/w/index.php?title=Wikipedia:Sei_mutig&oldid=222850911 (emphasis in original). See also "Wikipedia:Be bold," May 25, 2022, https://en.wikipedia.org/w/index.php?title=Wikipedia:Be_bold&oldid=1089804782.

Bibliography

All internet sources were last accessed on 8 August 2025.

Amberg. Comment on "Autoren." *Wikipedia*, September 5, 2019.https://de.wikipedia.org/w/index.php?title=Wikipedia_Diskussion:Relevanzkriterien&oldid=192308598#Autoren.

Anderson, Chris. "The End of Theory: The Data Deluge Makes the Scientific Method Obsolete." *Wired*, June 23, 2008. www.wired.com/2008/06/pb-theory/.

Ardis, James. "*Dictionary of non-notable Artists* by Gregor Weichbrodt [review]." *The Rumpus*, January 3, 2017. https://therumpus.net/2017/01/dictionary-of-non-notable-artists-by-gregor-weichbrodt/.

Arnold, Heinz Ludwig. "Arbeit am Mythos Kindler." In *Wertung und Kanon*, edited by Matthias Freise and Claudia Stockinger. Winter, 2010, 125–139.

Artmax. Comment on "Relevanz Sachbuchautoren jeglicher Art." *Wikipedia*, March 9, 2019. https://de.wikipedia.org/wiki/Wikipedia_Diskussion:Relevanzkriterien/Archiv/2019/Feb#Relevanz_Sachbuchautoren_jeglicher_Art.

Beutler, William. "Paid with Interest: COI Editing and Its Discontent." In *Wikipedia @ 20: Stories of an Incomplete Revolution*, edited by Joseph Reagle and Jackie Koerner. MIT Press, 2020, 71–85.

Biruitorul. Comment on "Wikipedia:Articles for deletion/Ștefan Hrușcă." *Wikipedia*, December 27, 2013. https://en.wikipedia.org/wiki/Wikipedia:Articles_for_deletion/%C8%98tefan_Hru%C8%99c%C4%83.

Bridle, James. The Iraq War. A History of Wikipedia Changelogs. Self-publ., 2010. 12 vols.

Bröckling, Ulrich. The Entrepreneurial Self: Fabricating a New Type of Subject. Sage, 2016.

Callahan, Ewa S. "Crosslinguistic Neutrality. Wikipedia's Neutral Points of View from a Global Perspective." In *Global Wikipedia. International and Cross-cultural Issues in Online-Collaboration*, edited by Pnina Fichman and Noriko Hara. Rowman & Littlefield, 2014, 69–84.

Callahan, Ewa S., and Susan C. Herring. "Cultural Bias in Wikipedia Content on Famous Persons." *Journal of the American Society for Information Science and Technology* 62, no. 10 (2011): 1899–1915.

Codrin.B. Comment on "Wikipedia:Articles for deletion/Ștefan Hrușcă." *Wikipedia*, December 27, 2013. https://en.wikipedia.org/wiki/Wikipedia:Articles_for_deletion/%C8%98tefan_Hru%C8%99c%C4%83.

Cooke, Richard. "Wikipedia Is the Last Best Place on the Internet." *Wired*, February 17, 2020. www.wired.com/story/wikipedia-online-encyclopedia-best-place-internet/.

Cordevilla, Edwin M. "Point of Clarification." *Facebook*, November 30, 2016. https://www.facebook.com/emcordevilla/posts/1308824182490620.

Cramer, Florian. "A Brechtian Media Design: Annemieke van der Hoek's Epicpedia." In *Critical Point of View. A Wikipedia Reader*, edited by Geert Lovink and Nathaniel Tkacz. Institute of Network Cultures, 2011, 221–225.

Dijck, José van. The Culture of Connectivity: A Critical History of Social Media. Oxford UP, 2013.

Ford, Heather. "The Missing Wikipedians." In *Critical Point of View. A Wikipedia Reader*, edited by Geert Lovink and Nathaniel Tkacz. Institute of Network Cultures, 2011, 258–268.

Goldsmith, Kenneth. *Facebook*, September 29, 2016. https://www.facebook.com/kenneth.goldsmith.739/posts/538599506325863 (no longer available online).

Graham, Mark. "Wiki Space: Palimpsests and the Politics of Exclusion." In *Critical Point of View. A Wikipedia Reader*, edited by Geert Lovink and Nathaniel Tkacz. Institute of Network Cultures, 2011, 269–282.

Graham, Mark, and Martin Dittus. *Geographies of Digital Exclusion. Data and Inequalities*. London: Pluto Press, 2022.

Hecht, Brent, and Darren Gergle. "Measuring Self-focus Bias in Community – Maintained Knowledge Repositories." In *Proceedings of the Fourth International Conference on Communities and Technologies*. ACM Press, 2009, 11–20.

Heydebrand, Renate von. "Probleme des 'Kanons' – Probleme der Kultur- und Bildungspolitik." In *Germanistik, Deutschunterricht und Kulturpolitik*, edited by Johannes Janota. Niemeyer, 1993, 3–22.

Janker, Karin, and Thomas Urban. "Die Besserwisserei." *Süddeutsche Zeitung*, October 5/6, 2019: 11.

Jannidis, Fotis. "Der Autor ganz nah. Autorstil in Stilistik und Stilometrie." In *Theorien und Praktiken der Autorschaft*, edited by Matthias Schaffrick and Marcus Willand. De Gruyter, 2014, 169–195.

Jungen, Oliver. "Der Wille zum Wissen. Die Kapitulation des Brockhaus." *Zeitschrift für Ideengeschichte* X, no. 2 (Summer 2016): 5–16.

Koerner, Jackie. "Wikipedia Has a Bias Problem." In *Wikipedia @ 20: Stories of an Incomplete Revolution*, edited by Joseph Reagle and Jackie Koerner. MIT Press, 2020, 311–321.

Lutzi, Tobias. "Exklusionisten gegen Inklusionisten – ein enzyklopädischer Bruderkrieg." In *Alles* über *Wikipedia und die Menschen hinter der größten Enzyklopädie der Welt*, edited by Wikimedia Deutschland e.V.. Hoffmann und Campe, 2011, 164–172.

Mandiberg, Michael. *Print Wikipedia*. Self-publ., 2015. 7,473 vols.

Mandiberg, Michael. *Print Wikipedia. About*, https://printwikipedia.com/#/about.

Mandiberg, Michael. "Making *Print Wikipedia*." In *Library of Artistic Print on Demand. Post-Digital Publishing in Times of Platform Capitalism*, edited by Annette Gilbert and Andreas Bülhoff. Spector Books, 2025, 512–521.

Manetas, Miltos. Comment on Kenneth Goldsmith. *Facebook*, September 29, 2016. https://www.facebook.com/kenneth.goldsmith.739/posts/538599506325863 (no longer available online).

Massa, Paolo, and Fiederico Scrinzi. "Manypedia. Comparing language points of view of Wikipedia Communities." *First Monday* 18 (2013): 1–7.

Orlowitz, Jake. "How Wikipedia Drove Professors Crazy, Made Me Sane, and Almost Saved the Internet." In *Wikipedia @ 20: Stories of an Incomplete Revolution*, edited by Joseph Reagle and Jackie Koerner. MIT Press, 2020, 125–139.

Ottenbacher, Jahna. "Our News, Their Events: A Comparison of Archived Current Events on English and Greek Wikipedia." In *Global Wikipedia. International and Cross-cultural Issues in Online-Collaboration*, edited by Pnina Fichman and Noriko Hara. Rowman & Littlefield, 2014, 49–67.

Øvrebø, Olav Gisle. Comment on Kenneth Goldsmith. *Facebook*, September 29, 2016. https://www.facebook.com/kenneth.goldsmith.739/posts/538599506325863?comment_id=538608692991611&comment_tracking=%7B%22tn%22%3A%22R9%22%7D (no longer available online).

Perlentaucher. "Wer wir sind." https://www.perlentaucher.de/wer-wir-sind/wer-wir-sind.html.

Perrak. Comment on "Wikipedia Diskussion:Relevanzkriterien/Archiv/2008/Sep, Autoren." *Wikipedia*, September 11, 2008. https://de.wikipedia.org/w/index.php?title=Wikipedia_Diskussion:Relevanzkriterien/Archiv/2008/Sep&oldid=178323078#Autoren.

Ruiin. Comment on "Wikipedia Diskussion:Relevanzkriterien/Archiv/2010/Mrz, Globales Relevanzkriterium en.Wikipedia.org." *Wikipedia*, March 24, 2010. https://de.wikipedia.org/w/index.php?title=Wikipedia_Diskussion:Relevanzkriterien/Archiv/2010/Mrz&oldid=77531028#Globales_Relevanzkriterium_en.Wikipedia.org.

Sambalolec. Comment on "Wikipedia Diskussion:Relevanzkriterien/Archiv/2008/Sep, Autoren." *Wikipedia*, September 16, 2008. https://de.wikipedia.org/w/index.php?title=Wikipedia_Diskussion:Relevanzkriterien/Archiv/2008/Sep&oldid=178323078#Autoren.

Sarkana. Comment on "RK Autoren." *Wikipedia*, December 31, 2016. https://de.wikipedia.org/w/index.php?title=Wikipedia_Diskussion:Relevanzkriterien/Archiv/2016/Dez&oldid=163562475#RK_Autoren.

Sarkana. Comment on "Relevanzkriterien für Autoren von Fachbüchern (erl., umgesetzt)." *Wikipedia*, April 22, 2008. https://de.wikipedia.org/wiki/Wikipedia_Diskussion:Relevanzkriterien/Archiv/2008/Mrz#Relevanzkriterien_f%C3%BCr_Autoren_von_Fachb%C3%BCchern_(erl.,_umgesetzt).

Sarkana. Comment on "Relevanz Sachbuchautoren jeglicher Art." *Wikipedia*, March 20, 2019, and April 1, 2019. https://de.wikipedia.org/wiki/Wikipedia_Diskussion:Relevanzkriterien/Archiv/2019/Feb#Relevanz_Sachbuchau toren_jeglicher_Art.

Scheuermann, Mario. Comment on "Schriftsteller." *Wikipedia*, January 15, 2007. https://de.wikipedia.org/wiki/Wikipedia_Diskussion:Relevanzkriterien/Archiv/2007/Jan#Schriftsteller.

User 84.118.96.92. "Wikipedia:Löschkandidaten/18. September 2016." *Wikipedia*, September 18, 2016. https://de.wikipedia.org/w/index.php?title=Wikipedia:L%C3%B6schkandidaten/18._September_2016#Gregor_Weichbrodt_(LAE).

Valentine, Jina, Eliza Myrie, and Heather Hart. "The Myth of the Comprehensive Historical Archive." In *Wikipedia @ 20: Stories of an Incomplete Revolution*, edited by Joseph Reagle and Jackie Koerner. MIT Press, 2020, 259–272.

Vrandečić, Denny. "Collaborating on the Sum of All Knowledge Across Languages." In *Wikipedia @ 20: Stories of an Incomplete Revolution*, edited by Joseph Reagle and Jackie Koerner. MIT Press, 2020, 175–188.

Weichbrodt, Gregor. *Dictionary of* non-notable *Artists*. Frohmann, 2016.

Weinberger, David. Everything is Miscellaneous: The Power of the New Digital Disorder. Holt Paperbacks, 2007.

"Wikipedia:Artikel in anderssprachigen Wikipedias als Relevanzkriterium." *Wikipedia*, October 2007. https://de.wikipedia.org/w/index.php?title=Wikipedia_Diskussion:Relevanzkriterien/Archiv/2007/Okt&oldid=128234063#Artikel_in_anderssprachigen_Wikipedias_als_Relevanzkriterium.

"Wikipedia:Articles for deletion/Log/Today." *Wikipedia*. https://en.wikipedia.org/wiki/Wikipedia:Articles_for_deletion/Log/Today.

"Wikipedia:Archived articles for deletion." *Wikipedia*. https://en.wikipedia.org/wiki/Wikipedia:Archived_articles_for_deletion_discussions.

"Wikipedia:Be bold." *Wikipedia*, May 25, 2022. https://en.wikipedia.org/w/index.php?title=Wikipedia:Be_bold&oldid=1089804782.

"Wikipedia:Belege." *Wikipedia*, 7 June 2022. https://de.wikipedia.org/w/index.php?title=Wikipedia:Belege&oldid=223508411#Wikipedia_ist_keine_Quelle.

"Wikipedia:Core content policies." *Wikipedia*, May 3, 2022. https://en.wikipedia.org/w/index.php?title=Wikipedia:Core_content_policies&oldid=1085939107.

"Wikipedia:Notability." *Wikimedia*, June 3, 2022. https://en.wikipedia.org/w/index.php?title=Wikipedia:Notability&oldid=1091359595.

"Wikipedia:Notability (books)." *Wikipedia*, September 2, 2019. https://en.wikipedia.org/w/index.php?title=Wikipedia:Notability_(books)&oldid=913584923#Non-contemporary_books.

"Wikipedia:Notability in the English Wikipedia." *Wikipedia*, April 14, 2022. https://en.wikipedia.org/w/index.php?title=Notability_in_the_English_Wikipedia&oldid=1082657701.

"Wikipedia:Prime objective." *Wikipedia*, February 10, 2022. https://en.wikipedia.org/w/index.php?title=Wikipedia:Prime_objective&oldid=1070972014.

"Wikipedia:Relevanzkriterien." *Wikipedia*, April 27, 2004. https://de.wikipedia.org/w/index.php?title=Wikipedia:Relevanzkriterien&oldid=1169003.

"Wikipedia:Relevanzkriterien." *Wikipedia*, May 3, 2022. https://de.wikipedia.org/w/index.php?title=Wikipedia:Relevanzkriterien&oldid=222583335._

"Wikipedia:Relevanzkriterien, 3.8 Literaturpreise." *Wikipedia*, May 3, 2022. https://de.wikipedia.org/w/index.php?title=Wikipedia:Relevanzkriterien&oldid=222583335#Literaturpreise.

"Wikipedia:Relevanzkriterien, 8.4 Autoren." *Wikipedia*, May 3, 2022. https://de.wikipedia.org/w/index.php?title=Wikipedia:Relevanzkriterien&oldid=222583335#Autoren.

"Wikipedia:Sei mutig." *Wikipedia*, May 13, 2022. https://de.wikipedia.org/w/index.php?title=Wikipedia:Sei_mutig&oldid=222850911.

"Wikipedia:Size in volumes," *Wikipedia*, July 1, 2022. https://en.wikipedia.org/w/index.php?title=Wikipedia:Size_in_volumes&oldid=1065930409.

"Wikipedia:Systemic bias." *Wikipedia*, June 19, 2022. https://en.wikipedia.org/w/index.php?title=Wikipedia:Systemic_bias&oldid=1093861193.

"Wikipedia:What Wikipedia is not," *Wikimedia*, July 1, 2022, https://en.wikipedia.org/w/index.php?title=Wikipedia:What_Wikipedia_is_not&oldid=1096046659.

"Wikipedia:WikiProject Countering systemic bias," *Wikipedia*, May 2, 2022. https://en.wikipedia.org/w/index.php?title=Wikipedia:WikiProject_Countering_systemic_bias&oldid=1085856665.

Sanker

Guy Bennett

If the title of this paper means nothing to you, it's because there's no reason it should. The person whose name it was has been all but excluded from the historical record save one fleeting mention in a brief narrative published in a journal that ceased publication 90 years ago. The piece in question, "Snowball battle in Dalton – Little Jimmy White," appeared in the first volume of the *Confederate Veteran* monthly in 1893. Its author is S.R. Watkins; Sanker was his slave. Here is the fleeting mention:

> This snow ball battle lasted all day. A good number of the boys were quite badly hurt. My little bedfellow, Jimmie White, a mere boy of fourteen years, was run over by a caisson and both his legs broken, and he was otherwise injured. Poor boy, tears rush to my eyes when I go back in memory to the death of the clever lad. I cry now when I think of him. Poor little fellow, how he suffered, and how he hated to die! Sanker, my negro servant, brought him and laid him on our bunk.[1]

While the name Sanker may not ring a bell, that of S.R. Watkins might. He wrote one of the most popular Civil War memoirs chronicling his service in the 1st Tennessee Infantry Regiment. Having been serialized twice, *Company Aytch*[2] knew two editions and some seven reprintings, and exists in multiple editions today. It was quoted extensively in Ken Burns' *Civil War* miniseries, the documentary director characterizing it as, "A memoir of staggering significance, wit, and beauty."

---

1 Sam Watkins, "Snowball battle in Dalton – Little Jimmy White," *Confederate Veteran* I, no. 9 (September 1893): 261-262, https://archive.org/details/confederateveter01conf/page/n291/mode/2up.

2 The full title is *"Company Aytch," Maury Grays, First Tennessee Regiment; or, A Side Show of the Big Show.*

Indeed it was in the Burns documentary that I first encountered the name Samuel Rush Watkins and heard excerpts of *Company Aytch*. I later acquired an audio version of the book and have listened to it many times, as I have other Civil War memoirs mentioned in the Burns miniseries.[3] Watkins' memoir is remarkable in that it covers the whole of the conflict from the point of view of a foot soldier who fought in and survived many of the bloodiest battles, Watkins having signed up in May 1861 and served throughout the war. It is also remarkable in that the word "slavery" appears exactly once, and that in reference to one of the many names given the war ("the war of secession, rebellion, state rights, slavery, or our rights in the territories, or by whatever other name it may be called," p. 12).[4] The word "slaves" likewise appears just one time, Watkins using it, without a hint of irony, to describe how poorly Confederate soldiers were treated by General Bragg ("We were tenfold worse than slaves...," p. 40).

Even to the non-historian that I am, this was a shocking omission: an entire book on the Civil War, written by one who had lived it no less, with nary a mention of slavery and no discussion of the central role it played in sparking the conflict? To be fair, the book does contain a number of allusions to slavery, but more often than not they are oblique, euphemistic, and merely suggest what could—and should—have been explicitly stated, for example: "the Federal army ... expected to march right into the heart of the South, *set the negroes free*..." (13), "Extra rations were issued to *negroes who were acting as servants*..." (108), and, following the passage of the "Twenty-Slave Law," "*Negro property* suddenly became very valuable..." (37; my italics all), etc.

At one point in the Burns documentary the narrator states, "Like most Rebel soldiers, Sam Watkins owned no slaves." Considering the latter's lack of candor on the subject I wondered: was this actually the case? A quick internet search revealed that in fact Watkins was born into a prosperous planter family, that in 1860 his father owned 108 enslaved African Americans and two plantations, that some 50 "Maury Grays" were accompanied in their military service and cared for by their enslaved manservants, one of whom, apparently, was Sanker.

3 Namely, Mary Chesnut's *Diary from Dixie* and Leander Stilwell's *The Story of a Common Soldier of Army Life in the Civil War, 1861–1865*.

4 The page numbers given here and below are from the 1900 edition published by Times Printing Company of Chatanooga, Tenn. It is accessible online at https://archive.org/details/coaytch00watk/page/n5/mode/2up.

That the latter may well have belonged to Watkins' father and not Watkins personally does not change the fact that he himself profited directly from slavery and that he and his family had an obvious stake in its preservation.

I took a look at Watkins' *Wikipedia* page: the words "slave" and "slavery" did not appear. The first section, "Early life and education," read simply:

> Watkins was born on June 26, 1839 near Columbia, Maury County, Tennessee, and received his formal education at Jackson College in Columbia.[5]

This was followed by brief narratives recounting Watkins' enlistment and military service ("The American Civil War"), his post-war life ("Later years"), and the legacy of his work ("In popular culture").

Wishing to correct what was at best an unfortunate lapsus I amended the "Early life and education" section to acknowledge the Watkins family's stake in the slave economy and thus the cause of the Confederacy so that it read as follows:

> Watkins was born on June 26, 1839 near Columbia, Maury County, Tennessee, to a wealthy, slave-owning family. He received his formal education at Jackson College in Columbia.[6]

I included a footnote with a link to a page on the National Park Services' website devoted to Watkins, and that mentions and provides references to his family's wealth in both property and slaves as documented in U.S. Census records from the time.[7]

Revisiting the Watkins *Wikipedia* page a year or two later I noticed that my amendation was gone. The page's revision history shows that it had been partially rewritten eight months later, the "Early life and education" section—and sole reference to slavery—deleted, and Watkins' life story encapsulated in a new section ("Biography") that stresses his valor, military service, survival, and the full military honors with

---

5 Accessible via the page's revision history at: https://en.wikipedia.org/w/index.php?title=Samuel_R._Watkins&oldid=696372709.

6 Ditto: https://en.wikipedia.org/w/index.php?title=Samuel_R._Watkins&oldid=696372709.

7 For the Watkins 1860 census slave schedule, see: https://www.familysearch.org/ark:/61903/3:1:33S7-9BS6-112?cc=3161105&personaUrl=%2Fark%3A%2F61903%2F1%3A1%3AWKTP-3PW2.

which he was buried.[8] The history also reveals that the revision was the work of a *Wikipedia* editor who seems a self-appointed custodian for this page, having edited it 86 times as of this writing (July 2022). The badges on their Wikipedia User page[9] indicate that they are a citizen of the state of Arkansas, a decorated war veteran, and the descendant of a soldier who fought for the Confederate States.

The removal of the reference to slavery stuck in my craw but at first I did nothing about it; it seemed pointless to re-introduce information that was sure to be deleted later. Eventually the idea occurred that I might create a *Wikipedia* page for Sanker himself, documenting what little is known about him and linking it to relevant pages both within and without *Wikipedia,* including of course the Watkins page, thus indirectly achieving my aim of qualifying the implication that Watkins had no personal stake in the preservation of slavery. The article would have the added benefit of drawing attention to the fact that during their service many Confederate soldiers were accompanied and cared for by their slaves who were often unnamed in the official record when they were mentioned at all, and whose daily lives and fate, like those of Sanker, were typically unrecorded. By extension, Sanker's story would likewise evoke the untold numbers of enslaved Africans who were for all intents and purposes excluded from the Book of Life as no written record of their existence as individuals was ever made.

I duly researched my subject and wrote the article, making sure to draw on what relevant, reputable sources existed, incorporating excerpts from them in my text alongside links to related webpages and giving full references in footnotes. I took pains to format the completed piece to *Wikipedia*'s specifications and, having verified that all was in working order by proofing the text on the *Wikipedia* sandbox page, I submitted a draft.[10] Six weeks later it was declined. The explanation read:

---

8 To this day (July 27, 2022) that section reads: "In May 1861, twenty-one year old Sam Watkins of Maury County, Tennessee, rushed to join the army when his state left the Union. He became part of Company H (or Co. "Aytch," as he called it), First Tennessee Regiment, and would fight from Shiloh to Nashville and was one of only seven men who remained in the company when it was surrendered to Major-General W.T. Sherman in North Carolina, April 1865. When he died at sixty-two, Watkins was buried with full military honors."

9 https://en.wikipedia.org/wiki/User:Lieutcoluseng.

10 See appendix 1.

> This submission is not adequately supported by [[reliable sources]].[11] *Reliable* sources are required so that information can be [[verified]]. If you need help with referencing see [[Referencing for beginners]] and [[Citing sources]].[12]

It continued:

> This submission's references do not show that the subject [[qualifies for a Wikipedia article]]—that is, they do not show *significant* coverage (not just passing mentions) about the subject in *published, [[reliable]], [[secondary]]* sources that are *[[independent]]* of the subject (see the [[guidelines on the notability of people]]). Before any resubmission, additional references meeting these criteria should be added (see [[technical help]] and learn about [[mistakes to avoid]] when addressing this issue). If no additional references exist, the subject is not suitable for Wikipedia.

Finally, there was a personal comment from the *Wikipedia* editor who declined the submission:

> This seems, to me, to fall at the first hurdle of [[WP:V]] verifiability, before even getting to [[WP:N]] notability. Or how can we possibly establish notability for a person who may or may not have existed, whose biographical details are unknown, and of whom there is no reliable record, written or otherwise; let alone no multiple records? And how are we to avoid [[WP:OR]]?[13]

So, at bottom, Sanker did not qualify for a *Wikipedia* page because his existence could not be verified or his notability as an individual subject established to that publication's satisfaction, yet in addition to affirming that he did live it is these very facts that beg to be

---

11 Double-square-bracketed words indicate internal *Wikipedia* links.

12 AUTHOR QUERY: AS THE DRAFT PAGE HAS BEEN DELETED FROM THE WIKIPEDIA SITE I CANNOT PROVIDE A LINK FOR IT. I DO HAVE A SCREEN-CAPTURE FOR IT, BUT HOW TO INCLUDE THAT IN THIS PAPER? (WERE IT TO BE REPRODUCED AS AN IMAGE, IT WOULD HAVE TO BE REDUCED IN SIZE SO AS TO BE ILLEGIBLE.) PLEASE ADVISE.

13 i.e. "No original research." The linked page begins: "Wikipedia articles must not contain original research. The phrase 'original research' (OR) is used on Wikipedia to refer to material— such as facts, allegations, and ideas— for which no [[reliable, published sources]] exist. This includes any analysis or synthesis of published material that [[serves to reach or imply a conclusion not stated by the sources]]. To demonstrate that you are not adding original research, you must be able to cite reliable, published sources that are *directly related* to the topic of the article, and *directly support* the material being presented."

acknowledged. Sanker was undocumented as an individual—a person with a name, a parentage, a recorded date and place of birth, etc.—because his personal identity was of no value in the slave economy into which he was born; the only identifiers given enslaved peoples in the census records of the time were age, sex, and race, i.e. physical characteristics which could help determine how much longer a slave might serve, what work they might be put to, and thus what their potential monetary value might be. To consider the slave an individual would be to recognize the common humanity they shared with their white owners and thus indirectly challenge the dehumanizing rationales ("curse of Ham," "Three-Fifths Clause," etc.) used to justify their enslavement in the first place. It seemed a cruel irony that *Wikipedia*'s inclusion standard would actually perpetuate the marginalization of underdocumented people such as Sanker, excluding them because they lack documentation intentionally denied them due to their supposed "less than" status.

I felt there was no point in pushing the matter further but was not undaunted—the rejection had sparked an idea: if I could not publish the Sanker entry in *Wikipedia* as I had hoped, why not publish it elsewhere, and not just the article but with it the comments from the editors who declined it? And why stop with Sanker? There were certainly other underdocumented people I had encountered in my readings and personal research whom I wished to draw attention to. I could write and submit several such pieces. Should they be published, I would have achieved my aim; should they not, as seemed more likely, I could publish them collectively afterwards, perhaps even as a volume of declined *Wikipedia* articles titled *Un-Imaginary Lives*, after Marcel Schwob.

I decided to pursue this idea, and next wrote about Meryem bent Ali, a member of the Algerian Ouled-Naïl tribe who had left a small but not insignificant mark on the French literature of the late 19th century. bent Ali was living in Biskra, Algeria in the mid-1890s, dancing and performing sex work to earn her dowery, as was the custom of her people. She would be a significant inspiration for the protagonist of Pierre Louÿs' *Les chansons de Bilitis*,[14] a famed literary hoax that had scholars of classical antiquity believing the book contained Louÿs' translations of poems by a 6th-century BCE Greek poetess, contemporary (and possibly lover) of Sappho, whose tomb and writings had

14 Pierre Louÿs, *Les chansons de Bilitis* (Paris: Librairie de l'art indépendant, 1895).

supposedly just been discovered in Cyprus. Several of these poems had been set to music by Claude Debussy, which is how I first encountered them, and I later read and reread the book, researched its writing, reception and author.

As it happens, Louÿs had learned of Meryem bent Ali from his childhood friend André Gide who, traveling in North Africa, had stayed for a time in Biskra and had his first sexual experience there with her. After his return to Europe, Gide recommended his friend follow suit and Louÿs did, meeting bent Ali in Biskra, then spending ten days with her in Constantine. While there he completely revised the manuscript of *Les chansons de Bilitis*, fashioning the poetess character after his companion and writing new poems incorporating things she said and did while they were together.

Unlike Sanker, bent Ali was not exactly unknown: she had apparently been a fixture in Biskra and as such figured in Jean Lorrain's *Heures d'Afrique*[15] and Gide's *Si le grain ne meurt ...*[16] Louÿs and traveling companion André-Ferdinand Herold also kept a travel diary while in Algeria—later published as the *Journal de Meryem*[17]—that recounted in detail their experiences and exchanges with her. She was discussed at length in epidemiologist Émile Laurent's 1893 essay "La prostituée arabe,"[18] which also includes a full-length drawing of her, and there are a few period photographs in which she appears as well. More recently, she was the focus of a 2016 article on sexual tourism and literature by social anthropologist François Pouillon.[19] Collectively, these elements would certainly satisfy the requirements of verifiability and notability as defined above. Or so I thought.

I wrote a draft of the article.[20] As I had done with Sanker's, I structured the text in *Wikipedia* fashion and formatted it to their specifications, "test driving" it on their sandbox page to make sure it presented as

---

15 Jean Lorrain, *Heures d'Afrique* (Paris: Bibliothèque-Charpentier, 1899).

16 André Gide, *Si le grain ne meurt...* (Paris: Éditions de la Nouvelle revue française, 1924).

17 Pierre Louÿs and André-Ferdinand Herold, *Journal de Meryem [1894], Suivi des Lettres inédites à Zohra Bent Brahim*, ed. Jean-Paul Goujon (Paris: A.-G. Nizet, 1992).

18 Émile Laurent, "La prostituée arabe," *Archives d'Anthropologie criminelle, de Criminologie et de Psychologie normale et pathologique*, VIII (1893): 315-322.

19 François Pouillon, "Tourisme sexuel et littérature," *La Revue* LXVIII (November-December 2016): 126-128.

20 See appendix 2.

intended, that all links were functioning, etc. When it was ready I submitted it. It was declined the following day. The explanation:

> This submission does not appear to be written in the formal tone expected of an encyclopedia article. Entries should be written from a neutral point of view, and should refer to a range of independent, reliable, published sources. Please rewrite your submission in a more encyclopedic format. Please make sure to avoid peacock terms that promote the subject.[21]

Thankfully, "peacock terms" was explained in a comment ("For example, 'Like the spectral image of a moving figure in a daguerreotype, Meryem bent Ali's presence was captured only fleetingly…'"); there was also a request that I remove all external links in the event I was planning to revise and resubmit the article, which seemed odd given the emphasis on verifiability.

I made the requested revisions and resubmitted the draft, but it too was declined the next day by another *Wikipedia* editor who repeated verbatim the explanation quoted above and followed up with a petulant, "Rewrite the article. Don't just resubmit it."

I contacted this latter editor via their talk page, explaining that I had made the requested revisions before resubmitting the draft, and asking what would constitute "a more encyclopedic format" or what, in the draft as then written, would be considered non-encyclopedic. They replied:

> It does not have the tone of Wikipedia, for example "Louÿs was taken with Meryem and under her spell revised…." is not the correct tone. The language is too informal and subjective. Perhaps more importantly though it is not clear why you think this person is even notable. There is no credible claim that they are significant enough to warrant an article.

I responded:

> As for M.b.A.'s notability, in my view it lies in the following:

21 https://en.wikipedia.org/wiki/Draft:Meryem_bent_Ali.

- she was the principal inspiration for Pierre Louÿs' *The Songs of Bilitis,* arguably his most well-known and best-loved work;
- she achieved a dubious notoriety in Biskra among western tourists, who frequented the cafés where she danced, some of them (like Émile Laurent and Jean Lorrain, whom I reference) writing about her in their work;
- she was an object of sexual tourism, and as such exploited—while still a child—by some of those same westerners, including figures such as Gide and Louÿs, who used her for their purposes then simply "moved on."

Through her contact with the above writers, M.b.A. left a mark—albeit a faint one—on western literary culture. Given her status as a colonial subject, woman, and child, this is no small feat and is worthy of recognition, hence the proposed article.

Quoth the raven:

> It would be worth you reading the full article on Wikipedia Notability (WP:N). Notability is established from reliable sources discussing the individual in a way that establishes notability. In particular, the General Notability Guidelines apply here. Nothing you've written implies notability in the Wikipedia sense I'm afraid.

Notwithstanding the tautological circularity of the argument whereby "Notability is established from reliable sources discussing the individual in a way that establishes notability," and begging to differ on the quality of my sources, as recommended I read the General Notability Guideline,[22] which is presented in a single, brief sentence, each italicized term being defined briefly afterwards:

> A topic is *presumed* to be suitable for a stand-alone article or list when it has received *significant coverage* in *reliable sources* that are *independent of the subject.*

Unless I am missing something here Meryem bent Ali seems to meet all of these criteria: she has been "covered" in numerous published, reliable, secondary sources having no affiliation with her, including a pair

22 https://en.wikipedia.org/wiki/Wikipedia:Notability#General_notability_guideline.

of canonized texts (*Les chansons de Bilitis* and *Si le grain ne meurt...*) by renowned writers (Louÿs and Gide). The one gray area, of course, is the word *presumed*. Here is the definition given:

> "Presumed" means that significant coverage in [[reliable sources]] creates an assumption, not a guarantee, that a subject merits its own article. A more in-depth discussion might conclude that the topic actually should not have a stand-alone article—perhaps because it violates [[what Wikipedia is not]], particularly the rule that [[Wikipedia is not an indiscriminate collection of information]].

This would seem to be a blanket justification for rejecting entries that meet all requirements but are undesirable for some other, unexplained reason. The idea that one would establish explicit criteria for inclusion, but suggest that subjects which fulfill them might still constitute "indiscriminate information" seems, frankly, duplicitous—wouldn't the provision of required documentation demonstrate the opposite? Isn't that its purpose? And if it isn't, then why is it required? What other reason(s) for it might there be? Is it to serve as a hurdle? A camouflage? An insinuation of due diligence? Something else?

I took a look at the page "what Wikipedia is not,"[23] paying particular attention to the section "Wikipedia is not an indiscriminate collection of information"[24]—not one thing listed there applies to the case of bent Ali (nor to that of Sanker, for that matter), so there must be a certain *je ne sais quoi* about her / them that just isn't right for The Free Encyclopedia. One wonders what that might be.

I suppose it's possible that the editors who declined these articles were loathe to them appearing in *Wikipedia* because they highlight injustices committed against marginalized, subjugated people of color by their white (colonial) masters, thereby laying bare the hypocrisy of those who would present the latter in such a way as to suggest that no injustices were occurring, or that if they were, "our people" were not

23 The following are listed as what *Wikipedia* is not: a dictionary; a publisher of original thought; a soapbox or means of promotion; a mirror or a repository of links, images, or media files; a blog, web hosting service, social networking service, or memorial site; a directory; a manual, guidebook, textbook, or scientific journal; a crystal ball; a newspaper; an indiscriminate collection of information; censored. From: https://en.wikipedia.org/wiki/Wikipedia:What_Wikipedia_is_not.

24 i.e. summary-only descriptions of works; lyrics databases; excessive listings of unexplained statistics; exhaustive logs of software updates. From: https://en.wikipedia.org/wiki/Wikipedia:What_Wikipedia_is_not#Wikipedia_is_not_an_indiscriminate_collection_of_information.

among those committing them. This may well have been the motivation of the self-appointed custodian of Sam Watkins' page. Yet it is no less possible that their rejections were sincere, unmotivated applications of *Wikipedia*'s inclusion standard as they know and understand or have been trained to use it. To give them the benefit of the doubt, let's assume this is the case. What does it suggest?

To me, one or the other of two things: either that some people, due to that above-mentioned *je ne sais quoi*, are simply unfit for inclusion in The Free Encyclopedia. They are *not significant enough*, to paraphrase the second rejector of the bent Ali draft. Perhaps no one can explain exactly why—that's the *je-ne-sais-quoi* part—hence ill-defined appeals to "encyclopedic format" and "peacock terms,"[25] and the bumbling pseudo-clarification that "notability is established [...] in a way that establishes notability."

The other is that inclusion standards are also necessarily exclusion standards, obviously, and they tend to function to the benefit of those who establish them, ensuring their access while keeping "undesirables" out, and protecting their interests and reaffirming their worldview as they do so. Perhaps *Wikipedia*'s criteria for inclusion need to be revisited and retooled in such a way that they are not skewed in favor of the already documented, but can also accommodate if not prioritize people who were not similarly valued and thus not afforded the same attention and respect. It is unrealistic, to put it charitably, to require equal documentation of those whose lives were not documented equally because it was assumed that they were simply *not significant enough*. Is it actually necessary to say this?

25 The quoted example of a peacock term in my draft does not even reflect Wikipedia's own definition of "peacock terms": "In Wikipedia, a *peacock term* is language that shows off the importance of a subject without giving any real information. For example...: *William Peckenridge, 1st Duke of Omnium (1602?–May 8, 1671) is considered, by some people, to be the most important man ever to carry that title.*" See: https://en.wikipedia.org/wiki/Category:Articles_with_peacock_terms.

Bibliography

Burns, Ken. dir. *The Civil War.* PBS, 1990.

Gide, André. *Si le grain ne meurt...* Paris: Éditions de la Nouvelle revue française, 1924.

Intellectual Reserve, Inc. "Watkins 1860 Census Slave Schedule." https://www.familysearch.org/ark:/61903/3:1:33S7-9BS6-112?cc=3161105&personaUrl=%2Fark%3A%2F61903%2F1%3A1%3AWKTP-3PW2.

Laurent, Émile. "La prostituée arabe." *Archives d'Anthropologie criminelle, de Criminologie et de Psychologie normale et pathologique*, VIII (1893): 315-322.

Lorrain, Jean. *Heures d'Afrique.* Paris: Bibliothèque-Charpentier, 1899.

Louÿs, Pierre. *Les chansons de Bilitis.* Paris: Librairie de l'art indépendant, 1895.

Louÿs, Pierre and André-Ferdinand Herold. *Journal de Meryem [1894], Suivi des Lettres inédites à Zohra Bent Brahim.* Edited by Jean-Paul Goujon. Paris: A.-G. Nizet, 1992.

Pouillon, François. "Tourisme sexuel et littérature." *La Revue* LXVIII (November-December 2016): 126–28.

Watkins, Samuel R. "Snowball battle in Dalton – Little Jimmy White." *Confederate Veteran* 1, no. 9 (September 1893): 261-262. https://archive.org/details/confederateveter01conf/page/n291/mode/2up.

Watkins, Samuel R. *"Co. Aytch," Maury Grays, First Tennessee Regiment; or, A Side Show of the Big Show,* 2nd Ed. Times Printing Company, 1900.

Wikipedia, "Samuel R. Watkins," last modified November 10, 2024, 01:41 (UTC), https://en.wikipedia.org/wiki/Samuel_R._Watkins.

Nota bene

While researching and writing this article I was surprised to see that, though declined by *Wikipedia*, my article drafts have been published on the mirror sites *EverybodyWiki* and *Wikitia*. I don't know why that occurred (these were drafts after all, not published pieces) nor how long they will remain up but as of this writing they can be found at: https://en.everybodywiki.com/Sanker, https://en.everybodywiki.com/Meryem_bent_Ali, and https://wikitia.com/wiki/Sanker.

Appendix 1

Draft: Sanker

From Wikipedia, the free encyclopedia
Submission declined on 20 July 2021 by DoubleGrazing.

This submission is not adequately supported by reliable sources. *Reliable* sources are required so that information can be verified. If you need help with referencing, please see Referencing for beginners and Citing sources.

This submission's references do not show that the subject qualifies for a Wikipedia article—that is, they do not show *significant* coverage (not just passing mentions) about the subject in *published, reliable, secondary* sources that are *independent* of the subject (see the guidelines on the notability of people). Before any resubmission, additional references meeting these criteria should be added (see technical help and learn about mistakes to avoid when addressing this issue). If no additional references exist, the subject is not suitable for Wikipedia.

Comment

This seems, to me, to fall at the first hurdle of WP:V verifiability, before even getting to WP:N notability. Or how can we possibly establish notability for a person who may or may not have existed, whose biographical details are unknown, and of whom there is no reliable record, written or otherwise; let alone no multiple records? And how are we to avoid WP:OR? DoubleGrazing (talk) 13:10, 20 July 2021 (UTC)

Sanker (birth and death dates unknown) was the enslaved manservant of Samuel R. Watkins, who fought in the American Civil War with the 1st Tennessee Infantry Regiment.

Contents

Life

Sanker was one of some fifty slaves to accompany their masters as body servants while the latter fought with the "First Tennessee"; only nine are known by name. Watkins, who survived the war and would later write about his experiences as a Confederate foot soldier, mentioned Sanker in a brief narrative entitled "Snowball battle in Dalton—Little Jimmie White", which was published in the first volume of the *Confederate Veteran Magazine* in 1893. Here is the passage in question:

> This snow ball battle lasted all day. A good many of the boys were quite badly hurt. My little bedfellow, Jimmie White, a mere boy of fourteen years, was run over by a caison [sic] and both his legs broken, and he was otherwise injured. Poor boy, tears rush to my eyes when I go back in memory to the death of the clever lad. I cry now when I think of him. Poor little fellow, how he suffered, and how he hated to die! Sanker, my negro servant, brought him and laid him on our bunk. (261–262)

This is Sanker's only appearance in the piece; indeed, it may well be the sole record of his existence as he is entirely absent from Watkins' popular and oft reprinted postwar memoir *Co. Aytch*. As Edward John Harcourt noted, "None of the previous editors of *Co. Aytch* (first serialized in 1881–82, again in 1901–02, and published in seven editions since) has acknowledged 'Sanker' or the Watkins family's slaveholding interests, though the 1893 piece and the 1860s federal census and county tax records are clear on this point." Even Ken Burns, who quotes extensively from *Co. Aytch* in his The Civil War (miniseries), states that Watkins "owned no slaves."

Death

While the post-war lives of some body servants have been documented, it is unknown whether Sanker survived the war and, if so, where he might have gone and what he might have done afterwards; the time, place and cause of his death are likewise unknown. His fleeting presence in Sam Watkins' writings bears testimony to the many body servants, and enslaved African Americans more generally, whose identities and stories have been lost to history.

References

1. See Body Servants of the 1st Tennessee.

2. "Confederate veteran" [serial]. Nashville, Tenn.: S. A. Cunningham. 1893.

3. "Co. Aytch". Chattanooga, Tenn.: [Times printing company]. 1900.

Watkins does mention in passing "the negro boys, who were with their young masters as servants" (p. 34), "the negros who were with us as servants" (p 39) and "the negros who were acting as servants" (p 108), and he twice referred (on pp. 119 and 183), to "the negro boy" of two different officers. Nothing more is said of them and none are named.

4. From footnote 17 of "Would to God I could tear the page from these memoirs and from my own memory: *Co. Aytch* and the Confederate Sensibility of Loss."

On the Watkins family's slaveholding interests, the National Park Service notes the following: "Census and tax records of antebellum Maury County show that Sam's father, Frederick, owned more than 100 enslaved African Americans on two plantations in the county. The Watkins family was the third wealthiest in one of the most prosperous counties in the state. Incredibly, Watkins was not an outlier in his company. Nearly half of the company with which he left Maury County in 1861 came from slave-owning households."

5. Perhaps Burns inferred this from the following passage, in which Watkins implies he was poor:

> A law was made by the Confederate States Congress about this time allowing every person who owned twenty negroes to go home. It gaves us the blues; we wanted twenty negroes. Negro property suddenly became very valuable, and there was raised the howl of "rich man's war, poor man's fight." The glory of the war, the glory of the South, the glory of the pride of our volunteers had no charms for the conscript. (p. 37)

6. See for example "Osbourne Cunningham, Body Servant to William Cunningham, 1st teen. Infantry Co. D. Williamson Grays, CSA" on the blog From Slaves to Soldiers and Beyond–Williamson County, Tennessee's African American History

<u>*External Links*</u>

- Sam Watkins page[26] on the National Park Services website
- Body Servants of the 1st Tennessee[27]

26 https://www.nps.gov/people/sam-watkins.htm

27 https://williamsongrays.com/body%20servants.htm

Not logged in Talk Contributions Create account Log in

WIKIPEDIA
The Free Encyclopedia

Draft Talk Read Edit View history Search Wikipedia

Main page
Contents
Current events
Random article
About Wikipedia
Contact us
Donate

Contribute
Help
Learn to edit
Community portal
Recent changes
Upload file

Tools
What links here
Related changes
Special pages
Permanent link
Page information

Print/export
Download as PDF
Printable version

Languages

Draft:Sanker

From Wikipedia, the free encyclopedia

Submission declined on 20 July 2021 by DoubleGrazing (talk).

This submission is not adequately supported by reliable sources. *Reliable* sources are required so that information can be verified. If you need help with referencing, please see Referencing for beginners and Citing sources.

This submission's references do not show that the subject qualifies for a Wikipedia article—that is, they do not show *significant* coverage (not just passing mentions) about the subject in *published*, *reliable*, *secondary* sources that are *independent* of the subject (see the guidelines on the notability of people). Before any resubmission, additional references meeting these criteria should be added (see technical help and learn about mistakes to avoid when addressing this issue). If no additional references exist, the subject is not suitable for Wikipedia.

- If you would like to continue working on the submission, click on the "Edit" tab at the top of the window.
- If you have not resolved the issues listed above, your draft will be declined again and potentially deleted.
- If you need extra help, please ask us a question at the AfC Help Desk or get **live help** from experienced editors.
- Please do not remove reviewer comments or this notice until the submission is accepted.

Where to get help [show]
How to improve a draft [show]
Improving your odds of a speedy review [show]
Editor resources [show]

Declined by DoubleGrazing 6 seconds ago. Last edited by DoubleGrazing 6 seconds ago. Reviewer: inform author.

Resubmit Please note that if the issues are not fixed, the draft will be declined again.

- **Comment:** This seems, to me, to fail at the first hurdle of WP:V verifiability, before even getting to WP:N notability. Or how can we possibly establish notability for a person who may or may not have existed, whose biographical details are unknown, and of whom there is no reliable record, written or otherwise; let alone no multiple records? And how are we to avoid WP:OR? DoubleGrazing (talk) 13:10, 20 July 2021 (UTC)

Sanker (birth and death dates unknown) was the enslaved manservant of Samuel R. Watkins, who fought in the American Civil War with the 1st Tennessee Infantry Regiment.

Contents [hide]

Life [edit]

Sanker was one of some fifty slaves to accompany their masters as body servants while the latter fought with the "First Tennessee"; only nine are known by name.[1] Watkins, who survived the war and would later write about his experiences as a Confederate foot soldier, mentioned Sanker in a brief narrative entitled "Snowball battle in Dalton – Little Jimmie White," which was published in the first volume of the *Confederate Veteran Magazine* in 1893.[2] Here is the passage in question:

> This snow ball battle lasted all day. A good many of the boys were quite badly hurt. My little bedfellow, Jimmie White, a mere boy of fourteen years, was run over by a caison [sic] and both his legs broken, and he was otherwise injured. Poor boy, tears rush to my eyes when I go back in memory to the death of the clever lad. I cry now when I think of him. Poor little fellow, how he suffered, and how he hated to die! Sanker, my negro servant, brought him and laid him on our bunk. (261–262)

This is Sanker's only appearance in the piece; indeed, it may well be the sole record of his existence as he is entirely absent from Watkins' popular and oft reprinted postwar memoir *Co. Aytch*.[3] As Edward John Harcourt noted, "None of the previous editors of *Co. Aytch* [first serialized in 1881–82, again in 1901–02, and published in seven editions since] has acknowledged 'Sanker' or the Watkins family's slaveholding interests, though the 1893 piece and the 1860s federal census and county tax records are clear on this point."[4] Even Ken Burns, who quotes extensively from *Co. Aytch* in his The Civil War (miniseries), states that Watkins "owned no slaves."[5]

Death [edit]

While the post-war lives of some body servants have been documented,[6] it is unknown whether Sanker survived the war and, if so, where he might have gone and what he might have done afterwards; the time, place and cause of his death are likewise unknown. His fleeting presence in Sam Watkins' writings bears testimony to the many body servants, and enslaved African Americans more generally, whose identities and stories have been lost to history.

References [edit]

1. ^ See Body Servants of the 1st Tennessee.
2. ^ "Confederate veteran [serial]". Nashville, Tenn. : [S.A. Cunningham]. 1893.
3. ^ "Co. Aytch". Chattanooga, Tenn. : [Times printing company]. 1900.
Watkins does mention in passing "the negro boys, who were with their young masters as servants" (p. 34), "the negros who were with us as servants" (p 39) and "the negros who were acting as servants" (p 108), and he twice referred (on pp. 119 and 183), to "the negro boy" of two different officers. Nothing more is said of them and none are named.
4. ^ From footnote 17 of "Would to God I could tear the page from those memoirs and from my own memory": Co. Aytch and the Confederate Sensibility of Loss."
On the Watkins family's slaveholding interests, the National Park Service notes the following: "Census and tax records of antebellum Maury County show that Sam's father, Frederick, owned more than 100 enslaved African Americans on two plantations in the county. The Watkins family was the third wealthiest in one of the most prosperous counties in the state. Incredibly, Watkins was not an outlier in his company. Nearly half of the company with which he left Maury County in 1861 came from slave-owning households."
5. ^ Perhaps Burns inferred this from the following passage, in which Watkins implies he was poor:

> A law was made by the Confederate States Congress about this time allowing every person who owned twenty negroes to go home. It gave us the blues; we wanted twenty negroes. Negro property suddenly became very valuable, and there was raised the howl of "rich man's war, poor man's fight." The glory of the war, the glory of the South, the glory and the pride of our volunteers had no charms for the conscript. (p. 37)

6. ^ See for example "Osborne Cunningham, Body Servant to William Cunningham, 1st Tenn. Infantry Co. D, Williamson Grays, CSA" on the blog From Slaves to Soldiers and Beyond - Williamson County, Tennessee's African American History

External Links [edit]

- Sam Watkins page on the National Park Services website
- Body Servants of the 1st Tennessee

Categories: AfC submissions by date/09 June 2021

This page was last edited on 20 July 2021, at 13:10 (UTC).

Privacy policy About Wikipedia Disclaimers Contact Wikipedia Mobile view Developers Statistics Cookie statement

Appendix 2

Rejected draft of "Meryem bent Ali"

Meryem bent Ali (born 1878) was a member of the [[Ouled Naïl]] tribe of [[Algeria]].

Life

While the exact date and place of her birth have not been recorded, the presence of Meryem bent Ali has been attested in [[Biskra]], Algeria in the 1890s, where with her cousin Mbarka she achieved notoriety as a belly dancer and sex worker. Émile Laurent[1] and Jean Lorrain[2] both wrote of her being there at the time, as did [[André Gide]], who had his first heterosexual experience with her in late 1893–early 1894 during a voyage to North Africa with painter [[Paul Laurens]]. Here is the description Gide gives of her in [[*Si le grain ne meurt...*]] [*If it die...*]:

> Meriem was amber-skinned, firm-fleshed. Her figure was round but still almost childish, for she was barely sixteen. I can only compare her to a bacchante – the one on the Gaeta vase, for instance – because of her tinkling bracelets too, which she was continually shaking. I remember having seen her dance in one of the cafes of the Holy Street, where Paul had taken me one evening. Her cousin En Barka was dancing there too. They danced in the antique fashion of the Oulad, their heads straight and erect, their busts motionless, their hands agile, their whole bodies shaken by the rhythmic beating of their feet.[3]

Having returned to Europe, Gide was undergoing a course of treatment in [[Champel]], Switzerland, in summer 1894, when his friend [[Pierre Louÿs]] came to meet him. Gide recounted his North African travels to Louÿs, including his experience with Meryem, and recommended that his friend follow suit. Louÿs, who was actually on his way to the [[Bayreuth Festival]], changed his plans and went instead to Biskra, intent on taking the young Algerian as his mistress. He and traveling companion [[André-Ferdinand Herold]] arrived in Algiers on July 17, and a week later made for Biskra, where they met Meryem on July 24.[4] Louÿs spent the night with her, and the following day set off with Herold for [[Constantine]] with the idea that Meryem would join them there, which she did on August 1.

They would live together in Constantine through August 12. Though their relations were turbulent, Louÿs was taken with Meryem and under her spell revised [[*Les chansons de Bilitis*]] [*The Songs of Bilitis*], which he was writing at the time. As he explained some six months later in a letter to his brother Georges Louis, Meryem "caused me to completely rework Bilitis in her image, from the day I first saw her.... She was a wonder of grace, delicacy and ancient poetry." To his brother he would also confide:

> Through the Arab women of the Algerian south (who are not Moorish), I understood, I saw the living women of antiquity, in 1894. That's why Bilitis is truer, more ancient and more alive than [[Chrysis]].

Louÿs completed *Les chansons de Bilitis* after returning to Paris in late August 1894. Published that December by the Librairie de l'Art Indépendant, the first edition bore a double dedication – "To ANDRÉ GIDE // M.b.A."[5] It was dated "Champel, 11 July 1894," four days before Louÿs and Herold set out for Algeria, retroactively foreshadowing of the influence she would exercise over the work.

<u>*Death*</u>

The date and place of Meryem's death have not been recorded; in fact, very little is known of her after her contact with Louÿs. According to Jean-Paul Goujon, the latter's biographer, she wrote to both Louÿs and Herold on September 1, 1894, following their return to France, and in early 1895 Louÿs telegraphed Gide who was back in Biskra, inquiring, "How is Meryem?" Gide replied: "She is waiting for you."[6] Thereafter she disappears from the historical record, joining the ranks of untold numbers of child sex workers whose lives and deaths have not been documented and whose names and stories remain unknown to us.

References

1. See « La prostituée arabe » in *Archives d'Anthropologie criminelle,*[28] de Criminologie et de Psychologie normale et pathologique, tome 8, 1893, pp. 315–322.
2. See *Heures d'Afrique,*[29] Paris: Bibliothèque-Charpentier, 1899, pp. 206–210
3. *If it die...,*[30] tr. Dorothy Bussy (Middlesex, England: Penguin Books, 1977), p. 255.
4. This chronology is based on the entries in *Pierre Louÿs : Journal de Meryem (en collaboration avec A.-F. Herold), suivi des lettres inédites à Zohra Bent Brahim,* J.P. Goujon, ed. (Paris: Librairie Nizet, 1992).
5. I.e. M[eryem]b[ent]A[li].
6. See *Pierre Louÿs : Journal de Meryem...,* pp. 19–21.

External Links

- François Pouillon. « Tourisme sexuel et littérature ». *La Revue,* 2016, pp. 126–128.[31]

28 https://criminocorpus.org/fr/bibliotheque/doc/8/?page=14

29 https://tinyurl.com/m7tdbe2y

30 https://archive.org/details/in.ernet.dli.2015.242430/page/n255/mode/2up

31 https://halshs.archives-ouvertes.fr/halshs-01510375/

A Framework
For Imagining an Abolitionist Special Collection Librarianship

Marshall Weber, Monica Johnson, Berlin Loa, T-Kay Sangwand, and Candace Weber

Land Acknowledgement

This text written on the unceded lands of the Munsee Lenape. I ask you to join us in acknowledging their community, their elders both past and present, as well as their future generations. We acknowledge that the current government and society occupying this land is founded upon exclusions and erasures of many Indigenous peoples, including those on whose land our homes are located. This acknowledgement demonstrates a commitment to beginning the process of dismantling the ongoing legacies of settler colonialism.

Terminology

I have tried to use current terminology as suggested by members of the communities referred to, acknowledging that there is no monolithic consensus in any community and that terminology changes, sometimes rapidly. I apologize for any offense that my description of any community might cause.

Disclosure

Though this Framework essay was coordinated and written by me, many of the concepts were solidified in conversations and correspondences with the staff of Booklyn, with the participants in a July 2022 California Rare Book School (CalRBS) workshop called "Using Artists' Books to Decolonize Special Collection Libraries"

Figure 1 Minneapolis police murder of George Floyd protests, Grand Army Plaza, Brooklyn, NY (June 20, 2020)

that was held at Booklyn's studios in Brooklyn, NY, and with numerous activists, archivists and librarians across the country and around the world.

For the last 23 years, I have worked with over a hundred special collection librarians in the capacity of a curator, distributor, maker, and publisher of artists' books and political ephemera. Through these relationships I have witnessed a wide spectrum of ideological and pedagogical approaches to special collections librarianship. For the last 50 years I have also been a social justice organizer and cultural diversity advocate and have worked with many activists, artists, and educators in diverse communities within academia and beyond.

In this free-form essay, I will correlate these two areas of experience and create a very basic framework that imagines what the practice of abolitionist special collections librarianship might look like, and what this practice would need to manifest in order for some of the conditions for the implementation of decolonization to be possible. In general the scope is limited to the Americas, and

Figure 2 LGBTQIA+ led weekly street march for social justice, mid-town Manhattan, NY (April 4, 2021)

to the academic special collections library system of the United States specifically. The spectrum of definition and practice regarding abolition, colonialism, and decolonialization on a global scale is too wide and complicated for this particular short essay to handle.

This essay is not a manifesto, a history, or an instruction manual, and I do not pretend to speak for anyone (or any social movement) other than myself. I represent these ideas as freely associated concepts, as suggestions, as provocations. I also make no claim that any of the ideas presented in this essay are new or original, or my property. I have had the opportunity and the privilege to study and work with many talented and committed people, and I hope to honor them with this written collage of their contributions to our society.

My optimism and my knowledge of these principles is inspired by my witnessing of programs that prove that many of the concepts discussed in this essay have, and are, being used across the field. I have seen many active programs, research provision, and curriculum and policy development led by special collection librarians and other activist educators in a wide variety of approaches both within and outside of any affiliation or identification with the current abolitionist movement. Whether it be the 'abolitionist' leaning programing around incarceration issues catalyzed by the Sr. Helen Prejean papers at the DePaul University Archives in Chicago, the comprehensive collection of artwork and protest material by the Justseeds activist printmakers collective held and programmed at the special collections library of Bucknell University, or the support of grassroots local human rights and union organizing culture by the special collection library at the University of Wisconsin, Milwaukee, there is a noticeable affiliation with progressive thought that is present in many aspects of special collections culture.

So despite the origins of the United States public and academic libraries being within colonial and imperialist culture, the library is still a potential locus for anti-capitalist and abolitionist thought. Special collection libraries are filled with instructive materials about both the 18th and 19th century abolition movement in the United States, and a valuable comprehensive record of all aspects of the American slave trade and European and American colonialism. The library is the place where you get services and resources for free. It is the center of both academic and social life at many universities and in many communities. And it is the data source for the informed electorate that makes democracy possible. Even in the fragmentation of the data-overload of current digital culture, the library symbolizes a place where truth resides and where data is managed. So the library, and specifically, the special collections library, is a place of contestation, a hub of possible resistance, and perhaps, because of the connection to institutional archives, the perfect laboratory for the development and dissemination of academic abolitionism.

Please note that we also have no intention to define or otherwise limit or, on the other hand, diffuse or dilute the concepts of abolition, decolonization, or librarianship. There are many leading public intellectuals who have articulately defined these movements with accuracy and eloquence (Mariame Kaba, Roxanne Dunbar-Ortiz and Angela Davis, Linda Tuhiwai Smith, come to mind.) This essay is a collage of the work of numerous activists, artist and academics, leaning more towards imagination than academic exposition or definition.

Figure 3 NYPD murder of Eric Garner protests, downtown Manhattan, NY (December 13, 2014)

Disclosure, Part 2

The majority (an estimated 80%) of academic librarians I have met are caucasian, Christian or Jewish, middle or upper-class in origin, presented hetero- and abled-normative identities, and their conversational vernacular implied capitalist economic beliefs. Their field of study, notwithstanding their job title or actual librarianship, was primarily (again 80%) in western European antiquity. So basically, minus the capitalist ethos and the focus on antiquity, these are people much like me, entitled (literally, some with many acronyms after their names, as if they were part of some kind of academic royalty), and privileged, settler colonists, whose vested class and political interests would directly conflict with abolitionist practices. I embody contradictions to abolitionist practice which have to be interrogated, deconstructed, and countered on a daily basis. Confronting and dismantling the powerful inherent biases and prejudices of one's settler colonist identity is an essential process towards any abolitionist practice and pedagogy. This process is never complete, like any other form of self- and health care or professional development, it is a life-long commitment.

It is apparent to me, that, at this time in academic history, it is the approximately 20% of academic librarians from diverse backgrounds who are the primary drivers of the implementation of abolitionist and social and environmental pedagogies and practices within special collections culture, while often being denied the politically powerful positions that would facilitate systemic change. Over the years numerous librarians have mentioned to me that progressive programing and policies are often adopted (sometimes with great fanfare) but then quietly under-funded. This is unjust, and an example of systemic racism that both blames the 'victim' and forces the 'victim' to implement solutions to 'the problem' that will not disrupt systemic inequities or diminish White skin privilege. In North America, at this time, White supremacy and colonialism are structures for White people to deal with, to acknowledge, to dismantle, and to make amends and reparations for. They are not metaphorical concepts to build performative allyship around while maintaining systemic inequities.

For example, the current National Endowment for the Humanities' (and other state agencies) diversity initiatives are delivering substantial funding for the acquisition and programming of books and art by BIPOC artists to many special collections libraries (and museums) across the country which are led by caucasian curators and librarians, without addressing the lack of diversity on those institutions' staffs and boards. Thus the illusion of performative diversity can be maintained while executive staff continues to support and embody the systemic racism of much of the academic, museum, and public library system. This "wanting the culture but not the people (or the leadership)" construct has got to go. (This critique does not diminish the encouraging fact that some of these recent diversity initiatives are also successfully delivering substantial resources to BIPOC cultural leaders and communities.)

An abolitionist practice demands that colonist-settlers, especially White male-identified ones, wield their privilege to redistribute power and resources, and pass the mic. Diversity funding should be predicated on diversity staffing within leadership positions. Participating in one's own disenfranchisement is difficult, but White middle-class Christian and Jewish cis-male identified people must consider that they have been either, or both, directly disenfranchising, and indirectly benefiting from the disenfranchisement of others, for centuries, so, again, please pass the mic.

In our primarily hetero-normative, cis-male identified society it is always instructive to maintain awareness of the relationship of patriarchy to colonialism and White supremacy. Abolition of both the patriarchy and the gender binary are necessary measures for social equity and justice. In United States the dismantling of these Christian western European constructs are crucial to creating the conditions for abolitionism and decolonization. While female-identified people are well represented in the field of special collections, as they are in the librarian occupation in general. But this representation diminishes in the upper echelons of the field, and patriarchal values remain entrenched in actual collection development, access, instruction, history, and archive preservation. For all the commendable advances in representation, access to leadership, and the development of feminist and LGBTQIA+ programming across the field, I persistently hear many stories from the field describing sexual harassment, plagiarism, White, cis-male-identified people failing upwards, and the normalizing of sexist and misogynist behavior and materials. An abolitionist practice is a feminist practice, an abolitionist practice is a LGBTQIA+ practice, and an abolitionist practice is a practice of disabled, differently abled, and neurodivergent people. Abolitionist thought demands a dismantling of "normativity" in the definition of individuality, in regard to sexuality and gender, ethnicity, physical and mental 'ability', 'race', and identity. An abolitionist librarian would "teach to the learner" at all times with an informed context regarding each learner's community.

Let us be blunt about this issue of personal disclosure: any White cis-male of middle or upper class origin could literally do nothing and still reap the benefits of White skin privilege, middle or upper class entitlement and cis-male hetero-normativity. It is important to realize that privilege is amplified by individual willful exploitation of these entitlements. Simply put, the hegemony of racial capitalist patriarchy rewards White cis-males for unethical and even violent behavior. (Do we even need to cite the various recent quotes from Donald Trump and others that exemplify this construct?) The more complicit that one is in capitalist colonialism, the more benefits one receives. An extreme, yet recently and frequently, reenacted example of this phenomenon is the overtly ritualized care police show right-wing, White male mass shooters when they are apprehended. This manifestation of alt-right terrorist theater is an evocation of the perverse respect for, and the continual normalization of, militarized White patriarchal power.

Figure 4 Sunrise Ceremony, Alcatraz Island, California (October 11, 2021)

Examining the combination of the privileging of substance-based addictive behavior in a consumerist society with the normalization of the behavioral-based addiction to using violence as a tool of social and political interaction in a police state explains many perplexing American behaviors. From the emulation of aspects of nazi culture and tactics shared by Republican party militias, and Jewish neo-conservative and Christian evangelical Zionists, (the Trump 'troika') to the escalating violence towards Asian-American, Native American female, and LGBTQIA+ identified people, the tropes of colonialism are recycled again and again into deadly, yet also symbolic, violence. Power directs powerlessness in an unending American civil war. The more violent and exploitative we behave, the more the racial capitalist patriarchy rewards us, makes us celebrities, appoints us as influencers, and denigrates our victims. An abolitionist pedagogy would address these dynamics constantly, consistently and explicitly with the goal of dismantling them completely.

In "Discipline and Punish" Michel Foucault writes about how violent ritual is a theatrical performance of power by those in power and the powerless. Angela Davis has spoken on how the State enacts itself through our bodies with enslavement and incarceration being two extreme examples. The personal realization of these forces and their role in the construction of our identities and behavior is a necessary component of abolitionist practice. Abolitionist practice involves deep meditation about, interrogation of, and ultimately a dismantling of this ego-entitlement-identity construct. White male-identified librarians need to be transparent about the personal and social sources of their entitlement in order to even begin the dismantling of that privilege that is necessary for an abolitionist practice.

Beyond Land Acknowledgement

1. An abolitionist practice in the United States must align with local, regional, national, and hemispheric decolonization and social justice movements. Decolonization in the Americas is a primary goal of many who share an abolitionist practice.

2. Special collection libraries are often paired with institutional archives and thus, often hold, access, and interpret the historical memories of an institution, including materials that evidence crimes again humanity within their own colonial histories. It is a difficult journey to go from being a simple vessel for institutional history to being the institutional consciousness of a school, but every special collections and archives should examine its holdings for evidences of crimes against indigenous American peoples and others, including other species and the land itself, and acknowledge, initiate investigations, seek resolution, and make amends for those crimes. This process is already happening in libraries across the country, an abolitionist framework is necessary for the process to progress.

3. Many, if not most, special collection libraries in proximity to Native communities have, and all should have, a designated Native American collection, and outreach, career development, and interdisciplinary studies programs developed in collaboration with local Native communities with respect to their needs and expectations. Programs like these should be coordinated and directed by Native American community members with input from other local and Pan-American Native communities. There are many successful examples of this kind of programming at institutions across the Americas, such as The Pitzer College/Western University's *Native*

American Summer Pipeline to College Program and various programs at California State University at Humboldt (now California State Polytechnic University, Humboldt).

4. Balanced outreach programs should include dialog with Native communities to identify education needs and develop partnerships or program that include free tuition and support scholarships for Native Americans, with the goal of increasing Native American student enrollment and employment, while also expanding remote, limited residency, and off-campus learning sites led by Native Americans. It is instructive to note that the Regents of the University of California have eliminated tuition for Native American students (who are California State residents) at all UC campuses.

5. Special collection libraries often have rare, personal, and distinctive material. The historical context for the educational use for this material and the related interpretive needs to be complex and nuanced. The lens of White supremacist thought is diminishing in the US and the abolitionist framework demands its complete dismantling. Some special collection libraries share these goals, simply put, it's the best use of the material. An abolitionist special collection practice would prioritize the reviewing, fact-checking, and providing of accurate interpretive material including the inclusion of Native perspectives. Special collection materials that contain an unbalanced collection of unsustainable agricultural, engineering, economic and environmental curricula and erroneous research materials (perhaps driven by extractive corporate interests) should contextualize this material with ecologically sustainable Native American science derived curricula and research resources.

6. Special collections should refocus on building collections that center sustainable and indigenous practices and collaborate with faculty to shift the curriculum towards this direction. This shift needs to happen both in institutional strategic planning as well as funding.

7. All holdings related to Native American tribes and communities held in special collections should be reviewed for proper ethical provenance and tribal authorization. Items not held legitimately with explicit permissions from Native stakeholders and originating communities should be returned to Native communities. Numerous programs and protocols within the field exist to facilitate this process, but political will is necessary to initiate and prioritize actions in regard to cultural returns. Tribal communities

Figure 5 Philonise Floyd's memorial service for his brother George. Cadman Park Plaza, Brooklyn, NY (June 4, 2020)

should also receive compensation for the temporary loss of the use of returned materials. Libraries should offer to provide long-term or permanent storage for materials as identified and requested by the community as a repository, and work with the community to ensure preservation and access per community needs both on and off campus.

8. Native items legitimately held in special collection should have interpretive material and provenance history provided by the originating Native community members and in the originating Native language and Native people providing these services should be compensated equitably. The burden of provenance research, proper translation, and proper presentation of interpretive material should be taken up by the special collection library not the Native community.

9. All special collection libraries should initiate programs to construct the conditions for decolonization. Evidence from university archives should be used to calculate reparations to Native communities for usages of their land and resources, to develop policy proposals regarding the return of colonized land, and for substantiating Native governance over university properties. What we do not imagine we cannot teach; what we cannot teach we cannot implement in our society. It is time to imagine and teach abolitionism and decolonization.

(Note that many of the above program points could be applied to other communities historically and presently disenfranchised by academic institutions such as BIPOC, LGBTQIA+, and disabled or differently abled communities.)

Conditions for an Abolitionist Pedagogy

We cannot effectively teach justice if our schools are run unjustly. We cannot truly teach democracy if our schools are run non-democratically. We cannot teach socialism and economic equity if capitalists control our curricula and finances. We cannot teach ecological sustainability if climate criminals control our schools' research funding. We cannot teach peace if our IT and engineering departments are controlled by weapons manufacturers and the Defense Department. An abolitionist practice demands economic, ethical, and pedagogical accountability. Abolitionist librarians reach back into their collections and expose the propaganda, lies, and bad science. They reveal and chip away at the corrosive influence of colonial and corporate narratives on their collecting and programming. The abolitionist pedagogy unapologetically arcs towards justice.

Parts of the academic special collections library culture, especially the rare books and manuscripts culture, still convey subtle and overt White supremacist values that need to be abolished. No bible is worth one million dollars. (Likewise, no annual digital academic journal subscription is worth $45,000.) The influence that primarily antiquarian, secondary-market private bookdealers and auction houses have on many academic special collections libraries evidences a power imbalance in the field. In general, special collections and rare book and manuscript expenditures on books and ephemera from Euro-centric antiquity (despite the aforementioned influx of cash for performative ally infused diversity initiatives) far exceeds expenditure on materials from living artists and activists. This persistent imbalance underfunds the collection and support of living artists, activist artists, diverse communities, and materials from important recent social movements. It anchors scholarship in the past, instead of in the present, where the attention of scholars is now urgently needed. It hobbles the process of diversifying both staff and collections, and it stymies community outreach and critical scholarship. The preservation, access and study of antiquity is important, but the antiquity (and to a similar extent the modern) book markets are inflated and rigged. It's time to flip the switch. It's intriguing that state and smaller universities and colleges that can't afford to play in the antiquity and modern book markets often have stronger collections of contemporary books, art, and social justice movement ephemera. These schools need to substantiate acquisitions with usage and curricular relevance, not with the maintenance of living wealthy patrons or the limitations of qualified endowments from long dead ones. The continued 'legal' validation of static limited endowment funds from dead patrons whose wealth was garnered from criminal colonization and extraction that needs to be dismantled.

This persistent valorization and commodification of imperial colonial antiquity and late colonial modern culture is evidenced in the inventory unconditionally offered by many of the members of the Antiquarian Booksellers' Association of America (ABAA). One of the primary book sources for academic libraries, the ABAA is a membership only organization whose membership policy statement harkens back to the coded language of old school New England White anglo-saxon protestant covenant agreements: *"Membership in the ABAA cannot be obtained simply by paying a fee or signing an agreement. Before being considered for membership, booksellers must prove that they are established, knowledgeable, and of excellent reputation. Prospective members must be sponsored by current members, and undergo a rigorous screening process. The average ABAA member has been in the antiquarian book business more than twenty years..."* [emphasis mine]. My critique of this aspect of ABAA culture is not meant to impugn any particular bookseller. It is based on first-hand experience of numerous association events, analysis of the membership, and by discussions with librarians and members across the field. The lack of diversity in the membership, the persistent uncontextualized marketing of racist and sexist materials, and the extraction and commodification of materials from BIPOC communities by primarily caucasian dealers, are topics that are frequently and openly discussed amongst members and in the field in general.

While I am aware of members who are sincerely concerned with addressing these systemic problems within and beyond the association, we must be realistic about the ability of personal change and institutional reform to secure the abolition of the systemic racism and inherent bias present in an exclusionary culture. Systemic problems need systemic solutions. An abolition practice demands accountability from patrons, venders, publishers, educators and users, and this demand should be honored by systemic anti-racist and diversity programs self-initiated by all institutions operating in the field.

The continuing emphasis on scholarship regarding and acquisition of anglo-European works prevents the support of work of indigenous and BIPOC communities and is a form of continued violence that, is often only addressed through 'diversity' programs (as mentioned above) that seek to purchase materials without critical approaches to the curriculum developed around them, or without a plan for implementing curriculum. These 'diversity' initiatives are often operated without representation by the BIPOC community that created the work collected. It is also instructive to note that many diversity programs are powered by temporary designated external funding, while standing institutional budget lines and expenditure on anglo-European work remains privileged.

Once I was at a special collections library showing an artists' book by a living artist that the curators were interested in acquiring but they told me that the $4,000 price "was not affordable for them". This is understandable for many different reasons and I did not question their sincerity at the time or now. The curators then asked if I would like to see their most recent antiquarian acquisition, a signature album from 16th century nobility that had been acquired at a Sotheby's auction for over 3 million dollars. A private family foundation had paid for the book which had been put up for auction by one of those seemingly ever-present members of the Getty family who seem to always be dumping some kind of antiquity treasure into the market at some point or the other. Admittedly within this particular cultural hegemony, this specific library had compelling reasons to acquire this book, even so I am unhappily impressed by the looping hermeneutic nature of the book's entire history. There is no interpretation I can imagine that supports the sky-high valuation of this particular book. Here we have a book created by nascent oligarchs about oligarchs, collected (and invested in) by oligarchs, re-sold by oligarchs, bought again by oligarchs, and then bequeathed to a public institution in an act of noblesse oblige. Thus the book functions more as a financial instrument (basically is actual, original intention in any case) across the centuries and has little inherent or general cultural or scholarly value. I do not deny the book has value, of course it does, but far less than the expenditure of funds substantiates. An entire outreach and diversity program could have been created by this level of expenditure that would have exponentially increased the educational impact of this particular library in the entire region where it is located.

This is just one of thousands of exchanges where a 'fake' economy is perpetuated by the global oligarchy and where antiquarian books from Europe command astronomical prices, that continuously substantiate elitist patronage systems. The inherent cultural bias of all the good librarians involved in the tail end of this fiscal arrangement obscured the irony of this entire machination. The momentum of the culture of this library will unconsciously drive all acquisitions policy until a major disruption occurs. An abolitionist librarian would have to call this out.

For a moment imagine you are standing in the rare book stacks of any major academic special collections library (if you are reading this essay than you probably even know the smell). The rows of fleshy incunabula, mostly biblical in content, silently rest in front of you, the epitome of grounded ponderous authority, quietude, and stasis. In fact you are looking at the blueprints for numerous genocides, the guidebooks for centuries of imperialism and White supremacy, and the source books for the 'moral' substantiation of manifest destiny, the right of discovery, misogyny, homo and transphobia, enslavement, and climate catastrophe.

With all this in mind I suggest the following moratorium, which will act as an opportunity to reset the priorities of special collections librarianship, completing the field's movement out of the 19th century and into the 21st century, while developing a pedagogy that focuses on the present and future at least as much (if not more) that it focuses on the past. We need special collection libraries in the United States to abolish the exclusionary mindset that insists on the comprehensive acquisition of, and uncritical scholarly focus on, the now completely commodified, imperial and settler colonist cultural propaganda of the last two millennia. White people are addicted to the entitlement of White supremacy, they get high on it; frequent and numerous interventions are necessary.

<u>*For Immediate Special Collections Library Action*</u>

1. Start an immediate three-year academic moratorium on the acquisition of antiquarian art, books, ephemera, photography, and prints from secondary market dealers and auction houses.

2. Focus academic acquisitions on the work of living, progressive, activist printmakers and collectives, and on current political ephemera (with funds going to makers and affiliated groups). Keep the above acquisition focus concentrated on the work of disabled, LGBTQIA+, BIPOC, and Native American makers and groups. Focus on building balanced, diverse, representative collections across time, geography, and culture.

3. Use acquisitions as a gateway to create programing and curricula with activist artists and groups, to train and hire staff from local grassroots organizations and develop collaborations between the special collection library (and other faculty and departments) and social and environmental organizations.

4. During the antiquity/secondary market acquisition moratorium do an audit of the history of the disbursement of acquisition funds and a statistical analysis of special collections. Identify and categorize holdings by book type, date, self-identified 'race'/ethnicity, self-identified gender/sexual orientation, and religion of the primary makers, religion (as subject matter), geographic origin, general subject matter, and economic ideology. Correlate the current acquisitions and access (cataloging, promoting, programming) budgets for these categories.

5. Using this data, plan an equitable collection development policy that balances disbursement of funding of antiquarian and contemporary titles, that reflects both campus and local community diversity, and actively steers all curricula and programs toward sustainable social and environment justice policy and practice.

An abolitionist librarian would also advocate for the following listed policies that would create the conditions that will enable social and environmental justice to be teachable in our schools and applicable to our society.

For Immediate University Action

1. End all university contracts with police forces (municipal, county, state, and other) and armed security providers on campuses, using money saved from those contracts for student social and medical services and unarmed community-based security provision.
2. End all university contracts with any businesses involved in public and private incarceration facilities.
3. Forgive all student loans immediately. (We're on the right track!)
4. Divest all academic funds from the nuclear and fossil fuel industries, from apartheid Israel, from weapons manufacturing of any kind, from any corporation with a record of infringing on Native American sovereignty.

Long Term Goals

1. Make all colleges and universities public and free. Open all academic libraries to local public use.
2. Unionize all academic university, students, staff, and faculty.
3. Use direct and universal democratic electoral processes to elect university leadership, including representatives from local communities.
4. Make all private universities redistribute their endowments, with a focus on reparations to descendants of communities that were exploited by these institutions. Especially address the Ivory Tower/Island phenomenon where extremely wealthy universities whose endowments were created in part via earnings from slavery and whaling, are surrounded by disenfranchised communities. (Yale and Columbia Universities come to mind.)
5. Dismantle academic institutes that have a record of fostering and harboring war criminals, human rights violators, and dictators, (like the Hoover Institute at Stanford University).

Figure 6 Cadman Park Plaza, Brooklyn, NY (June 4, 2020)

Student Class Consciousness

An abolitionist librarian would have complete solidarity with all students. They would acknowledge the existence of a student class, would identify student class interests, and would integrate the development of student class consciousness as a primary tenet of their pedagogy and librarianship. It is obvious that at this point in history student class interests are dramatically in conflict with their parents' class interests at almost all class levels except the poor and lower working class. Many working-class parents have abandoned, or have been abandoned by, any form of union protection and thus workers globally have suffered a diminishment of both job and family security. Many middle-class and upper-class parents have ubiquitously embraced both capitalism and authoritarian oligarchies as models of global governance. Besides the existential dilemma of losing the entire planet and their future, most students have little to lose materially, by engaging with abolitionist and decolonizing movements and opposing the suicidal racial capitalist ideologies of their parents.

Figure 7 NYPD murder of Eric Garner protests, downtown Manhattan, NY (December 13, 2014)

In this particular moment it seems crucial to double down on teaching students about class structure and culture and about their very unique status as members of a class that is volatile and uniquely temporal and has historically been a great engine of social change. While, ultimately, one abolitionist goal would be to dismantle class structure entirely, at this juncture in time, the amplifying of the class conflict between the student class and other static class identities is part of an important strategy for the rescuing of the world from climate catastrophe. Interfering with the imbued class cultures (and identities) of individual entitlement and rights to property could prepare the conditions for a global shift of consciousness that could change the paradigm of human behavior dramatically enough to prevent a near future human species extinction event.

Abolitionist Librarianship and Artists' Books

Over the last decade an important academic movement to 'decolonize' and activate collections and archives, and to build inclusionary and diverse bibliographies, has produced both valuable scholarship and facilitated positive social change in numerous communities. This is a large cultural shift with leadership coming primarily from BIPOC archivists and librarians, like the Blackivists collective, and the participants in Black Bibliographica conference of the Center for Material Culture at the university of Delaware. Some people in this movement also have affiliations with current abolitionist culture and are leading projects such as the "living archives," "community-based archives," and archival research regarding Native American treaties, contracts, and sovereignty, that often share abolitionist goals. As stated at the beginning of this essay, institutional archives contain many records of colonial crimes, contracts, treaties, and documentation of provenance and production, that could further abolitionist projects and prove the validity of abolitionist stances on numerous issues including enslavement, Land Back, incarceration, and policing. Special collection library archives are also filled with profound histories of resistance and ideas, tactics, and strategies to spark social change that are unidentified or just underused. Applying critical lenses to the archival holdings of any institution can produce revelatory histories. In 2021 genealogist Nicka Smith found documentation in the Amherst Colleges archive that one of their College Trustees, Israel E. Trask, had enslaved members of her family. Smith's presentation at Amherst College on this matter is instructive and evocative, and part of the college's attempt to build a racial history that, in the most optimistic possibility, could lead to reparations and perhaps even abolitionist governance.

This Framework has touched on major systemic, institutional, and personal issues that provide a context for imagining an abolitionist librarian's practice. It has also mentioned some specific policies and practices that are informed by abolitionist pedagogy and librarianship. I will end with one more example of the kind of affective teaching practices an abolitionist librarian and educator could use in the class and in library programming.

In July of 2022, during part of the time this essay was being written I was also facilitating the previously mentioned CalRBS "Using Artists' Books to Decolonize Special Collections Libraries" class. (I think I would add a conditional phrase to this title if I were to use it again.) The fact that CalRBS Director Robert Montoya would invite an outlier like me to teach illustrates the ideological and pedagogical shift in the field of rare books from the focus on antiquity and oblique scholarship, to a more balanced and activist curricula. The participating archivists and librarians in the class were progressive, critical, and self-aware, and involved in many projects that addressed (across a spectrum of failure and success) diversity, social justice and critical pedagogical issues.

Despite the successes we all had enjoyed in our work and saw reflected in the field, all of us had also encountered (and some of the group were the target of) sexist and racist micro-aggressions and strong institutional resistance to any kind of systemic change. Noting this, some participants suggested that any optimism we had could be countered by practical observations, garnered from personal experiences, that large academic institutions are corporations that cannot be reformed. Perhaps this is true, but I believe there is a spectrum of ideological and systemic change possible at different institutions. I think that reform, dismantling, political maneuvering, organizing student and faculty resistance, and parallel abolitionist programming that reaches out into the community (or is performed behind the closed classroom doors) should and must proceed until the conditions for completely dismantling and reconstructing conventional academic institution are created.

During this class we looked at 50 artists' books and catalogs (listed in the addendum) and considered how these books could be used as catalysts of learning that would inspire the creation of the conditions that could further the abolitionist and decolonization movements. Since most artists' books collections are held in special collections libraries and/or shared with art libraries, artists' books are an accessible resource for teaching from an abolitionist perspective and with abolitionist goals.

Late 20th and 21st century artists' books often have a component of self-referential, and sometimes, critical, subjectivity. (The books of Leopoldo Bloom come to mind.) This 'biblio-subjectivity' can amplify, integrate, and/or contrast, the books material form with its subject matter. Within that biblio-existential 'condition,' an artists' book sitting on the library shelf can also interrogate, not just the other books around it, but can also extend into a systemic critique of the library that houses the book, the institution that houses the library, and the society that created the institution. These ripples widen infinitely and affectively; artist engraver and bookmaker

Anton Würth has suggested that many artists' books are inherent critiques of conventional typography and language itself. This linguistic critique can be expanded into a abolitionist and decolonial perspective, as done by Nigerian activist and musician Fela Aníkúlápó Kuti, who often lectured about how written languages are tools of colonial oppression.

Another extension of the 'biblio-subjectivity' of artists' books is something I call 'active materiality,' the artists' book is often a first person testimony made in an activist modality where experience is prioritized over imagination, where the books' materials and form reflects the books' content and function, and the immediate social goals of the content and form are self-evident. A large body of book works, exhibition, and scholarship suggests that the genre, in recent practice, often tends towards social engagement and explicitly documents cultural and political affiliations. This is not due to any inherent material or structural quality, (refutations of both modernity and objectivity are ubiquitous in the genre), but to tendencies in the current global social aesthetics and practice of the form. Simply put, the artists' book often seems to strive not to be about 'some-thing' but to be that 'thing', to be part of 'that thing.' (For example, Alisa Banks' artists' books and art often incorporate materials that are also the subjects of their texts, ranging from human hair, plant material, and cotton.)

These above tendencies make artists' books useful tools in deconstructing White supremacist, patriarchal, ableist, and colonialist histories. But there are other factors that further amplify the usefulness of artists' books as research materials across disciplines.

1. Artists' books are antidotal to the "shallow" reading inherent to screen based electronic devices and media. Research on the tactile and experiential elements of touching, reading, and seeing materially based information has proven again and again, that cognitive processing of books and other data infused materials (textile, objects, etc.) provokes more neurological activity across the brain and prompts both more comprehension and more recallable memory. Simply put, our body and brains like touching things and perceptual elements such as the touch, sound, smell, and three-dimensional motion of data bearing materials provoke more cognitive activity and support more embodied and affective learning.

2. Some members of the artists' bookmakers and/or printmakers communities are often publicly affiliated with general social justice movements and specific organizations. Some use the term activist/artist to underline this focus outside of the corporate or academic artworlds. Their artists' books and prints exemplify and model activist solidarity and commitment to social change and justice. As both student class and ecological consciousness and teacher unionization increase, many academic and public library collections are focusing on providing research materials and textbooks from diverse activist perspectives. Many living activist/artists see art and creative publishing as part of a public activist culture, so the introduction of their creations into a collection can also initiate a direct, ongoing and productive relationship with the artists and the organizations they work with.

3. We live in a world with complicated environmental and social justice problems, where most people (perhaps the majority of students) are immersed in visual social media culture. The level of visual and media literacy in the general population demands teaching and research support material that can provide sophisticated and efficient infographic data delivery across all disciplines. Artists' books are an essentially interdisciplinary, and multi-disciplinary, genre where important experimentation in language, text/image integration, typography, visual culture, and data delivery is happening on a daily basis. The genre is a locus of design and material exploration and experimentation and is a valuable and discrete resource for both digital and analog/material cultural production.

4. The environments in which artists' books are usually first encountered, classroom settings or library reading rooms, are model spaces for social engagement. Libraries are one of the last social locations in American culture where one is neither expected to buy something, or to be selling something. The library models crucial elements of democratic culture, the free (and /or at least, sustainable) exchange of information and culture. Since many libraries now offer facilities to also make books (or align their programming with such facilities), there is an opportunity for any person to participate in that exchange as both a user and maker. Thus passive models of library function

> and librarianship are maturing into activist models that get us closer to creating the conditions for an abolitionist practice.

It is a major convenience that these artists' books are already in the libraries. They just need to be activated in the context of abolitionist practices and ideologies so that their utility as critical consciousness raising tools can be implemented. Many special collections and art libraries are using artists' books to catalyze student engagement with other printed material and other library resources as a counter to the fake and soft news and data found on many social and other on-line data sources. An abolitionist librarian would share these goals but would also utilize the affective and material qualities of artists' book as a way to teach students to also engage in dismantling systemic issues of injustice in their institutions and personal lives. The multi-media combination of emotional entanglement, intellectual engagement, visual stimulation, and tactile sensation, being used to convey the subject matter makes artists' book an important resource for presenting complex abolitionist perspectives.

Figure 8 Covid Memorial Fence, Greenwood Cemetery, Brooklyn, NY (June 17, 2020)

Our global library system is the brain of the world, a planetary nervous system, a neural network of knowledge. Special collections libraries can be imagined as the amygdala of that brain, a place with deep, profound, memories and knowledge that are at the root of cognition and emotion. The experiential impact, and the amplification of learning, that many people experience, when they have the opportunity to handle the historical material and original artwork in special collections, is known to most librarians. Those teaching moments need to be focused on creating the social conditions and equity to address abolishing all aspects of injustice and colonization and diminishing the climate catastrophe those forces have created. We are in crisis. We should be in crisis mode. This is an emergency. We do not have the luxury of spending most of our time studying history at our or anyone else's leisure. (And most people on the planet have never had this luxury.) It is time to make history.

The End Run: One Reason Why it is Possible to Imagine an Abolitionist Future

The science is clear on the matter of climate catastrophe, we do not have much time to address this matter. The connection between saving the planet, abolishing capitalism, and seriously engaging in decolonization, has never been more obvious than at this historical moment. Many will say that abolition and decolonization are impossible tasks. That they are dreams or fantasies. But we have recently seen massive and rapid social change enacted on a global scale. Fortunately, global capitalism has already provided us with the action model to quickly change our world. Let's imagine using the global capitalist nation-states' and oligarchies' 2020 agreement to shut down much of the world economy during the Covid pandemic as a model to shut down the global oligarchy itself, and then transfer that wealth into a global fund for decolonization, reparations and climate change amelioration. If the capitalists can close up shop for more than three months and still make an astronomical amount of money, the citizens of the planet can close down the oligarchs forever. This is a possibility not a fantasy. This is a scaling up of something we have experienced. We can lockdown against the capitalist virus until everybody has been inoculated with the abolitionist vaccine.

Figure 9 Occupy Wall Street encampment, Zuccotti Park, Manhattan, NY (October 9, 2011) Photography, Marshall Weber

Addendum

Books discussed and/or reviewed at "An Assembly Using Artists Books to Decolonize Special Collections."

Global Indigenous Peoples

- Katie West, Melbourne, Australia
  Decolonist, 2016, edition of 100, inkjet, dyed cloth.
- Stephen Dupont, Scarborough, Australia
  Guns and Arrows, 2007, #2 of 15, 30 silver gelatin prints, 18" x 24".

American Imperialism

- Stephen Dupont, Scarborough, Australia
  Kill Them All, with Marshall Weber, 2018, edition of 12, ink jet.
- Fred Rinne, San Francisco, CA
  Zombies USA, 2022, unique, acrylic.

- Beldan Sezen, Brooklyn, NY
  Home of the Brave, 2019, edition of 15, monoprint.
- Dana F. Smith, San Francisco, CA
  1863, 2021, edition of 45, a variable set of 5 screenprints and 5 inkjet prints. 7. *1861*, 2022, edition of 45, a variable set of 7 screenprints and 7 inkjet prints.
- Scott Williams, San Francisco, CA
  Horses West, 2004, with Fred Rinne, hand painted book, airbrush stencils, edition of ten.

Artists' Books

- Booklyn, Inc., Brooklyn, NY
  Diamond Leaves, CAFAM, 2011, offset.
  Freedom of the Presses, 2019, editor Marshall Weber, second edition of 3,000, offset. 11. *The Booklyn Ed. Manual,* 2021, second edition, free PDF down-load.

Black America

- Tia Blassingame, Claremont, CA
  Mourning/Warning: Numbers and Repeaters (M/W2), 2018, edition of 26, inkjet.
- Booklyn, Inc., Brooklyn, NY
  Mariame Kaba Zine Box Set, 2020, edition of 5.
- Catherine Carnahan, Murphys, CA/Marshall Weber, Brooklyn, NY
  I of the Storm, 2018, edition of 12, inkjet.
- Kyle Goen, Maplewood, NJ
  Black Panther Party Stamp Book, 2021, edition of 100, offset.
- Sauda Mitchell, Savannah, GA
  Never Forget, Volumes #2, 2021, a variant series with volumes in editions of 10, linoleum print.

Collective Healing/Sexual Violence

- FORCE: Upsetting Rape Culture, Baltimore, MD & Mexico City
  The Monument Quilt Project, 2020, edition of 10, a box set with ephemera, and a section from the original quilt.

Collaborations

- Booklyn, Inc., Brooklyn, NY
  Booklyn Bridge #6, 2022, 21 various artists, a variant edition of 21 artists' books, acrylic, calligraphy, collage, hand-painting, ink, inkjet, laser print, marker pen, offset print, photography, risograph, screenprint, wood block.
  Streetopia: North Beach volume (the limited-edition), 2011, Chris Johanson, Barry McGee, various, edition of 30
- Nicholas Lampert, Milwaukee, WI / Marshall Weber, Brooklyn, NY
  Intersectional Wall, 2022, unique, collage, screen-print.
- Marshall Weber, Brooklyn, NY
  The Invisible Army of Love, 2020, unique, blood, calligraphy, ink, inkjet, monoprint, wax, Hosho paper.

Ecology

- Bullet Space, New York, NY
  Fracktured Lives, 2021, edition of 100, offset, screen print, sheet metal covers.
- Roger Peet, Portland, OR
  Seven Elemental Forces, 2021, edition of 15, hand-carved letter-pressed linoleum relief prints.
- Eliana Perez, New York, NY
  COCA, 2022, edition of 10, collage, ink, gauche.

Incarceration

- Erik Ruin, Philadelphia, PA
  Letter from Isolation, 2019, text by Ulrike Meinhof, edition of 9, silkscreen.
- Vikki Law, New York, NY
  Tenacious Box Set, 2021, edition of 15,44 facsimile issues, machine copy.

Latina/Latino American

- Guillermo Gomez Pena, Mexico City/San Francisco
  New World Order, 1992, edition of 15, wood, cloth, glass, etching, bronze, engraving.
- Interference Archive, Brooklyn, NY
  Armed by Design / El Disenoa Las Armas, 2015, 10 screen prints, prospectus, catalog.
- Justseeds, Pittsburgh, PA, The School of Popular Culture of the Revolutionary Martyrs of 1968, Mexico City
  Territorio y Libertad, 2018, edition of 100, screenprint.
- Laura Langa Martínez, Ariel Arango Prada, Malcolm Linton, Bogotá, Colombia
  Sin Cesar and Metamorphosis, 2019/2021, bundle edition of 100, Sin Cesar ed. 1,000/Metamorphosis ed. 250, inkjet, offset.
- Erica Mena, Fiskars, Finland
  Gringo Death Coloring Book, 2022, limited deluxe edition of 5, letterpress.
- María Verónica San Martín, Santiago, Chile/Brooklyn, NY
  In Their Memory, 2019, second edition of 20, silkscreen, woodcut.

LGBTQIA+

- Shana Agid, Brooklyn, NY
  Call a Wrecking Ball to Make a Window, 2012, about David Wojnarowicz, edition of 40, letterpress.
- Leopoldo Bloom, Portland, OR
  How to Transition of 63 Cents a Day, 2013, edition of 163, collage, letterpress, offset.

Linguistics

- Ryoko Adachi, Tokyo, Japan
  Language of Shape, 2021, edition of 15, inkjet, letterpress, lithograph, hand sewn.

Figure 10 LGBTQIA+ led weekly street march for social justice, mid-town Manhattan, NY (April 4, 2021)

- Candace Hicks, Nacogdoches, TX
  Common Threads (various), 2019-2020 1, unique, hand-embroidered cotton canvas.

Middle-East

- Booklyn, Inc., Brooklyn, NY
  A House without a Roof, 2016, edition of 700, offset.
- Friends Peace, and Sanctuary, Swarthmore, PA
  Friends Peace, and Sanctuary Catalog, 2019, edition of 700, offset.
- Librarians and Archivists with Palestine, Brooklyn, NY
  Librarians and Archivists with Palestine, 2014, edition of 40, digital, risograph.

Native American

- Brian D. Tripp (Karuk), Orleans, CA
  Collection of Native Californian Posters.
  Standing In Line, (undated, 1992-94/2022), unique, newspaper interventions, drawings, acrylic, ink, marker pen.
  Would You Rather Fish or Cut Bait, (undated, 1992-94/2022), unique, newspaper intervention drawings, ink.
- Minneapolis Institute of Ats, MN
  Hearts of Our People, 2019, Teri Greeves, Jill Ahlberg Yohe, various, exhibition catalog.
- Organik, Brooklyn, NY
  Turtle Island, 2022, unique, collage, offset set lithography, rubbing.

Neurodivergent

- James Enos, Portland, OR
  KID ADALT STUFF The Little Rascals In Young Arthur and Other Leguns Where Dreams n nightmares come true, 2019, 16.5 × 12.75 × 1 inches (closed), 120 pages.

Russian Imperialism

- Ken Campbell, Bristol, England
  Ten Years in Uzbekistan, 1994, David King, Aleksandr Rodchenko, edition of 45, letterpress.

Sustainable Economies

- Aaron Sinift, Cambridge, MA
  5 Year Plan, Francesco Clemente, Yoko Ono, et al, 2010, ed of 180, cloth, screen & block print.
  OTHER IMAGININGS, 2016, edition of 100, cotton, screenprint.

Union Organizing

- Art Build Workers, Milwaukee, WI, Los Angeles, Oakland, CA
  When We Fight We Win, A Public Advocacy Tool Box, 2021, edition of 25.

Veterans / Anti-war

- Iraq Veterans Against the War (IVAW)/About Face, New York, NY *War is Trauma,* 2011, edition of 130, screenprint, 30 prints.

Figure 11 StrikeMoMA event, mid-town Manhattan, poster design by Kyle Goen (May 22, 2021)

Artists' Books and the Space of Collective Memory

Beldan Sezen

Intro

When I create my books I enter a space in which the landscape of a page is at once a sculptural and a narrative place.

To open an artists' book is to enter a given space. A world unfolds, its shared memory being triggered by form, the (sequential) composition of image and text, the book's weight, size, touch, sound, texture, and smell of materials.

Our conscious lived experience rules the present but in this lived experience we incorporate subconscious phenomena[1] that influences our understanding—yet without our knowing. Artists' books have the ability to interrupt the conscious and resurface the subconscious by the physicality of the experience. In comics, the reader participation happens in the "empty" space between the frames—one frame showing a gun, the frame after showing a dead body next to a smoking gun, it's the reader's mind that pulls the trigger in between those two frames and as such commits the murder.[2] In artists' books the space and tension between two drawn or printed lines shapes the reader's engagement. In this 'empty' space between those two lines, the reader

1 See: Jane Turner, "Embodiment, Balinese Dance Theatre, and the Ethnographer's Predicament" in: *Performance and Spirituality* Volume 2, Number 1 (Spring 2011), 7.

2 As Scott McCloud puts it: "Every act committed to paper by the comics artist is aided and abetted by a silent accomplice. An equal partner in crime known as the reader", in: Scott McCloud, *Understanding Comics*, 68.

has the possibility of getting involved in the subtext and actively connecting to the material.

Any moment of comfort or discomfort triggered through the engagement with the material can interrupt unconscious routine. By such interruption, artists' books allow us to expand the boundaries of our learning, our perception of words and texts, our acceptance of form and space, and our acceptance of what is seemingly a given. Stepping out of the given can change how we perceive the world, one that we may have never noticed, took for granted, or simply clung to out of habit. We engage in a space with a shared pool of memories, knowledge and information that either unite or divide us. We enter such a collective space with our individual bodies with thoughts and feelings which are embodied within an individual's sensory motor experience. Those individual bodies are simultaneously part of embodied collective.[3] How do artists' books create such a space of collective memory and as an art form what is their contribution and advantage in advocating conversation, and perhaps change and development?

The Construction of Identities: Entering a Collective Space

What am I but a painful reminder of someone once beautiful and kind?

I'm often interested in looking at the emotional usage to construct an identity. In my book *Wetrocities* I focus on the construction and implantation of the 'white' identity. Over the years people I've met have shared memories and stories that were crucial at one point in their lives. Many were elders who no longer care if and how their stories will be judged. For them, it was important to talk about "happenings" that for too long were shushed away, met with disbelieve or indifference or tabooed. These seemingly small incidents triggered life changing decisions which resulted in inner betrayal and then living in this betrayed form.

3 Two ways in which the body phenomenologically can be experienced: "individuation of the psychological self and the instantiation of dualism in the conceptualisation of human being" (1995, 7). Within Western culture we often assume that the body is objectified and individual, and as a consequence do not acknowledge the possibility of the body being perceived as both individual and part of a collective: "diffused with other persons and things in a unitary, sociomythic domain." in: Jane Turner, Embodiment, Balinese Dance Theatre, and the Ethnographer's Predicament in: *Performance and Spirituality* Volume 2, Number 1 (Spring 2011), 13.

Wetrocities is the fictionalized story of two elderly people unrelated to each other. Both at one point had been confronted with the consequences of a "chosen" White identity. One person as a young child still unaware of the rules and demands of their privilege told me this story:

> I was perhaps four years of age when I dropped my toy onto the streets of my hometown. An elderly man would pick it up and hand it back to me. As I was told by my parents I said: "Thank you, Sir". Only this time my parents would tell me otherwise. Once back home I'd get spanked for calling him 'Sir'. You see, he was not 'We' and you never say 'Sir' to a 'colored' person. Never. Not 'We'. I was corrected to never forget. I was to stay the perpetual brat.

The other person at a rather late moment in life, having already lived with the consequences of a 'White' identify said thus:

> It took me a life time to understand my helpful politeness to ease your pain as ignorance. To listen to you, to grant you my ear, to grant me your heart means to connect with my atrocities. The corruption I complied to, all in the jolliest, friendliest spirit.

Both stories show the demands for loyalty of a constructed groups' behavior, in this case 'Whiteness'. Their honesty and willingness to speak of their pain and regret permitted me to have insight on how this group identity is coerced and implemented from early on.

A child can get complimented or punished for their same good behavior. When implementing identities it depends to whom the behavior is addressed. Being praised or being punished is the very moment one chooses to comply or rebel. One results in being loyal and complicit to a group's behavior; the other in the loss of love and social 'death,'[4] a sometimes life-long struggle of being an outcast and 'Nestbeschmutzer,' a traitor to their 'own.'

I thought I would lose everything dear when the slapping hand struck. The shame I felt after I called you 'Sir'. It was easier to betray myself.

Any deviation to this racial identity concept bears the possibility of being branded as a 'rootless cosmopolitan,' as a 'parasite within healthy national bodies,' terms that Hitler as well as Stalin have used and can

4 Best expressed in James Baldwin's *Blues for Mister Charlie*.

be equally heard in today's political climate. All of us who aren't an 'out & proud' racist or a self-aware White nationalist live with these unaware and murky implantation of constructed identities through our upbringings.

Identity is fluid. It adapts to situations and can be constructed and developed. Then why do we hold on to any of those foisted upon us? In *Wetrocities*, after the implantation of a 'White' identity, I ask what happens when we relate to others, to 'the other'.

As we enter a collective space it is an opportunity to ask ourselves: *How do we (choose to) exit?*

Dissolving a Fixed Identity by Physically Entering a Book

Solitary Confinement and *Spielraum* are artists' books in which the reader can be completely enveloped. I was curious if I could create a book through which a reader could be physically enclosed in the pages of a book and its subject; to enter a world of a book not only in their mind but also with their body.

Similar to *Wetrocities*, in these 'walk-in-books' the reader engages with this imaginative leap in a full sensory experience. People who stepped into the book and confined themselves for a certain amount of time experienced unexpected emotions and memories being triggered. Surprised by this, a conversation unfolded afterwards wherein they shared what was buried not only in their subconscious mind but also subconscious body.

The first walk-in-book, *Solitary Confinement*, focuses on the extremely painful repercussions of involuntary isolation and confinement. I've met people who were confined by authoritarian forces. I've listened to their stories, their attempts to explain how it feels, what it does to you when you are isolated, when your ability to move and your free will is taken away. I wondered what is it like to be trapped in a book? How long could one stand in such a confined space willingly? *Spielraum*, the second book, is an examination of Anton Wilhelm Amo, who at the beginning of the eighteenth century came to the court of the Dukes of Brunswick-Wolfenbüttel as a child and is considered the first European philosopher of African descent. It focuses on the notion of inner confinement—What is it like to be confined to your own memory and cultural context? According to Amo, the human body with its sensory system merely exists but does not live[5] when isolated from its environment. To survive the mind relies on reactivating emotional experiences through memories. How long can a spirit and, according to Amo, a soul feast on the positive memories of a 'free' life? How free are our thoughts when the body is, voluntarily or involuntarily, isolated from its surroundings?

How many dreams and memories do you have left? Or are they outnumbered by those confined days?

Solitary Confinement and *Spielraum* are made of thin, yet strong, almost translucent paper, prompting readers to feel a disconnect from civilization while also being surrounded by a hazy, outside world that is out of reach. The longing for a connection is kept alive only by memory. The 'fragility' of my artists' book, at first, reflects a certain solitude and beauty shown in the lightness of the slowly fluttering pages, a lightness that ends the moment the pages come together and turn the book into a solid, concrete-like form.

The pages open up into all directions with the middle page becoming the top part which can be attached to the ceiling, turning a flat surface into a cubic space. The remaining pages fall down sideways and create the space that then can be entered. The once easy accessible text that could be read page by page now is in all directions with light, height and transparency interfering with the usual way of consuming knowledge. Bending our bodies to regain access is made almost impossible due to the confined space. This is intended to be disorienting and can result in the loss of the all defining horizontal line.

"Our traditional sense of orientation—and, with it, modern concepts of time and space—are based on a stable line: the horizon line. Its stability hinges on the stability of an observer, who is thought to be located on a ground of sorts, a shoreline, a boat—a ground that can be imagined as stable, even if in fact it is not." [...] "This disorientation is partly due to the loss of a stable horizon. And with the loss of horizon also comes the departure of a stable paradigm of orientation, which has

---

5 Anton Wilhelm Amo, Die Apatheia der menschlichen Seele, 1734 in: Anton Wilhelm Amo's Philosophical Dissertation on Mind and Body, Stephen Menn and Justine E.H. Smith, Oxford University Press, 2020

situated concepts of subject and object, of time and space, throughout modernity."[6]

Steyerl argues that the horizontal line is key to the implementation and stabilization of our identity. With the horizontal line gone or disturbed how will the perception of one's relationship to the world be affected? In artists' books[7] and in *Solitary Confinement* and *Spielraum* dissolving the horizontal line is an opportunity to question a fixed identify, a 'fixed' world.

Reconstructing a Collective Space Through Memory Fragmentation

We know about Marsha P. Johnson and Sylvia Rivera because of the shattering effect the Stonewall riots had—pulling the LGBTQ+ movement out of the societal closet and into visibility. 'Out and Proud,' paving a way for every gay, trans, and lesbian. To be seen as we are, instead of having us silenced into invisibility by "excusing" gay men as eternal bachelors, lesbians as spinsters and scolding, nay shaming trans people as fake woman and men. The pain and effort butch women had to endure to become more feminine either by resisting or complying to a society's seemingly eternal construct of heteronormativity. The *Kitchen Table Diaries* are a diary of collages with materials of 'underground' queer and leftist spaces from Europe, Turkey and the US which I collected and preserved on my kitchen table in the nineties and beyond. My memory about these times is fragmented and reflected in the sparse and incomplete imagery and text fragments. Where there is a gap—of lost imagery or text—a white space shows up.

Constructed as a double sided boustrophedon the books can be paged in both directions. Folded out, they turn into a two sided imagery with one side revealing the Alice Walker quote: "No person is your friend (or kin) who demands your silence or denies your right to grow and

6 Steyerl, Hito *In Free Fall: A Thought Experiment on Vertical Perspective in The Wretched of the Screen* (2012)

7 Marshall Weber's *Eleven* documents the environment of New York City in the weeks after 9/11, by having to turn the book in random direction to 'access' the pages. Dissolving the horizontal line through spiraling the book succeeds in loosing a compass point and recreating a loss of direction. Ken Campbell's *Tilt: The black-flagged streets* and María Veronica San Martin's *Colonia Dignidad/ Dystopic Utopia* disturb the horizontal line to challenge fixed versions in how to read a book.

be perceived as fully blossomed as you were intended."[8] The quote is printed on pages from Arthur Miller's *The Crucible*. Unfolded, the other side becomes a large tapestry with a red line winding through.

Creating artists' books[9] through such memory fragmentation aims to reconstruct a collective space that is no longer accessible. Marginalized histories are not necessarily on the forefront of societal mainstream. I use absence to evoke curiosity. The embodied memory is triggered by recognition of a shared invisibility. To pursue a lost idea or person or identity, you must first know that it is lost—which is both a tragedy and irony. How do you know what to ask or who to ask, if that entire space is gone but you do not know this? You have to know that such spaces existed, which often were and still are at the forefront of change, before you can search for them in archives. You have to know that someone experienced this to ask for stories about them should you end up sitting next to an actual eyewitness.

Collective Memory as a Counter-Voice in Dominant Cultures

In the moment of a happening, there is a moment of chaos which I think is a moment of unaltered truth. All that is said, talked about, reported, eye-witnessed, requested and observed is spontaneous unfiltered. It takes time to alter reality.

I've documented the killing of a Turkish prosecutor after an escalated hostage situation. I navigated a highly political situation that resulted in the prosecution of people branded as 'terrorists.' Contained in this story were uncensored thoughts and stories deleted from the collective space.

Memory Patches is an attempt to preserve those 'unofficial' voices. I sew 'patches of information' to a visual blanket as a counterbalance to the implemented versions of all those 'alternative truth' seekers. Not because the version I depict is the 'right one' but because owners of a de facto totalitarian system do their best to control our judiciaries,

---

8 Alice Walker, In *Search of Our Mothers' Gardens*: Prose, 1983

9 Sauda Mitchell in her work *Finding Aid* as well as *Timbuktu* implements QR codes into her artists' books which 'teleports' the reader into archives where the 'whole story' or documentation can be found. The created physical artists' book itself triggers a fragmented collective recognition through the use of material and imagery and combined with digital technology in the same moment connects to geographically distant places.

executive orders and news outlets shutting down inconvenient or embarrassing versions of reality.

The first part of this work is voices a day after the incident. The second part shows what's left of the incident by now, years later. In times where news stories can be altered into a 'he said/she said' situation with fact-checking websites ending up as yet another weapon for governments, I ended up focusing on the question 'Who benefitted from the incident?' rather than 'Who shot the prosecutor?'

Memory Patches was my first attempt to use comics as eyewitness.[10] While we may not be fluent in the idiosyncrasies of a country or culture, or a specific group of people, comics through their usage of abstraction have the ability to translate even the most complex narratives in a manner that can be universally accessible.

Evoking Collective Memory through Sound and Repetition

The German word 'Brandstifter' describes someone who intentionally or negligently ignites a fire. A real fire or verbally by fueling people's mind to inflict harm or to wage wars.

In *I Kill You in Dreams* I use gel transfer, acrylic medium and oils to create pages for a book that make a sound when paged. I wanted to evoke a collective symbol by creating the sound of a match being lit to trigger the memory of an ignition. The physical activity of the paging arm, its repetitive movement creating the sound over and over again taps into embodied memory. Dancers memorize their movements by storing them in their bodies through repetition. During German fascism repetition of words and physical movement was used to implement national-socialistic ideas and identity. By paging my book (repetition) the actively created sound can trigger emotions, allowing memories to enter our consciousness. When closing the book the heavy lead covers put weight on the pages and after a while they stick together again. The next time when the book is reopened the pages have to be torn off again and the sound is recreated.

---

10 My work on *Memory Patches* became the basis for co-creating "Cypher Zine," a digital comics magazine that brings audiences into the radical lives and dangerous work of human rights defenders around the world.

Outro: The Importance and Advantages of Artists' Books

What is a book? When we read a traditional book, we enter a world created by words. When we read an artists' book, words, images, touch, size, weight, and sound extend this world to a sensory one. The way we have to engage with artists' books, its physicality (lifting and turning pages) and sensorial experience—our fingertips feel the structure of the pages, we smell the paint or ink, we absorb the size and composition visually, what sound does the weight of the page make? Simply by a casual gesture with or without knowledge of the body in space, we have an embodied experience.[11] Such an experience has the ability to disrupt normative behavior and trigger curiosity to explore and reflect.

It's in the artist's creative imagination to draw a yet not existing reality that allows us to question situations, to change perspectives and contexts. For me, by defying the laws of physics, the drawing of a brick floating on water is real—I drew it, therefore it exists—and coexists with the impossibility of our present reality. Yet it is in this stated impossibility that the curiosity of an explorative mind gets triggered. Can it be true? And if not, are there ways to make this true? What is a non-literal interpretation of this? How we access words, our almost automated reading directions, contribute to how our brain works: "We incorporate knowledge through the physical behavior of our bodies and thus our learning is constantly active and our behaviors constantly in a process of being modified."[12] Artists' books ability to interrupt the process of given can change the way we read, perceive a story, words, text and perhaps how we identify in the world we created. Herein I see their significance.

11 "The term embodiment is understood as a particular aspect of knowledge that tacitly includes lived experiences that go beyond the everyday." in: Jane Turner, "Embodiment, Balinese Dance Theatre, and the Ethnographer's Predicament" in: *Performance and Spirituality* Volume 2, Number 1 (Spring 2011), 12

12 in: Jane Turner, "Embodiment, Balinese Dance Theatre, and the Ethnographer's Predicament "in: *Performance and Spirituality* Volume 2, Number 1 (Spring 2011), 6; Such a change in perspective does have the effect of challenging our own sense of habitus and can enable us to mentally and/or physically engage with different approaches to performance practice.

Authors' Bios

Annette Gilbert is Associate Professor in Comparative Literature at Friedrich-Alexander Universität Erlangen-Nuremberg in Germany. As literary scholar, she is particularly interested in phenomena at the boundary between art and literature. The focus is on avant-garde, experimental, conceptual, and postdigital literature and art, which contribute to the discussion of fundamental questions of art and literary theory such as the concept of the work, authorship, originality, literature, medium, and publishing. Her publications include *Library of Artistic Print on Demand. Post-Digital Publishing in Times of Platform Capitalism* (with Andreas Bülhoff, Spector Books, 2025, see also https://apod.li), *Literature's Elsewheres. The Necessity of Radical Literary Practices* (MIT Press, 2022), *Digitale Literatur II* (with Hannes Bajohr, Text + Kritik 2021), *Under the Radar. Underground Zines and Self-Publications 1965–75* (with Jan-Frederik Bandel and Tania Prill, Spector Books, 2017) and *Publishing as Artistic Practice* (Sternberg Press, 2016).

Devin Fitzgerald A specialist in western and East Asian book history and a bibliographer, Devin completed their Ph.D. in History and East Asian Languages at Harvard University. Devin was a 2015 Andrew W. Mellon Fellow in Critical Bibliography and received additional training at both the University of Virginia and California Rare Book Schools. They are currently working on a monograph on the global history of the paper codex.

Robb Hernández is a Professor of English and Director of Fashion Studies at Fordham University. He is a public advocate for queer and trans artists of color and serves these communities as a curator, oral historian, arts juror, lecturer, and scholarly advisor to museums, libraries, and archives. His book project, *Transplanetary: Speculative Arts of the Americas* examines Latinx artist responses to the modern space program by fielding different historical epochs, celestial happenings, and cosmologies of the ancient Americas. He is the author of *Archiving an*

Epidemic: Art, AIDS, and the Queer Chicanx Avant-Garde (NYU Press, 2019), which offers a queer of color retelling of AIDS' devastation on Latinx artist communities in Southern California. His research has been awarded fellowships and grants from The Andy Warhol Foundation, National Gallery of Art, Smithsonian American Art Museum, and Crystal Bridges Museum of American Art.

Johanna Drucker is Distinguished Professor and Breslauer Professor Emerita, Department of Information Studies, UCLA. She is internationally known for her work in the history of graphic design, typography, experimental poetry, fine art, and digital humanities. Recent work includes *Visualization and Interpretation* (MIT Press, 2020), and *Iliazd: Meta-Biography of a Modernist* (Johns Hopkins University Press 2020), and *Inventing the Alphabet* (University of Chicago Press, 2022), a history of knowledge about the origin of the alphabet. She received her BFA from California College of Arts and Crafts (1973); MA in Visual Studies, (1982), and PhD in Écriture (1986) both from UC Berkeley in 1986. She has received Mellon, Getty, and Fulbright Fellowships, AIGA's Steven Heller Award, and was inaugural Distinguished Humanities Fellow at Yale's Beinecke Library in Spring 2019. Drucker's artist's books, widely represented in museum and library collections, were subject of a retrospective, *Druckworks: 40 years of books and projects* (2012). *The Century of Artists' Books*, Granary Books,1994, remains the defining text in the field. Her art exhibit, *Graphic Animism*, was held in Los Angeles in 2025. In 2014 she was elected to the American Academy of Arts and Sciences and is Chair of the Humanities, Arts, and Culture Advisory Committee. In 2023 she was elected to the American Philosophical Society, Other recent work includes *Diagrammatic* Writing (Onomatopée, 2014), *The General Theory of Social Relativity*, (The Elephants, 2018), and *Downdrift: An Eco-fiction* (Three Rooms Press, 2018). *Affluvia: The toxic off-gassing of affluent culture* was published by Bridge Books in May 2025.

Jonathan Furner received his BA from the University of Cambridge, and his PhD from the University of Sheffield. He is currently a professor in the Departments of Information Studies and English, and an affiliate of the Center for Digital Humanities, at the University of California, Los Angeles (UCLA). In this capacity, he serves as a researcher, educator, and administrator; he is also known as a writer, collector, and bibliographer. His field is library and information science (LIS), and he is particularly interested in taking historical approaches to the study of scholarly communication. He has written over a hundred papers on related topics—including information retrieval (IR), knowledge organization (KO), and philosophy of information (PI)—and his book, *Information Studies and Other Provocations*, came out in 2021. He is a chartered member of CILIP: The Library and Information Association in the UK, and was chair of the Dewey Decimal Classification's Editorial Policy Committee (DDC EPC) from 2014 to 2019.

Kate Crowe (she/her) is Professor and Curator of Special Collections and Archives at the University of Denver, where she oversees archives and rare materials-based acquisition, processing, teaching, exhibits, and outreach, and has published widely on these topics. As Curator, Kate has developed teaching and collecting partnerships with faculty in and outside of the library and across the disciplines, working with them to acquire and use archival and manuscript collections to support critical information literacy-based instruction and research.

Marshall Weber is an artist and curator known for his charismatic teaching, exuberant artists' books, his passionate advocacy for diversity in the field, and his publishing work with social justice organizations such as: Interference Archive, Iraq Veterans Against the War, Librarians and Archivists with Palestine, Occupy Wall Street, and Voces de La Frontera. He received an MFA from S.F.A.I. in 1981, in 1982 he co-founded and became Director of Artists Television Access in San Francisco. In 1999 he co-founded Booklyn, Inc. in Brooklyn, NY, where he is currently the Directing Curator. Weber has major bodies of work in artists' books, collage, poetry, photography, video, and performance art. Significant collections of his art are in the La Jolla Athenaeum Music and Arts Library, the Boston Athenaeum, the German National Library, the Library of Congress, the New York Public Library, and the State Library of Queensland. Weber is an archivist of radical culture and has curated and placed numerous archives in institutional collections across the USA, including: V. Vale's *Search and Destroy* archives (UCLA), the René Yañez Archives (UC Berkeley), the Ruth Lingen Archives (Clark Library UCLA), the Fly, and the Seth Tobocman Archives (Columbia U.), the Booklyn, Inc. archives (LoC), and part I of the Erica Dawn Lyle archive (U. of Miami). Weber has curated dozens of major exhibitions of artists' books notably co-curating (with Xu Bing) the first "Diamond Leaves" Triennial exhibition at the Central Academy of Fine Arts Museum in Beijing in 2012. He has authored numerous critical texts regarding artists' books including co-editing the "Diamond Leaves" exhibition catalog (Guangxi Normal University Press, 2013) and editing "Freedom of the Presses" (Booklyn, 2018). He was the recipient of the 2019 Herzog August Bibliothek Artists' Book Prize and received Interdisciplinary Arts Fellowships from the New York Foundation for the Arts and the McKnight Foundation.

Peggy Keeran, Professor Emeritus, was the Arts & Humanities Librarian until January of 2024, when she retired after 35 years of service to the University of Denver. She is the coeditor, with Carrie Forbes, of *Successful Campus Outreach for Academic Libraries: Building Community through Collaboration* and, with Bowers and Crowe, the coauthor of the *Collection Management* article "'If You Want the History of a White Man, You Go to the Library': Critiquing Our Legacy, Addressing our Library Collections Gaps." Keeran's research interests during her tenure included: library services for graduate students, integrating digital and physical primary source research into the curriculum, and visual literacy for students in non-arts disciplines.

Robert D. Montoya is the Martin and Bernard Breslauer Endowed Professor in Bibliography; Chair and Associate Professor in the UCLA Department of Information Studies; Director of UCLA California Rare Book School, and Director of the UCLA Library, Ethics, and Justice Lab. Montoya's research trajectory focuses on special collections and rare books; book history; knowledge organization; international library development and publishing; information representation and positionality; and critical, ethical, and justice-oriented LIS work.

Sean Pessin is a writer, editor, and educator whose work bridges creative writing, digital humanities, and sustainability studies. He teaches at California State University, Northridge, where his courses invite students to engage critically and creatively with literature, games, and multimodal storytelling. He mentors students in publishing through The Northridge Review, the university's long-running literary magazine. His pedagogy emphasizes writing as both an art form and a social act. Beyond the classroom, Pessin develops innovative digital projects that explore the intersections of narrative, technology, and community. His scholarship and teaching often foreground sustainability and ethical inquiry, guiding students to consider the material and social dimensions of creativity—whether through supply-chain mapping assignments, diagramming the fields of various forms of literary production, or environmental case studies. As an editor and advocate for small press publishing, Pessin champions process-oriented approaches that highlight the collective labor behind literary production. He is committed to supporting emerging voices, fostering inclusive workshop practices, and cultivating spaces where writing and publishing become vehicles for discovery, dialogue, and social engagement. Whether in print, digital form, or the classroom, his work reflects a dedication to craft, community, and the imaginative possibilities of language in shaping more connected and sustainable futures.

Beldan Sezen is an artist, curator and independent publisher with a Diploma in Political Sciences. Her main focus is creating books that confront themes of war, confinement, and human resilience. In 2015 she was awarded with a Global Arts Fund by the Astraea Lesbian Foundation for Justice for exploring questions of survival, freedom and possibility in regard to Queer bodies through her guerrilla art project BUTCH IT UP! in Istanbul, Turkey. She has created comics reportages and cartoons for i.a. Front Line Defenders, an international human rights organization with the specific aim of protecting human rights defenders at risk; the Human Resource Development Foundation (HRDF) in Turkey focusing on human trafficking victims, child labour and child marriage; the European Union and the University of Amsterdam for their project on gender equality and hate speech. She is also the co-founder of Cypher Zine, a digital comics magazine that introduces audiences to human rights defenders around the world. She received a 'book as art' development grant by the City of Amsterdam and was awarded the 2022 Herzog August Library Artists' Book Prize for exploring questions of inner confinement based on the work by German Black philosopher Anton W. Amo. Her books are collected privately and by institutions, with exhibition at places such as the Getty Research Institute (GRI), The Bainbridge Museum of Art, Herzog August Bibliothek and the Bronx Community College. As a curatorial member of Booklyn she aims to continuously broaden the canon of the artists' book world.

Index

www.ingramcontent.com/pod-product-compliance
Lightning Source LLC
LaVergne TN
LVHW010612100826
845148LV00014B/2936